# MUSIC AND MOVEMENT

SEVENTH EDITION

# MUSIC AND MOVEMENT

## A Way of Life for the Young Child

Linda Carol Edwards
*Professor Emerita, College of Charleston*

**PEARSON**

Boston   Columbus   Indianapolis   New York   San Francisco   Upper Saddle River
Amsterdam   Cape Town   Dubai   London   Madrid   Milan   Munich   Paris   Montreal   Toronto
Delhi   Mexico City   São Paulo   Sydney   Hong Kong   Seoul   Singapore   Taipei   Tokyo

**Vice President and Editorial Director:** Jeffery W. Johnston
**Senior Acquisitions Editor:** Julie Peters
**Editorial Assistant:** Andrea Hall
**Vice President, Director of Marketing:** Margaret Waples
**Senior Marketing Manager:** Christopher D. Barry
**Senior Managing Editor:** Pamela D. Bennett
**Senior Project Manager:** Linda Hillis Bayma
**Senior Operations Supervisor:** Matthew Ottenweller
**Senior Art Director**: Diane C. Lorenzo

**Cover Designer:** Wanda Espana
**Cover Images:** (clockwise from top): © Elena Schweitzer / Shutterstock; © MarcusVDT / Shutterstock; © Gelpi / Shutterstock; © Vladimir Melnikov / Shutterstock; © Victoria Buckle / Dorling Kindersley
**Full-Service Project Management:** Kelli Jauron, S4Carlisle Publishing Services
**Composition:** S4Carlisle Publishing Services
**Printer/Binder:** Edwards Brothers
**Cover Printer:** Lehigh Phoenix/Hagerstown
**Text Font:** Times LT Std Roman

Credits and acknowledgments for materials borrowed from other sources and reproduced, with permission, in this textbook appear on the appropriate page within the text.

Every effort has been made to provide accurate and current Internet information in this book. However, the Internet and information posted on it are constantly changing, so it is inevitable that some of the Internet addresses listed in this textbook will change.

**Photo Credits:** Shirley Zeiberg/PH College, p. 1; Annie Fuller/Pearson, pp. 5, 10, 105; L. Morris Nantz/PH College, p. 7; © Kim Gunkel/iStockphoto.com, p. 18; Silver Burdett Ginn, p. 28; Katelyn Metzger/Merrill, pp. 31, 37, 65, 185; Jane Schuler, p. 40; © Maria Teijeiro/OJO Images Ltd/Alamy, p. 43; Krista Greco/Merrill, pp. 44, 67, 84; © Jim West/Alamy, p. 50; Scott Cunningham/Merrill, pp. 53, 63, 66; Anne Vega/Merrill, pp. 55, 61, 77, 87, 94, 126; Julie Peters, p. 71; Teri Leigh Stratford/PH College, pp. 72, 91, 123; Laima Druskis/PH College, pp. 74, 129; Todd Yarrington/Merrill, pp. 97, 117, 125, 160; Phyllis Gates, pp. 103, 108; Ryan McVay/Getty Images, Inc.-Photodisc/Royalty Free, p. 112; © Paul S. Conklin/PhotoEdit, p. 116; © Tom McCarthy/PhotoEdit, p. 121; Barbara Schwartz/Merrill, p. 133; © Glowimages RM/Alamy, p. 137; Bob Daemmrich/PhotoEdit, p. 144; © Martinapplegate/Dreamstime.com, p. 163; David Mager/Pearson Learning Photo Studio, p. 177; Patrick White/Merrill, p. 178; Julie Cudahy, p. 188; Anthony Magnacca/Merrill, p. 190; © NOVASTOCK/PhotoEdit, p. 193

Library of Congress Cataloging-in-Publication Data was not available at the time of publication.

**PEARSON**

ISBN-13: 978-0-13-265716-7
ISBN-10:    0-13-265716-3

*This book is dedicated to my teacher, Ben Timpson.*

# About the Author

**Linda Carol Edwards** is a professor emerita of early childhood at the College of Charleston, Charleston, South Carolina, where she taught both graduate and undergraduate courses in the visual and performing arts. Her degrees include a BA from Pembroke State University and an MEd and EdD from the University of Massachusetts at Amherst. Before moving to the college level, she taught kindergarten for 12 years in the public schools of North Carolina.

Dr. Edwards is the author of *The Creative Arts: A Process Approach for Teachers and Children* (Pearson), which is now in its fifth edition. She has been published in *Young Children, Science and Children, Journal of Early Education and Family Review, Dimensions in Early Childhood,* and the *Kappa Delta Pi Record.* She also serves on the advisory board of *Annual Editions: Early Childhood Education.* In addition, Dr. Edwards's experience allowed her to create undergraduate and graduate programs in early childhood education that have received NCATE/NAEYC approval.

As an advocate for arts education for young children, she takes the opportunity to present at local, state, and national conferences about the importance of the visual and performing arts in the lives of young children.

# Preface

Music is our universal language, the language of our imaginations, of musicians and dancers, composers and performers, orchestras and operas. Movement is the rhythmic language of the dancing 5-year-old using her body to re-create the graceful movements of a swimming dolphin. Music is the lullaby of a father singing to his infant while communicating tenderness and love. The language of movement is revealed through the dancers who choose not to be restrained by convention as they represent their understanding of space, time, and form in ways that are personally satisfying and pleasing. Music is the language of children adding original lyrics and new melodies to a familiar song.

This new edition presents a comprehensive and up-to-date survey of professional research while continuing to provide links between theory and practice. It encourages teachers and caregivers to attend to the importance of research and contemporary thought regarding music and movement education. At the same time, the narrative frames theoretical ideas in meaningful ways for the adult who has chosen teaching as a profession.

The songs, ideas, suggestions, and music and movement concepts are time tested. Parents, teachers, student teachers, caregivers, and students have aided in compiling and assessing the contents of this edition. Musical concepts and activities appropriate for each age level have been included to accompany some of the songs and rhythms. Movement and dance concepts are also presented in age-specific content. I do not believe, however, that music and movement experiences provided for young children must always be used to teach them something. Children's awareness and understanding of the concepts and skills presented should grow out of natural encounters with the musical selections and movement activities. At each age level, enjoyment of music and movement should be paramount, and teachers are encouraged to use music and movement in creative ways. I encourage you to actively participate in all the movement activities. They were designed with children in mind, but that doesn't mean adults can't enjoy the fun as well. Become an advocate for music and movement in the lives of young children. Even though you may feel you lack experience, just begin! Young children are not critics of your expertise with music and movement; they enjoy, participate, and thrive as you do the same.

Throughout the book, the word *teacher* is used to describe the adult who is charged with the care and well-being of children. This includes the preservice college student enrolled in a teacher education program, the student teacher embarking on a teaching career, practicing teachers, master teachers, college professors, and other professionals who are dedicated to enriching the lives of children.

## NEW TO THIS EDITION

In this edition, I have expanded and enriched the emphasis in a number of areas. Most specifically, this seventh edition provides a comprehensive look at music, movement, and physical activity. Here are some of the specifics:

- Updated references throughout the book, including recent research that emphasizes the need for and multiple roles of music, movement, and physical activity in the lives of young children
- New information from the National Association for Sport and Physical Education, including the National Standards and the National Standards for Movement and Dance
- New focus on the Head Start: I Am Moving, I Am Learning goals and guidelines
- Guidelines for the national Let's Move obesity campaign program
- The most recent developmentally appropriate practice (DAP) guidelines for physical development
- Feature focusing on the Early Childhood Environment Rating Scale-Revised with a focus on music and movement, diversity, gross motor activities, and children with disabilities
- More songs for infants and toddlers
- Sample lesson plan
- How to use visual documentation

## SPECIAL CONTENT COVERAGE

All chapters present overviews of important components of the learning environment in today's classrooms.

### Music and Movement for Children with Special Needs

Chapter 3 provides an overview of how children with special needs can be actively involved with both music and movement. It includes a review of the research that demonstrates how music and movement curricula can be inclusive and designed to provide for each child's unique needs. The chapter addresses different special needs, and these are divided into specific categories. Also included in this chapter is an in-depth discussion on the least restrictive environment.

### Movement for Young Children

The seventh edition includes a broader focus on music, movement, dance, and physical activity. Chapter 2 addresses a wide range of current issues, such as childhood obesity and physical inactivity. Included in this chapter is information from the National Association for Sport and Physical Education, the National Standards for Movement and Dance, Head Start: I Am Moving, I am Learning goals and guidelines, and the Let's Move obesity campaign program. This chapter also includes the most recent DAP guidelines for physical development and the Early Childhood Environment Rating Scale-Revised.

### Songs for Toddlers

Chapter 4 has been expanded to include more action songs and lullabies, including lullabies from around the world for 2-year-olds.

### Music and Movement for 3-Year-Olds

Chapter 5 includes a sample lesson plan based on the National Standards for Music Education and the National Standards for Physical Education. The sample lesson plan is designed to address standards, objectives, procedures, guided practice, closure, materials and equipment, and assessment.

### Music and Movement for 4-Year-Olds

Chapter 6 has been expanded to include additional information on the National Standards for Music Education. In addition, this chapter addresses the developmental characteristics of 4-year-olds.

### Music and Movement for Kindergarten and Early Primary

Chapter 7 includes and acknowledges the importance of music and movement throughout kindergarten and the early primary years. The chapter includes the National Standards for Music Education for 5-year-olds. In addition, this chapter addresses the developmental characteristics of children from 5 to 8 years old. Musical notations on the treble-clef only provide an opportunity to learn melodies of new and/or unfamiliar songs.

### Talks with Teachers

The seventh edition retains the feature titled "Talks with Teachers" in which I profile individual teachers who recommend practical methods or strategies for implementing music and movement with children of particular ages. In addition, Chapter 6 presents a new section, an interview with the director of a local preschool in which she describes the process of visual documentation and how teachers and children use it throughout the school year.

### Music from Around the World

Music is suited to address the wonderful diversity of children in today's schools. Music provides teachers with a multicultural context for seeing diversity from viewpoints different from their own and provides some of the tools needed to meet the different learning modalities of children. An expanded focus on viewing music through a multicultural context is included in each chapter in this seventh edition. "Music from Around the World" highlights music's great potential as a resource for musical and movement expression, and an awareness of the diversity of music.

## Music and Movement: An Interdisciplinary Approach

Chapter 8 describes how music and movement can be interwoven into other disciplines, such as mathematics, science, reading and the language arts, and multiculturalism and social studies. Examples of national standards are included to facilitate lesson planning. This chapter presents many ideas for the integration of music and movement using the boundless enthusiasm and spontaneity of children.

## Other Features of This Text

### *Summary and Conclusions*
Each chapter ends with key ideas, a summary of the content, and questions to consider. Included in these chapters are suggestions for song collections and recommendations for recordings.

### *Multiple Intelligences Theory*
Howard Gardner's intelligences theory has implications for music and movement education. In this edition, the coverage of musical, bodily-kinesthetic, and logical-mathematical intelligences is integrated into the content of the age-specific chapters.

### *National Standards for Music and Dance Education*
Sections on the National Standards for Music Education and the National Standards for Dance Education are included throughout the chapters.

### *Research*
Each chapter is rich in current and relevant references. More than ever before, research studies and theoretical contributions provide a comprehensive view of why music and movement are integral components of education for all learners, especially children. Current and relevant research is included in this edition to provide the foundation for continued study of music and movement. Also cited are practical articles and references to which teachers can refer for additional information.

### *Developmentally Appropriate Practice*
The term *developmentally appropriate practice* (DAP), as reported by the National Association for the Education of Young Children, focuses on the ways in which teachers implement the curriculum, the organization of the classroom environment, the materials and equipment, and the children's interactions with the teacher and with one another. This edition presents new information on DAP as it relates to music education for young children.

### *Quotations*
The powerful words of philosophers, musicians, and dancers at the beginning and end of each chapter promote new ways of thinking about music. Some quotations are presented to provoke serious thought, while others use humor to convey a musical message. All provide inspiration to teachers for including music education in the lives of young children.

## ORGANIZATION AND STRUCTURE

Chapter 1 of the seventh edition presents an overview of the central themes and ideas about music and movement that are woven throughout the book. Chapter 2 focuses on the role of music and movement, singing as a support to movement, and children and dance in the classroom. Chapter 3 focuses on children with special needs. Chapters 4, 5, 6, and 7 focus on specific age levels and children's growth and development in music and movement education. Chapter 8 emphasizes music and movement in an integrated curriculum, with suggestions, songs, and movement activities suitable for other content areas, including language arts, mathematics, science, multiculturalism, and social studies. Musical notations are included throughout the chapters as an aid to learning melody.

### Appendixes

The extensive appendixes at the end of the book provide a wealth of additional resources and information. **Appendix A, "Music Terminology and Approaches to Music Education,"** introduces musical concepts, a glossary of terms, grand staff and piano keyboards, music fundamentals, and information on the Orff and Suzuki approaches to teaching and learning to play musical instruments. **Appendix B, "Resources for Teachers in Early Childhood Classrooms,"** provides a quick reference for professional organizations, newsletters, and journals; sources for ordering instruments; books on making instruments; songs for listening and music appreciation; an extensive list of recordings appropriate for encouraging movement and music in the learning environment; and a list of wonderful children's books that involve music. **Appendix C, "Learning Autoharp® and Guitar for the Classroom,"** introduces the basics of playing the autoharp and guitar. There is also a fingering chart for the guitar. **Appendix D, "Instruments for the Classroom,"** provides an overview of percussion, melody, and chording instruments.

## NEW! COURSESMART eTEXTBOOK AVAILABLE

CourseSmart is an exciting new choice for students looking to save money. As an alternative to purchasing the printed textbook, students can purchase an electronic version of the same content. With a CourseSmart eTextbook, students can search the text, make notes online, print out reading assignments that incorporate lecture notes, and bookmark important passages for later review. For more information, or to purchase access to the CourseSmart eTextbook, visit www.coursemart.com.

## ACKNOWLEDGMENTS

Many people inspired me as I was writing this seventh edition, and it has been enhanced by the combined efforts of a talented team of professionals at Pearson. I want to thank Julie Peters for her valuable assistance, support of my writing, and her commitment to music and movement education. I wish to thank Linda Bayma for her careful attention to detail, valuable feedback and for securing permissions; Carol Sykes and Lori Whitley for selecting beautiful and appropriate photographs for this edition; and Andrea Hall for keeping the communication lines open. I would also like to thank the talented team at S4Carlisle Publishing Services, especially Kelli Jauron. It has been a pleasure and an honor to work with such a wonderful group of professional women.

In addition, I appreciate the input from the following reviewers, who provided timely and helpful reviews of the manuscript: Debra Brodowski, Aiken Technical College; Kelly Jennings, University of Central Florida; Carole Outwater, Central Piedmont Community College; Bob Sasse, Palomar College; Carol Sigala, Rio Hondo College; and Olivia Wagner Wakefield, Central Carolina Community College.

I appreciate and wish to acknowledge the support of friends and colleagues who provided guidance during the writing process: Dr. Candace Jaruszewicz, director, and Mary White, Phyllis Gates, Deanna Satzger, and Stephanie Johnston, master teachers at the N. E. Miles Early Childhood Development Center on the College of Charleston campus (www.cofc.edu/~child/).

I wish also to thank my graduate assistant, Kathleen Malmgren, for her masterful technical skills and tireless work on this edition. Finally, I owe much to Karen Paciorck for her friendship and guidance throughout the process.

*Linda Carol Edwards*

# Brief Contents

# Contents

# Statement of Beliefs

Music is a vital part of daily living. It becomes a part of life as opportunities are provided for experiences in singing, responding physically to different rhythms, creative expressions, playing instruments, and quiet listening. A well-organized musical environment provides for a wide range of musical activities and experiences adequate to meet the needs and interests of all children. It also supports and strengthens learning in the other areas brought into the unified experience. Music helps children understand other people and their cultures and gives increased opportunities for social and emotional development. Music also provides a means for the aesthetic enrichment and growth of every child.

**I BELIEVE**

## Young Children Have a Right to

- have a variety of musical and movement experiences that will bring pleasure and enjoyment throughout their lives
- experience musical activities and materials that are appropriate to their age level and developmental needs
- engage in musical and movement experiences that are based on an action art, not a performing art
- be guided to the fullest development of their musical potential
- have the opportunity for support and/or extension of content areas throughout the medium of music
- express themselves musically in an atmosphere of freedom and trust, where divergent and creative interpretation is encouraged
- be involved in the full gamut of musical experiences, regardless of physical, social, emotional, or intellectual limitations
- have sufficient time provided each day for the exploration of musical experiences

## Adults Working with Children Will

- provide both planned and spontaneous musical and movement activities as a part of each child's day
- offer opportunities for listening, creating, singing, moving rhythmically, and experimenting with sound
- place emphasis on the child's enjoyment of the musical and movement experience rather than on an expected outcome
- provide musical and movement activities that will enhance other learning, such as acquisition of language, listening skills, auditory discrimination, and social understanding
- arrange an environment in which children will feel free to explore and engage in a variety of musical experiences that represent contributions from a variety of ethnic groups and cultures from around the world
- recognize and plan for well-balanced musical experiences for all children, adapted to physical, social, emotional, and intellectual capabilities

## Because

- one of the main goals for music and movement is to make children's lives richer through musical experiences that will help develop their aesthetic senses
- a balance of musical and movement activities can contribute to the development of all children according to their individual patterns of growth and development
- music and movement can support concepts and skills that children are developing, but enjoyment of music should hold priority
- children are natural musicians and dancers and, given the opportunity, will express themselves musically in a variety of creative ways

In 1898, Sarah E. Sprague, State Institute Conductor and Inspector of Graded Schools for Minnesota, wrote:

Life's Song, indeed would lose its charm,
Were there no babies to begin it;
A doleful place this world would be,
Were there no little people in it.

Sarah Sprague concluded,

Home, nature and school are the three influences in a child's life, and when these are harmoniously blended it is the "World Beautiful" realized for him, wherein he may grow, as a plant does, always toward the light.

## CHAPTER ONE

# Beginning the Music and Movement Journey

*We are the music makers,*
*And we are the dreamers of dreams . . .*

Arthur O'Shaughnessy (1881)

*It was time for the annual holiday program. Because I had a background in music, my principal appointed me chair of the program committee. I was excited. This was my first year teaching, my first class of 5-year-olds, and the principal wanted me to be in charge of the program. I decided that our whole K–3 school would perform* The Nutcracker Suite, *complete with costumes, music, props, and all the embellishments. I was eager to impress the parents and the other teachers, so I decided to teach my kindergarten girls the ballet "The Waltz of the Flowers," and my kindergarten boys "The Dance of the Toy Soldiers." For weeks I taught these children perfect steps, perfect timing, turn right, stand still, curtsey, and step and turn. At first my kindergartners seemed to enjoy it, but as the days and weeks went on, they started resisting going to practice or would actually beg not to have to do "the program" again. On several occasions, some complained of being tired, while others had great difficulty with self-control . . . disrupting, acting inappropriately, hitting, and being generally unhappy; however, we did make it to the big night. The parents loved the performance. We all congratulated ourselves on a wonderful program. I remember talking with a first-grade teacher about how much the children loved it and what a good time they had. The truth is that the children were exhausted. They were fidgety and irritable, tired and pouty. Some even fell asleep before the program ended.*

*After a long weekend, the children returned to school and seemed to be the happy, well-adjusted children they had been before I had this brilliant idea of producing* The Nutcracker. *Young children, as we all know, are so resilient. In the weeks that followed, they didn't want me to play any music during center time. I would put on a Hap Palmer album, and they would argue about the right and wrong way to "get up in the morning." Why would kindergartners turn against the sacred Hap Palmer? I tried playing more of their favorites, Prokofiev's* Peter *and the* Wolf *and Debussy's* La Mer *and, of course, the music from* The Nutcracker. *My children didn't want to hear the music from the ballet; they didn't want me to play any music at all. Just the mention of the word* dance *or* costume *or* program *would change the mood of our whole classroom environment. Although it took some time—several weeks as I remember—my children finally came back to music. By early spring they were again requesting their favorite music and especially enjoyed listening to the "Spring" movement from Vivaldi's* Four Seasons *(Edwards & Nabors, 1993, p. 78).*

*When thinking about how to begin this chapter, the story you just read seemed most appropriate. These events actually took place in a kindergarten classroom. This was obviously a performance-based experience, or product-oriented approach, to music in early childhood.*

*These little children had been forced to perform (under the name of "music" and, more specifically, "dance") in ways that were totally inappropriate for children their age. Not only were these children involved in inappropriate practice, but teacher-centered ideas had been imposed on these children, forcing them to become waltzing flowers and toy soldiers without regard as to how they might interpret or create their own ideas, thoughts, images, or forms of expression.*

How do you feel about expressing your ideas through music, creative movement, or dance? Are you musical? Do you enjoy singing "Happy Birthday" to loved ones or dancing with friends when the music is so good you just can't sit still? Have you ever noticed yourself tapping your foot in rhythm with a great band or standing to applaud for an encore at the end of a beautifully orchestrated symphony? Most of us probably have some of these musical competencies, while others have a deeper connection with music either as consumers or performers. Whatever our current level of musical involvement, any effort we make toward increasing our musical abilities and talents certainly falls under the broad definition of being creative.

In her classic and memorable words, Chenfeld defines a creative teacher as "a person who is open, flexible, willing to try new things and risk their failing, honest, responsive to people and situations, and welcoming of new experiences" (1978, p. 39). Most of us who have chosen teaching as a profession are willing to venture into new and different situations. In this case, the adventure involves exploring music. After all, musical happenings occur spontaneously as we hum a familiar melody or sing along with a favorite recording artist.

However, if you are saying to yourself, "I really can't sing," don't worry. A beautiful singing voice is not a requirement for bringing meaningful musical experiences to young children. You can recite or chant fingerplays and action songs. The rhythm is more interesting to children than the melody. You can use recordings, simple instruments such as an autoharp or melody bells, or the talents of a musical volunteer. If your body just doesn't feel rhythm in movement or dance, begin slowly by experimenting with the different types of movement presented in this book, and open yourself to the possibility of discovering something new about yourself and your musical creativity. Your children will respond to you, their teacher, and your enthusiasm, interest, and spontaneity. If you trust yourself enough to try, your children and their responses will help build your confidence.

Now let's take a look at how children respond to music and movement. More specifically, how do young children enjoy music and movement?

## MUSIC AND MOVEMENT: ENJOYMENT AND VALUE FOR CHILDREN

Young children are action oriented. Not only are singing, moving, and dancing fun, but they also provide young children opportunities to listen, respond, imitate, and use their voices, fingers, hands, arms, and bodies in ways that are creative and uniquely theirs.

In his timeless book, *Teaching the Child Under Six* (1981), Hymes writes about the "style and swing" of the young child in one of the clearest, most articulate descriptions ever written. Hymes must know more about the qualities of young children than most people in our profession. He reminds us of the following ways in which young children "flow" differently from their older brothers and sisters:

- Young children are not good sitters.
- Young children are not good at keeping quiet.
- Young children are shy.
- Young children are highly egocentric.
- Young children want to feel proud, big, and important.
- Young children have their private dream world.
- Young children are very tender.
- Young children are beginners.
- Young children are hungry for stimulation.
- Young children are earthy, practical, concrete-minded.
- Young children are acquiescent.
- Young children are illiterate. (pp. 38–46)

Hymes also says that our capacity and willingness to live with these qualities makes the crucial difference between a good classroom (and teacher) and one that does not fit the age or provide child-appropriate experiences for young children.

How does Hymes's description of the style and swing of young children apply to music and movement? The answer lies in our approach and our attitude toward developing musical experiences for children who are action oriented. They need room to move both indoors in the classroom and outside in the play yard. Dancing, rhythmic movement, and action songs all provide ample opportunity for action. A former graduate student coined a phrase that seems especially appropriate here: "Sitting still and being quiet is not a marketable skill" (R. W. Cain, personal communication, 1984). Since young children are not good at being quiet, they need the freedom to make a joyful noise by singing, playing instruments, and making up sing-songs and chants as they play and work.

Shy children should be given opportunities to play with musical ideas in small groups. Hymes calls these groups "safe personal clusters." When you see or hear shy children gingerly exploring the properties of a triangle and mallet or singing quietly to themselves during center time, remember that they are tentative in their efforts and may not yet be ready to join the whole-class activities.

The egocentric nature of young children will show in their excitement when they stop you in the middle of an activity and say, "Watch me do the little rabbit song all by myself," "I can move just like a butterfly," or "I went to the circus, and they had a band that played clown music." They begin their sentences with *I*, and the sensitive teacher takes time to listen to the musical news children bring to the classroom.

The main purpose of including music and movement in the classroom is enjoyment. Through music and movement, young children express themselves, explore space, develop language and communication skills, increase sensory awareness, and express themselves through rhythm, gesture, time, and space.

## Four Important Reasons for Including Music in the Classroom

Van der Linde (1999) outlines six reasons why the importance of music and movement activities should not be underestimated. Among these are four that are particularly relevant here:

1. *Mental capacity and intellect.* There is a connection between music and the development of mathematical thinking. Mathematical concepts are developed as children sing counting songs.
2. *Mastery of the physical self.* Children develop coordination, which aids muscular development. They begin to understand what they can do with their bodies as they run, balance, stretch, crawl, and skip.
3. *Development of the affective aspect.* Through music and movement, children learn acceptable outlets to express feelings and relieve tension. Music may also convey a specific mood through which children reveal their feelings and emotions.
4. *Development of creativity.* Music can create an imaginary world that stimulates a child's creativity. A box can become a drum, a stick can be transformed into a horn, or a broom can become a dance partner. Children make up songs or give new words to old songs for pure enjoyment. (pp. 2–5)

It is sometimes all too easy to miss the opportunity to expand on the music and movement experiences of a child's budding musical awareness. The imaginary world, the

Keep a camera handy so you can capture a creative moment in progress.

dream world, is a private place where children can sort out ideas before actually implementing those ideas. They can imagine how a butterfly moves from flower to flower before re-creating their own interpretation of pretending to fly like a butterfly. Teachers must encourage imagery and fantasy throughout music and movement activities. They are natural resources that children bring with them to the classroom, which encourage the development of musical processes that are foundational to future thinking and perceptual organization. Tender children who are just beginning to discover their ability to soar like an eagle, dance with the flowers, sing for the pure joy of hearing their own voices, or pretend to gallop swiftly like a pony look to their teacher to provide a safe place where they can explore all the possibilities their bodies, minds, and voices hold for musical and bodily-kinesthetic development.

Young children love to repeat things. They want to "sing it again!" and "move like a zigzag!" They are hungry for ideas that tap into their curiosity of how the Eensy-Weensy Spider goes up the water-spout; they want to move and dance when the spirit strikes them. They need teachers who will design a variety of rich musical experiences to help them test out things for themselves. We can play a recording by Hap Palmer or Raffi, but we must give children permission to test out their own ways of interpreting what they hear in ways that are right and personal to them.

A good classroom is geared to music. A sensitive teacher celebrates the clumsy and often awkward beginnings children make in their attempts to move rhythmically. When we care about the whole child we honor all aspects of their musical expression. An awareness of the values of musical encounters provides the wise teacher with many choices and worthwhile possibilities for immersing children in a rich variety of songs, fingerplays, and other musical experiences.

A child's awareness of music begins very early. Infants can be comforted by quiet singing, music boxes, and musical toys. As they make cooing sounds and begin babbling, infants experiment with different tones and rhythmic patterns. Typical toddlers can frequently be observed clapping, dancing, or parading around the room, trying out different ways of moving to musical beats and rhythmic patterns. Young children are sensitive to musical sound and respond freely and joyfully to different tempos and beats. At the same time, they discover new and different ways to use their bodies and voices.

Throughout the childhood years, children's major accomplishments in musical development in turn support many developmental milestones. One important by-product of exploration of music and movement is language development. Communication for the very young child is largely nonverbal, and music and movement can enhance and expand the child's repertoire of communication skills and abilities. Children experiment with familiar word patterns as they combine words with a tune. They imitate rhythmic patterns and combine these with physical activity as they communicate through movement or dance. Children play with words as they change the lyrics to familiar songs or make up chants to accompany their play activity. Verbal and motor cues help children remember new words or sequences of words. They experience regular beats, changes in tempo, accents, and synchronization, all of which are an integral part of communicating in words and sentences.

As with all areas of the curriculum, developmentally appropriate music and movement activities will be successful only if you, the teacher, understand why music and movement are important tools for assisting children in constructing knowledge about their world and helping them make sense of their experiences. Admittedly, music and movement *can* be used in an integrated curriculum to enhance other subject areas, such as the language arts, but as Metz (1989) cautions, "Simply using music in an educational setting does not insure that children's musical perceptions are developing. . . . We need to focus on music as 'an end in itself'" (p. 89).

We further believe that, as teachers, we must be well versed in not only *how* to bring musical experiences to children, but also *why* music is so essential to the young child's overall development. One way to facilitate our understanding of the "why?" is to look at the perspective that developmental theory has to offer. The next section provides some insight into why children need music in their lives and why music stands alone as an important subject area.

## BEGINNING THE PROCESS OF PLANNING

Children need to be provided with the circumstances for the development of all of their capabilities. When nurturing children's musical intelligence, we should provide a variety of experiences to support musical expression. For example, sing simple songs or let your children hear you humming, listen to music throughout the day, and play instruments to signal transition periods or to announce special happenings. Play background music in the classroom, and play special recordings regularly during specific times, such as after lunch or just before the children leave at the end of the day. Select many different varieties of musical compositions and styles to encourage your children to use their imaginations to see musical imagery. Introduce musical concepts that focus on the great classical composers and how classical compositions sound different from, for example, commercial musical jingles. Use music to help children relax after a period of high-energy activity. Play Debussy's *La Mer* (The Sea) before reading *One Morning in Maine*, or play a lively jazz recording just before you read *Ben's Trumpet*.

Educators have intuitively emphasized musical and physical activity as a part of children's learning experiences, but until recently, we have perhaps failed to realize fully the musical and bodily-kinesthetic learning that can take place when we purposely and systematically offer activities and experiences that nurture and support these two important areas of learning and knowing. The theory and educational philosophy supporting

Babies enjoy listening to songs sung by a loving adult.

every person's capacity to develop a wide range of human intelligence reflects the influences of Howard Gardner. Curricula designed to facilitate the development of musical and bodily-kinesthetic intelligence must be promoted through child-appropriate learning activities and teaching methods. At a very early age, children can begin to form concepts of music, movement, and dance that will serve as the base for later intellectual growth. Moreover, all children deserve opportunities to learn in ways that suit their individual and highly personal modes for knowing, learning, and processing information.

## The Tourist Approach

The early childhood classroom is the perfect place to begin increasing children's awareness of a variety of cultures, and it plays a key role in affecting children's long-term beliefs (Boutte, 2000). However, Saul and Saul (2001) caution teachers to move away from the "tourist approach" (p. 38) to teaching multicultural education wherein we "visit" different cultures, never to discuss them again. Multicultural experiences for young children should become a part of the child's music awareness throughout the whole year.

---

**MUSIC FROM AROUND THE WORLD**

Early childhood educators know that children's concept of space is generally limited to the child's home, the neighborhood, the ride to school, and other familiar locations within children's frame of reference. We also know that children's concept of space is developed by their own actions. What children see from their own perspective is of interest to them, but they will not be aware and will pay little attention to those things beyond their vantage point. Therein lies one of the challenges when introducing young children to music from cultures around the world. However, as Puckett and Diffily (1999) remind us, the children of today are growing up in a culturally diverse society, regardless of the children's immediate neighborhood or the ethnic composition of an individual class.

---

## CULTURAL DIVERSITY THROUGH MUSIC AND MOVEMENT

Most classrooms include children who are from cultures outside of the United States. The opportunities presented to the teacher/caregiver to use music and movement to promote communication and participation among these children are many. Seefeldt (2005) recommends that teachers begin with the children's families to gain information and to become more aware of family backgrounds and traditions. Celebration of special holidays of ethnic groups, using folk songs, demonstration of musical styles of different cultures, exposure to a variety of traditional instruments—maracas, castanets, bagpipes, drums, flutes, dulcimers, lute, harpsichord, and mandolin, to name a few—will create excitement and develop appreciation for the richness of the many family groups in our midst. Some schools have children from Christian, Jewish, Muslim, Buddhist, and nonreligious families. It is important for teachers to recognize cultural differences and design music and movement activities that can encourage young children to respect others. Songs can be learned to help celebrate special occasions. For example, at Chanukah, children can learn the "Dreidl Song" (Various artists, 1994). There is a wonderful collection of lullabies by Sara Jordan entitled *Lullabies Around the World* (2001). This collection includes songs that are in Russian, Mexican, Yiddish, Italian, Mandarin, Polish, German, Lingala, Japanese, French-Canadian, and English. Young children can also learn about other cultures by singing songs in other languages, or just learning to say hello in a variety of languages informs children of the variety of languages spoken around them.

Language differences and dialects also find a place in musical selections. It is important to remember that most of the behavior patterns children learn are related to the family and to the culture. Keep in mind that children labeled "verbally deficient" may simply be using language in their own way to fit the situation. The adult who is well informed about the backgrounds of children in the group will understand passivity on the part of some, nonverbal responses from others, fear of failure, and bilingual exchanges. Some will seldom volunteer and others will not look directly at adults. Children bring with them a wide range of family and cultural expectations. Learning to sing or play an instrument can have significant long-term value to a child with limitations in language or social functioning.

Music is everywhere, and therein lies its appeal. It can cross the boundaries that separate cultures and nationalities; it can transcend emotional differences. There is some form of musical expression attractive to each child. We need to develop awareness of both cultural differences and similarities. Often adults in the community can be used as resource persons to share the folk music, dances, musical instruments, and even some of the rhythms of a language "strange" to the ears.

Young children learn quickly and are eager for new experiences. If made to feel comfortable, they will often participate willingly in small groups. They strive to please. The culturally different child can thrive and blossom in the nonpunitive, nonthreatening atmosphere music provides.

Deiner (1983) provides us with timeless insight into the true nature of culture: "Just as there is no one White American culture, there is also no one Asian American, Black American, Hispanic American, or Native American culture" (pp. 242–243). The great Ella Jenkins discusses her role as an educator. She says, in part, "As an educator, it's important to me to share my excitement about cultures with children. When I do—and you do, too—we help them appreciate the varied peoples, places, songs, words, dances, rhythms, and rhymes in their own communities and around the world" (1995, p. 40). In an interview with Reninger (2000), Jenkins talks about chants: "Children in most countries like chants, even if they have to be translated. I use little chants that have a verse and a lot of rhythm and a lot of rhyming. Children are fascinated by rhyme. Sometimes, if they're singing and they forget the words, they try to make up their own rhymes" (p. 41). Jenkins recommends that one way of introducing children to chants and rhymes in languages different from their own is to teach them how to extend a greeting to someone who lives in a different place. In the previous section, we talked about toddlers "snatching" parts of a chant just as they are beginning to talk. Even 2-year-olds can chant "Hola, hola, hola" as a greeting in Spanish. Jenkins's classic album, "You'll Sing a Song and I'll Sing a Song," introduces many of her songs and chants. This recording and many others are available through Jenkins's website, www.ellajenkins.com.

It is important that the classroom environment, including materials and activities, reflect all the children's cultures without stereotyping them. In other words, if we want children to have a sense of belonging the environment must be inclusive of multiple cultures that give all the children an increased awareness and appreciation of how cultures can be different. Early childhood teachers use the guidelines in Developmentally Appropriate Practice (Copple & Bredekamp, 2009) to ensure the learning environment addresses cultural, linguistic, and other differences among children. These guidelines are summarized as follows:

- Teachers create a classroom that reflects the diversity of the community and society.
- Teachers involve every child's home culture and language in the shared culture of the group.
- Teachers promote children's positive self-identify and help them to respect and appreciate similarities and differences among people by showing that each child's family, culture, and language are valued.
- Teachers include parents in selection of multicultural materials, photographs, books, play themes, songs, and stories.
- Teachers ensure that everything presented to the children is authentic and that there are no offensive stereotypes anywhere in the room or curriculum (p. 152).

## Early Childhood Environment Rating Scale Revised

This important document, the Early Childhood Environment Rating Scale Revised (Harms, Clifford, & Cryer, 2005) will increase your understanding of how to measure quality in early childhood settings and is designed for preschool, kindergarten, and child care classrooms serving children 2½ through 5 years of age. It is a widely used program quality assessment instrument designed for program directors for supervision and program improvement. It is also used by teaching staff for self-assessment, by agency staff for monitoring, and in teacher training programs. It contains rubrics to check your program or classroom's practice on seven key scales of program development. This scale can also help you assess how you promote acceptance of diversity in your classroom as you review the following indicators.

- Inclusion of diversity is part of the daily routine and play activities. For example, ethnic foods are a regular part of meals/snacks; music and songs are from different cultures.
- Activities are included to promote understanding and acceptance of diversity. For example, parents are encouraged to share family customs with the children; many cultures are represented in holiday celebrations.

Providing props and open-ended materials is the teacher's responsibility. The availability of a variety of materials enables children to make choices.

- Many books, pictures, and materials are accessible showing people of different races, cultures, ages, abilities, and gender in nonstereotypic roles. For example, both historical and current images are provided, and males and females are shown doing many different types of work including traditional and nontraditional roles.
- When historical cultural traditions are represented, the images must be balanced with nontraditional modern representations. For example, if traditional African tribal cultures are represented in materials, then current representation must also be included. If stereotyping or violence is shown with regard to any group, such as some "Cowboy and Indian" toys, or you ask the children to "sit Indian style" you would not get a passing score under the ECERS-R (p. 57).

The role of the teacher is to discover differences, appreciate them, and incorporate such learning into the daily lives of children. Music can be a valuable aid in achieving such goals. Music is particularly useful in enhancing adult–child and peer–peer interaction. Teachers: Study the materials you are using for music and movement to see if they truly reflect the diversity of the children in your classroom. Do the materials include a reflection of the diversity of family structure and/or multigenerations? Do you present an unbiased portrayal of religion? Does your music and movement program include all the children, even those from differing socioeconomic levels?

## GARDNER'S THEORY OF MULTIPLE INTELLIGENCES

Harvard University psychologist Howard Gardner, author of *Multiple Intelligences*, believes that human beings possess nine intelligences, including the "musical intelligence," "bodily-kinesthetic intelligence," and "logical-mathematical intelligence." Children possess a natural awareness and sensitivity to musical sounds. They explore music with more spontaneity than any other age group, and they venture forward into music and movement activities with their voices, their bodies, and their emotions. The whole child is involved. The child's affective, cognitive, and psychomotor responses to a musical encounter are the hallmark of creativity.

Gardner (1973) provides us with a very perceptive observation that paints a lovely picture of children and their music:

> The child attending to a piece of music or a story listens with his whole body. He may be at rapt attention and totally engrossed; or he may be swaying from side to side, marching, keeping time, or alternating between such moods. But in any case, his reaction to such art objects is a bodily one, presumably permeated by physical sensations. (pp. 152–153)

## Musical Intelligence

Musical intelligence involves the ability to perceive, produce, and appreciate pitch (or melody) and rhythm, and to appreciate the forms of musical expressiveness. Composers, performers, musicians, conductors, and "the child attending to a piece of music" all possess a great deal of musical intelligence. Conductor and composer Leonard Bernstein, composer and performer Ray Charles, classical composer Igor Stravinsky, conductor Zubin Mehta, the world's "First Lady of Song" Ella Fitzgerald, renowned 20th-century pianist Arthur Rubinstein, and guitarists and songwriters James Taylor and Eric Clapton are all examples of individuals with immense musical intelligence.

## Bodily-Kinesthetic Intelligence

The ability to control one's body movements and to handle objects skillfully are the core components of bodily-kinesthetic intelligence. Gardner specifies that bodily intelligence is used by dancers, choreographers, athletes, mimes, surgeons, craftspeople, and others who use their hands and bodies in a problem-solving kind of way. Classic examples of individuals whose skills are embodied in this form of intelligence include American dancer and choreographer Alvin Ailey; Isadora Duncan, the pioneer dancer of this century; Katherine Dunham, the first choreographer and dancer to bring African dance to the American stage; Charlie Chaplin and Buster Keaton, the great silent clowns of the past; and contemporary masters of humorous characterizations, such as Robin Williams and Bill Cosby. Athletes like Venus and Serena Williams and Michelle Kwan also excel in grace, power, and accuracy.

## Logical-Mathematical Intelligence

Mathematicians, scientists, and composers certainly have this form of intelligence, which involves sensitivity to and a capacity to discern logical or numerical patterns (including rhythm, meter, time signature, and note value) and the ability to handle long chains of reasoning. Some examples of people who demonstrate highly developed logical-mathematical intelligence include Johann Sebastian Bach, scientists Albert Einstein and Madame Curie, biologist Ernest Everett Just, and botanist George Washington Carver. The capacity to explore patterns, categories, and relationships can be heard in the four-part harmony and counterpoint music from the baroque period.

An example of logical-mathematical intelligence in composers is revealed in Bach's colossal work, *The Art of Fugue*, often referred to as a transmission of a purely abstract theory. In any case, *The Art of Fugue* is an excellent example of logical-mathematical intelligence, carrying pure counterpoint to its height. Read the following description of

*The Art of Fugue*, and you may agree that Bach's work is as complex as any mathematical problem you have ever tried to solve.

> It starts with four fugues, two of which present the theme, the others presenting the theme in contrary motion (that is, back to front). Then there are counter fugues, in which the original subject is inverted (turned upside down) and combined with the original. There are double and triple fugues, several canons, three pairs of mirror fugues. To make the mirror reflection doubly realistic, the treble of the first fugue becomes the bass of the second fugue, the alto changes into a tenor, the tenor into an alto, and the bass into a treble, with the result that No. 12:2 appears like 12:1 standing on its head. (Schonberg, 1981, p. 43)

Certainly, few readers will understand what all of that means, but it does make a good case for including logical-mathematical intelligence in this chapter on music and movement!

The concept of musical, bodily-kinesthetic, and logical-mathematical intelligences suggests that our ability to produce and appreciate rhythm, pitch, and timbre while appreciating the many forms of musical expression and our ability to use our bodies and to handle objects skillfully, deserve to be nourished so that we can function at our fullest potential as human beings. According to Gardner, our success as adults in musical, bodily-kinesthetic, and logical-mathematical competency may have been helped or hindered by experiences during our early childhood years. Gardner challenges educators to recognize these separate intelligences and to nurture them as universal intelligences that serve important functions in children's cognitive, affective, social, and physical development.

## SUPPORTING CHILDREN'S INTELLIGENCES

As you prepare to guide young children in these areas of intelligence, remember to plan for a broad range of hands-on learning activities. Introduce your children to Marcel Marceau and the great tradition of mime. Show them how the artistic form of mime integrates body movement and the ability to use the body in expressive, nonverbal ways. Give your children crayons and paper, and encourage them to "draw" Pachelbel's *Canon in D*. Provide opportunities for children to use their bodies as a medium of expression. Let them dramatize or role-play stories or different outcomes to traditional folktales. Introduce physical awareness exercises, and use kinesthetic imagery to increase body awareness. Videotape the dances of your children, and allow them to watch and reflect on the dances they have created.

### Gardner's Message to Teachers

If we, as teachers, are to be committed to the development of all of a child's intelligences, we must provide music and movement activities as a means of fostering these important areas of human potential. To do anything less is to deny children an opportunity to function at their fullest. In a 1991 interview, Daniel Gursky (1991) quotes Gardner as saying, "To get teachers to think deeply about their strengths, their students' strengths, and how to achieve curricular goals while taking those strengths and different profiles seriously is a huge job. Teachers can't be expected to become 'multiple intelligence mavens' but they should know where to send students for help in, say, music or dance" (p. 42). Gardner's statement does not give us permission to assign musical and bodily-kinesthetic development solely to the music, dance, or physical education specialist. Music, movement, dance, physical awareness, and physical activities deserve the same natural assimilation in the early childhood curriculum as do storytelling and nap time.

## BASIC STAGES OF EARLY MUSICAL AND MOVEMENT DEVELOPMENT AND THE NATIONAL STANDARDS

Before you begin thinking about ways to plan and implement music and movement experiences for young children, it is important to have an understanding of the basic stages of early musical development and the national standards for music education. Figures 1–1, 1–2, and 1–3 provide a descriptive overview of musical development from birth through 5 years. Following these figures you will find the Music Educators National Conference (MENC) belief statement concerning the musical learning of young children.

### Figure 1–1   Listening and Moving to Music

**Birth to 4 Months**
*Awareness of music starts almost immediately.* The baby may show his early awareness by responding differently to different kinds of music; he quiets himself to a soothing lullaby and becomes more active when lively music is played.

**4 to 8 Months**
*Musical awareness becomes more active.* The baby now enjoys listening intently to all types of sounds in her environment. She begins showing more active awareness of musical sounds by turning her head or face toward the source of the music.

**10 to 18 Months**
*Expression of musical preferences begins.* The infant may begin indicating the types of music he likes best—many at this age prefer vocal to instrumental—as well as showing clear displeasure at music he does not like. He rocks or sways his hips to a familiar tune, although not necessarily in time with the music, and claps his hands to a pleasing song.

**18 Months to 2 Years**
*Exploration of musical sounds increases.* Sounds in her environment continue to captivate the toddler. Her developing language skills and increasing mobility allow her to seek out sounds that please her most. She may especially enjoy music on daily TV or radio programs or commercials and may watch with fascination as a family member plays a musical instrument.

**2 to 3 Years**
*Dance begins.* The toddler now attempts to "dance" to music by bending his knees in a bouncing motion, turning circles, swaying, swinging his arms, and nodding his head. He especially likes a marked rhythm, so band music, nursery songs, or catchy TV jingles may be favorites. He shows an increasing ability to keep time and to follow directions in musical games, which he loves. You'll also notice that he can now pay attention for longer periods. While easily distracted in the past, he can now lie or sit down quietly and listen for several minutes at a time.

**3½ to 4 Years**
*Self-expression through music increases.* At this stage, a very significant change takes place. As the child listens, she is increasingly aware of some of the components that make up her favorite music. She may love to dramatize songs and may also enjoy trying out different ways of interpreting music (for example, experimenting with different rhythms). She shows marked improvement in keeping the beat, although she is still not always entirely accurate. (Music is now an important means for her to express and communicate ideas and emotions that may be beyond her developing language skills.)

**4 to 5 Years**
*Ability to discuss musical experiences expands.* By now, the child can talk about what a piece of music suggests to him, and he is able to tell you in greater detail what he is hearing. This is the stage of the "active listener." With encouragement, the child's desire to listen to music will increase.

**5 to 6 Years**
*Actual coordinated dance movements begin.* The child's increased motor control and ability to synchronize his movements with the rhythm of the music are evident as one watches his attempts to dance. He can actually synchronize hand or foot tapping with music and can skip, hop on one foot, and make rhythmic dance movements to music. He may begin to show an interest in dance lessons.

## Figure 1–2    Singing

**Birth to 4 Months**
*Crying is a baby's first "musical" sound.* A baby's cries are her first and most important means of expressing early needs and feelings. They vary in pitch, loudness, and rhythmic patterns, making them musical in a very real sense. Gradually, she begins to experiment with other sounds; she coos, gurgles, squeals, and begins to "babble," repeating long strings of sound, such as "ba-ba-ba."

**6 to 18 Months**
*Babbling increases, taking on more pronounced musical characteristics.* As the baby continues to experiment with his voice, babbling becomes a favorite activity. As the infant's range of pitch, tone, and voice intensity widens, this activity comes to resemble song. Don't be surprised if at some point the baby is able to repeat the pitches you sing to him on exactly the same notes.

**18 Months to 3 Years**
*Real singing begins.* The baby's tuneful jabbering during play now sounds more like real song. She may chant a catchy rhyme, using nonsense syllables or even her own name as she plays, but she is still unable to sing a song like "Farmer in the Dell" completely accurately. She may join you in favorite nursery rhymes or songs; she especially enjoys familiar tunes and asks you to sing them repeatedly (Although she'll sing along with you or a family member, she's still hesitant to sing in front of other children and may balk at a solo performance in preschool.)

**3½ to 4 Years**
*Accuracy in matching simple tunes begins.* Now the youngster starts to approximate adult singing. He may spontaneously make up his own songs, although the words are often repetitive and the tune may closely resemble one he already knows.

**4 to 5 Years**
*Singing accuracy increases.* The child shows increased voice control and a closer approximation of pitch and rhythm. She may sing an entire song accurately. Sometimes she creates songs during play and may use these songs to tease others. She shows more responsiveness in group singing and may even enjoy taking a turn singing alone. She takes great pride in her ability to identify favorite melodies.

**5 Years and Older**
*Song repertoire expands; recognition and appreciation increase.* Most children now produce simple tunes accurately. The child's expanded vocal range should allow him to reach higher notes more easily, and his rhythmic accuracy is noticeably improved. He pays more attention to a song's "dynamics" and tempo and is able to add subtleties to its rendition, expressing meaning and emotion with his voice.

*Source:* Reprinted by author permission. Originally published in the March 1982 issue of PARENTS® Magazine reprinted with permission from Cohen, M.A. & Gross, P.J. (1979) THE DEVELOPMENTAL RESOURCE, VOL 2. New York: Grune and Stratton, Inc. 1979 Copyright. All rights reserved.

This overview of early musical development provides you with an important framework for developing goals for music and movement experiences with your children. Another very important point for you to consider in this process is the National Association for the Education of Young Children's position statement on developmentally appropriate practice.

## National Standards for Music Education

### Prekindergarten (Ages 2–4)
The years before children enter kindergarten are critical for their musical development. Young children need a rich musical environment in which to grow. The increasing number of child care centers, nursery schools, and early-intervention programs for children with disabilities and children at risk suggests that information should be available about the musical needs of infants and young children and standards for music should be established for these learning environments as well as for K–12 settings.

## Figure 1–3   Playing Musical Instruments

**6 to 9 Months**
*Baby enjoys creating sounds with any object available.* The infant's eye-hand coordination is rapidly improving. She loves to manipulate objects within reach and is fascinated with her newfound ability to make sounds with objects. She will tap, kick, or hit almost all objects with which she comes in contact, delighting in the sounds she creates.

**18 Months to 2 Years**
*Toddler seeks special objects to make sounds.* You may notice the toddler's repeated efforts to locate particular objects—pots and pans, cups, bowls, and other utensils—for his sound-making activities.

**2 to 3½ Years**
*Interest in real musical instruments increases.* At this stage, when the youngster is beginning to show interest in listening to musical instruments and recordings, provide her with toys that make interesting musical sounds, such as toy xylophones, drums, pipes, tambourines, or maracas. Musical toys needn't be expensive. In fact, you can easily make your own coffee-can drums, bottle-cap tambourines, soup-can shakers, or pot-cover cymbals.

**4 to 5 Years**
*A child begins experimenting with real musical instruments.* At this stage, the youngster can identify certain sounds made by selected instruments and can play many rhythm instruments, both to accompany songs or instrumental pieces he hears and to create tunes of his own. He may also enjoy trying out some of the instruments he has seen others play.

*Source:* Reprinted by author permission. Originally published in the March 1982 issue of PARENTS® Magazine reprinted with permission from Cohen, M.A. & Gross, P.J. (1979) THE DEVELOPMENTAL RESOURCE, VOL 2. New York: Grune and Stratton, Inc. 1979 Copyright. All rights reserved.

### MENC's Belief Statement[*]

1. All children have musical potential.
2. Children bring their own unique interests and abilities to the music learning environment.
3. Very young children are capable of developing critical thinking skills through musical ideas.
4. Children come to early-childhood music experiences from diverse backgrounds.
5. Children should experience exemplary musical sounds, activities, and materials.
6. Children should not be encumbered with the need to meet performance goals.
7. Children's play is their work.
8. Children learn best in pleasant physical and social environments.
9. Diverse learning environments are needed to serve the developmental needs of many individual children.
10. Children need effective adult models.

## Curriculum Guidelines

A music curriculum (National Association for Music Education, 1994) for young children should include many opportunities to explore sound through singing, moving, listening, and playing instruments, as well as introductory experiences with verbalization and visualization of musical ideas. The music literature included in the curriculum should be of high quality and lasting value, including traditional children's songs, folk songs, classical music, and music from a variety of cultures, styles, and time periods.

Play is the primary vehicle for young children's growth, and developmentally appropriate early music experiences should occur in child-initiated, child-directed,

---

[*]From *National Standards for Arts Education.* Copyright © 1994 by Music Educators National Conference (MENC). Used by permission. The complete National Arts Standards and additional materials relating to the Standards are available from MENC—National Association for Music Education, 1806 Robert Fulton Drive, Reston, VA 20191.

teacher-supported play environments. The teacher's role is to create a musically stimulating environment and then to facilitate children's engagement with music materials and activities by asking questions or making suggestions that stimulate children's thinking and further exploration.

Children also need group music time to experience the important social and musical aspects of sharing music and making music together. Ideally this should be delivered by either early childhood arts specialists employed as staff members in child care centers and preschools or by visiting music specialists with training in child development to provide musicality and creativity and to serve as models and consultants for the child care staff.

Effective music teaching should do the following:

1. Support the child's total development—physical, emotional, social, and cognitive
2. Recognize the wide range of normal development in prekindergartners and the need to differentiate their instruction
3. Facilitate learning through active interaction with adults and other children as well as with music materials
4. Consist of learning activities and materials that are real, concrete, and relevant to the lives of young children
5. Provide opportunities for children to choose from among a variety of music activities, materials, and equipment of varying degrees of difficulty
6. Allow children time to explore music through active involvement

## Assessment

Assessment provides special challenges. A substantial body of music education research has determined that young children know and understand much more about music than they can verbalize. Also, young children have not yet developed the ability to respond in a paper-and-pencil testing format. Another factor that affects their assessment is the very wide range of individual developmental differences displayed by young children.

Because of these characteristics, methods of assessment that are most appropriate to assess young children's music knowledge, skills, and attitudes include:

1. Checklists or anecdotal reports completed by teachers, parents, or aides to record and describe verbal and nonverbal behavior
2. Systematic observation documenting such behavior as time on task, number of instances of an event or behavior, and participation tendencies over time
3. Rating scales to provide data related to quality of responses, such as degrees of accuracy, originality, or involvement[*]

Finished products and correct solutions are not the only criteria for judging whether learning has occurred. Audiotaping and videotaping are recommended methods of gathering samples of children's musical behavior for assessment and of examining growth and development over time. In order to develop a profile of each child's musical responses, representative samples of assessment materials should be placed in a music portfolio that is maintained for each child, beginning with the child's entrance into an educational/child care setting and culminating with entrance into kindergarten.

---

*From *National Standards for Arts Education.* Copyright © 1994 by Music Educators National Conference (MENC). Used by permission. The complete National Arts Standards and additional materials relating to the Standards are available from MENC—National Association for Music Education, 1806 Robert Fulton Drive, Reston, VA 20191.

# DEVELOPMENTALLY APPROPRIATE PRACTICE

The concept of developmentally appropriate practice provides a clear description of appropriate practice for programs serving the full age span of early childhood. A summary of these important guidelines, as they relate to music, dance, and other musical experiences, is provided in Figure 1–4. Use this information to further your understanding of the role you play in providing musical experiences that match your children's developmental levels.

Remember that these developmentally appropriate practices represent the minimum that we should be doing to expand children's musical and movement experiences.

## Early Childhood Environment Rating Scale Revised

This important document, The Early Childhood Environment Rating Scale Revised (ECERS-R) (Harms et al., 2005) includes sections on gross motor play and music and movement. These are used to gauge program practice and where your program stands on providing indoor and outdoor gross motor play and encouraging development of singing, movement/dancing, and creativity. It mentions specific strategies such as making music available as free choice and group activity, inviting children to play instruments and encouraging children to make up new words to songs and move to music in new and creative ways.

# SELECTING SONGS, FINGERPLAYS, AND INSTRUMENTS

Singing songs, moving to music, and transforming little fingers into birds, rabbits, or falling rain form the basis for many types of musical expression. Young children who have positive and pleasurable experiences with rhythm and movement will want to repeat these experiences. Young children sing spontaneously while they play. They make up nonsense chants and songs as they experiment with variations in rhythm, pitch, and volume: Jane listens as her teacher magically transforms his fingers into

### Figure 1–4    Developmentally Appropriate Practice

- Teachers must sing with the children, do fingerplays, and take part in acting out simple stories like "The Three Bears" with children participating actively.
- Adults have to structure the physical environment to provide plenty of space and time indoors and outdoors for children to explore and exercise such large-muscle skills as running, jumping, galloping, or catching a ball. We also need to stay close by to offer assistance as needed. The old days of the teacher sitting in a chair during outdoor activity has, fortunately, disappeared.
- Adults in the classroom provide many experiences and opportunities to extend children's language and musical abilities. We introduce children to nursery rhymes and fingerplays; encourage children to sing songs and listen to recordings; facilitate children's play of circle and movement games such as "London Bridge," "The Farmer in the Dell," and "Ring Around the Rosie;" and present simple rhythm instruments as real instruments.
- Children must have daily opportunities for aesthetic expression and appreciation through hearing a variety of musical forms and compositions.

*Source:* From C. Copple and S. Bredekamp (Eds.), 2009, *Developmentally appropriate practice in early childhood programs* (Rev. ed.). Washington, DC: National Association for the Education of Young Children.

Drums are usually children's favorite instrument. One child told me that she feels special playing the drums.

two little blackbirds, one named Jack and one named Jill. She attends to the story line and the actions of this fingerplay and begins to respond with a few words and finger movements of her own. When she moves to the outdoor classroom, she lifts her arms and flies around the play yard singing, "This is Jack, and this is Jill!"

This 4-year-old finds intrinsic pleasure in learning a new fingerplay, and the enthusiasm of her teacher and his seriousness about the process have transcended circle time. A simple fingerplay has become a part of this child's universal experience—in this case, that of flying around the play yard.

## Singing with Young Children

Songs for toddlers should be short, easy to sing, and have a steady beat. Songs should also have a lot of repetition, as these children will often remember the chorus of a song long before they learn all the words to the verse. When pitching songs for young children, be sure that the range is well within their vocal abilities. Try pitching songs in the range between middle C up to G, a fifth above. If you don't know where middle C is located on the piano keyboard, find someone in your class who can find middle C on a piano, or ask your professor to show you how to find a middle C chord on an autoharp. Or find a piano and, beginning at the far left of the keyboard, count the white keys until you get to the 24th white key—this is middle C!

As children develop their singing voices, their range extends, sometimes by as much as an octave above and below middle C. Remember that even if you don't like your singing voice, you can still introduce and sing songs with your children. There are not many of us who have beautifully trained singing voices, so if you don't relish the idea of strumming a guitar as you sing to a group of children, you are most likely in the majority! Your children will always be more interested in the interaction than they are in your perfectly pitched, or unpitched, singing voice.

Young children enjoy a variety of songs and especially seem to like songs that have personal meaning, such as songs about their names, body parts, clothes, feelings, and special occasions like birthdays. Songs about children's interests—home and family, things that happen at school, and animals and pets—are appealing. Songs about animals, in which children can imitate or make animal sounds, capture children's interest and encourage them to become involved in singing activities.

It is very important for you to have a large repertoire of songs and chants available "in the moment." Teachers must constantly search for new songs and fingerplays, as they are an invaluable resource in the day-to-day happenings in the early childhood classroom.

## Selecting Songs for Singing

Out of the hundreds of songs that you can introduce to children, several categories of songs are used most often in the early childhood classroom. You might consider learning songs from the following categories before your singing debut with young children. For your children, singing and moving must be a purely pleasurable experience and not a "teaching method" for activating budding young composers or maestros.

### Old Traditional and Folk Songs

Many traditional and folk songs come to us from all around the world, and most tell a story or convey a simple message that children can understand. Some favorites include the following:

**WHERE IS THUMBKIN?**

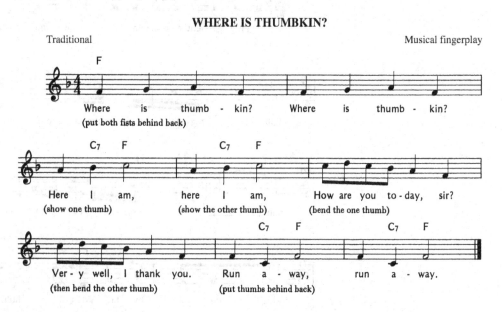

2. Where is pointer? (forefinger)
3. Where is tall man? (middle finger)
4. Where is ring man? (ring finger)
5. Where is pinkie? (little finger)

*Movement concept:* Development of small muscles
*Musical concept:* Matching measures that sound the same

## HEY, DIDDLE, DIDDLE

Mother Goose                                                                 J. W. ELLIOTT

Hey, did-dle, did-dle, The cat and the fid-dle, The cow jump'd o-ver the moon;  The

lit-tle dog laughed to see such sport, And the dish ran a-way with the spoon.

The Mother Goose rhyme is full of good humor. Hold the child, and gently sway back and forth while singing the rhyme. On the word *jump'd*, take one jump. On the phrase "And the dish ran away with the spoon," take running steps in time to the music.

## FROGGIE WENT A-COURTIN'

American folk song                                                    Arranged by K. BAYLESS

Frog-gie went a-court-in' and    he did ride,  uh    huh,      uh

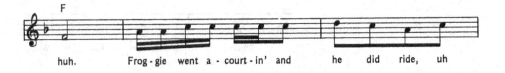

huh.       Frog-gie  went a-court-in'  and       he  did  ride,  uh

huh,_____      Frog-gie went a-court-in' and      he did ride____

Sword  and  pis-tol    by  his  side, uh   huh,    uh   huh.

**2**
He rode right up to Miss Mouse's door, uh huh, uh huh.
He rode right up to Miss Mouse's door, uh huh.
He rode right up to Miss Mouse's door,
Where he'd been many times before, uh huh, uh huh.

**3**
He took Miss Mousey on his knee, uh huh, uh huh.
He took Miss Mousey on his knee, uh huh.
He took Miss Mousey on his knee,
And said, "Miss Mousey will you marry me?" uh huh, uh huh.

**4**
"Without my Uncle Rat's consent, uh huh, uh huh . . .
I wouldn't marry the President," uh huh, uh huh.

**5**
"Where shall the wedding supper be?" uh huh, uh huh . . .
"Way down yonder in the hollow tree," uh huh, uh huh.

**6**
"What shall the wedding supper be?" uh huh, uh huh . . .
"Two green beans and a black-eyed pea," uh huh, uh huh.

**7**
First one in was a bumblebee, uh huh, uh huh . . .
Who danced a jig with a two-legged flea, uh huh, uh huh.

**8**
They all sailed off across the lake, uh huh, uh huh . . .
Got swallowed up by a big black snake, uh huh, uh huh.

**9**
There's corn and cheese upon the shelf, uh huh, uh huh . . .
If you want more verses just sing them yourself, uh huh, uh huh.

### Nursery Rhymes

The melodies of nursery rhymes are always favorites of young children. Because of their simple and catchy melodies, they are easy to sing and most appropriate for the young child.

## TWINKLE, TWINKLE, LITTLE STAR

Traditional

The moon and the stars are wonders to be enjoyed at an early age. Young children are particularly fascinated to look out of a window and see the yellow moon and shining stars. This is a delightful rhyme to sing at nighttime.

Show the child how to wiggle the fingers as the song is sung. In time, the child will imitate the movement. On the words "Up above the world so high," point a finger to the stars in the sky.

## LONDON BRIDGE

Mother Goose

English singing game
Arranged by K. BAYLESS

Happily

1. Lon - don Bridge is fall - ing down, fall - ing down, fall - ing down,

Lon - don Bridge is fall - ing down, my fair la - dy.

2. Build it up with iron bars,
3. Iron bars will bend and break,
4. Build it up with gold and silver,
5. Gold and silver I've not got,
6. Here's a prisoner I have got,

7. What'll you take to set him free,
8. One hundred pounds will set him free,
9. One hundred pounds we have not got,
10. Then off to prison he must go,

Two children are chosen to make an arch; they raise their arms above their heads to make a bridge for the other children to pass under. These two children secretly decide which one represents silver and which one gold. The other children then pass under the bridge as the song is sung. At the words "My fair lady," the bridge falls. The child who is caught is asked which he prefers, gold or silver. This child then stands behind the one who represents his choice. The game continues until all the children have been chosen.

### *Lullabies*

Lullabies are wonderful for quieting and calming children after active periods or before nap time. They are also useful when encouraging children to imagine that they are rocking a little bunny or a baby doll to sleep. It's very special to sing lullabies to children and watch their sweet eyes close for some much-needed sleep.

## HUSH LITTLE BABY

Alabama Folk Song

1. Hush lit - tle ba - by don't say a word,
(or baby's name)

Ma - ma's gon - na buy you a mock - ing bird.

2. If that mocking bird won't sing, Mama's gonna buy you a diamond ring.
3. If that diamond ring turns to brass, Mama's gonna buy you a looking glass.
4. If that looking glass gets broke, Mama's gonna buy you a billy goat.
5. If that billy goat won't pull, Mama's gonna buy you a cart and bull.
6. If that cart and bull turn over, Mama's gonna buy you a dog named Rover.
7. If that dog named Rover won't bark, Mama's gonna buy you a horse and cart.
8. If that horse and cart fall down, You'll be the sweetest girl in town.

### Fingerplays and Action Songs

Fingerplays are, in a sense, a type of rhythmic improvisation. They have strong appeal to young children because there is usually repetition of melody, words, and phrases. There seems to be some magic in transforming a tiny finger into a "Thumbkin" or a rabbit, or "shaking all about" during "The Hokey Pokey." In fingerplays and action songs, the words provide suggestions or directions on what, how, when, and where to move. In general, children enjoy the continuity of hearing and playing with the fingerplays and action songs from the beginning to the end. If the fingerplays are short (or led by a teacher) and action songs are simple and repetitive, children can learn the actions or movements after doing them a few times. With longer action songs and fingerplays, it is still important that children first hear the entire song. When children are familiar with the content, lyrics, and melody, you can always divide the song or fingerplay into smaller, more manageable parts. Echo chants and fingerplays, such as "Let's Go on a Bear Hunt," are very easy for children to respond to because they are led by the teacher. The teacher chants a phrase, and the children chant it back. Echo chants are popular among young children because all they have to remember is one short line or simple phrase.

Fingerplays and other action songs can relate to curriculum development and can be used to enhance a young child's understanding of concepts. For example, the action chant "Let's Go on a Bear Hunt" reinforces the concepts of under, over, around, and through. At the same time, action songs and fingerplays that directly relate to the children can provide personal, concrete experiences that are relevant and meaningful to the young child. "Where Is Thumbkin?" is an all-time favorite of young children. It is their fingers and arms that are the center of attention and the stars of the play.

Fingerplays and songs that encourage full-body movement are also helpful when it comes to transition times. "Teddy Bear, Teddy Bear, Turn Around" can be used to redirect children's energies when they need help to calm them down during transitions. The movement is fun, and children pick up cues from the words and move through transitions with ease and pleasure. The process is so much gentler to young children than ringing a bell or switching the lights off and on.

*"Teddy Bear, Teddy Bear"*

Teddy Bear, Teddy Bear,
Turn around,
Teddy Bear, Teddy Bear,
Touch the ground.
Teddy Bear, Teddy Bear,
Tie your shoe,
Teddy Bear, Teddy Bear,
That will do.
Teddy Bear, Teddy Bear,
Climb the stairs,
Teddy Bear, Teddy Bear,
Say your prayers.
Teddy Bear, Teddy Bear,
Turn off the light,
Teddy Bear, Teddy Bear,
Say Good Night.

The traditional song "Come Follow Me in a Line, in a Line" is a delightful little tune that can also be used to assist children through transition periods. The teacher moves through a group of children while singing or chanting the verse in Pied Piper fashion and, one by one, touches the head of each child. As the children are touched, they join one hand and follow the teacher until they are all in a long, connected line. This is especially effective for moving children into a circle or a different area of the classroom. This calm process of forming a line and moving to a repetitive song allows you and your children to gather together or form a circle without the confusion that this request often causes!

### COME FOLLOW ME IN A LINE, IN A LINE

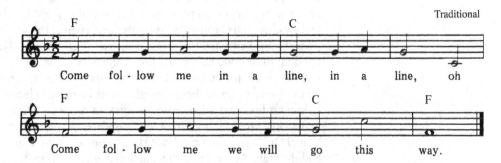

It is very important that we not limit the use of fingerplays and action songs to very young children. Children's abilities to elaborate and expand their movements, actions, and singing abilities increase with age and experience. Three-year-olds may sing or chant short melodic songs informally as they move through an activity. These young children may not remember all the words or even understand the exact meaning of some words, but they often remember the feeling they experienced during a song or fingerplay.

For the older child, fingerplays and songs offer great potential for learning new words, rhyming, and alliteration; developing language and verbal skills; and forming concepts. Teachers can also use songs and fingerplays to expand children's awareness of tempo, accent, rhythmic patterns, and intensity, all of which are part of the language and reading process.

Before using fingerplays and action songs with young children, you must learn and practice the words and movements until they are committed to memory. Fingerplays, especially, should involve a warm, intimate exchange between you and your children. This atmosphere can be lost if you have to read or refer to written notes during the play. You must be enthusiastic about sharing fingerplays and action songs with your children and must be involved with both the play and your children. Learn and practice a few fingerplays until you are totally familiar with the words and actions. Once you are comfortable with the words and actions, you can present them with the warmth, naturalness, and spontaneity needed to give them excitement and life.

Feel free to change or revise the basic forms to create your own versions or to accommodate the ages or abilities of your children. Approaching action songs and fingerplays from this perspective will allow you to use your own creative abilities and should limit the potential stereotyping of having all of your children doing the exact same thing at the same time. Your children should make their "Eensy Weensy Spider" move the way they want it to move. And, if you'll think about it, all children shake their "Hokey Pokey" in individual and different ways!

# MUSIC INSTRUMENTS FOR YOUNG CHILDREN

Making music by playing instruments can be one of the most exciting parts of the musical experience. Children are responsive to musical instruments, and they love to experiment with the different sounds and tone qualities of sticks, drums, cymbals, bells, and a variety of other instruments. Rhythm instruments, which are real musical instruments, provide rich and varied opportunities for young children to focus on creative exploration. Each instrument is different, they are simple to use, and they can be played in many interesting ways.

## Appreciating Musical Instruments

While it is important for children to be free to manipulate and experiment with instruments, it is equally as important that we, their teachers, provide guidance and structure when introducing instruments. One of the first things that we must do is adopt the attitude that percussion and tuned instruments are real instruments. All major symphony orchestras use drums, triangles, bells, and other instruments in the traditional early childhood rhythm band sets.

Each instrument in your commercial rhythm band set can produce a distinctive and unique sound quality. Tuned instruments, such as resonator bells, have their own particular rich and resonating tone qualities. Young children stand ready to model our behavior and take our word on things, and our treatment of instruments and our attitude toward them can have a lasting effect on the way children handle and play all instruments.

Introduce one instrument at a time. If possible, have several identical instruments so that all of your children can explore and discover what sounds the instrument can make and how to produce these sounds. Young children are not good at waiting. They want to play the instrument now! Encourage your children to try different ways to produce sounds. Give them the time they need to get to know the instrument. If you have only one set of instruments, try placing an instrument in a music center and introducing it as a small-group activity.

By introducing instruments one at a time, you allow your children to develop a musical sensitivity to each instrument gradually. When children have experimented with several instruments, you can encourage them to make rhythmic patterns or melodies. Give your children this type of respectful introduction to musical instruments. You will be opening an avenue for them to respond to rhythm, tone, melody, and harmony—an avenue to music. Figure 1–5 illustrates and explains the rhythm instruments that are appropriate for use with young children.

While the music and movement ideas presented earlier are good ways of getting you and your children started on the road to a music program, you should also consider some of the excellent recordings available. One advantage of using compact discs is that the songs are usually grouped and classified for specific purposes. It would be impossible to provide you with a complete list of what is suitable and available for use in the early childhood classroom, but you will find many suggestions throughout the book.

Give children music made all around the world as a way of beginning a lifetime discovery of other cultures and countries, from the reggae of Jamaica to the jigs and reels of Ireland to the zydeco of Louisiana. A wide variety of music and movement from across the globe can be a springboard for children's introduction to multicultural education in the classroom. Later in this book, you'll be introduced to many music and movement activities from cultures on opposite sides of the globe.

**Figure 1–5    Instruments for Young Children**

 *Triangles* are suspended from a cord so they hang freely. Strike them gently with a metal striker. The triangle produces a lovely, bright sound.

 *Claves* are thick, polished sticks made of hardwood. Place one clave in the palm of your hand, and strike it with the other clave.

 *Rhythm sticks* are played in pairs. They can be smooth or serrated. Play them by holding one rhythm stick and striking it with the other, or rub one along the ridges of the other. Rhythm sticks are wonderful for keeping time or, when appropriate, helping children maintain a steady beat.

 *Wood blocks* are small, hollow blocks of wood that produce a resonant sound. Strike the wood block lightly with a wooden or hard rubber mallet.

 *Maracas* are made from gourds (or hard plastic) and are filled with seeds or pebbles. Shake them sharply, at intervals, to produce rhythm. Maintain steady shaking for continuous sound.

 *Drums* produce many different sounds, depending on how they are played. Drums can be played with your fingers, hand, or knuckles or with a drumstick or mallet. Drums sound best when struck with a quick bouncy touch so that the drumhead can reverberate.

 *Sand blocks* are small wooden blocks covered with coarse sandpaper or emery cloth. Hold them by the handle or knob and rub them together.

 *Jingle bells* mounted on sticks can be shaken vigorously or tapped rhythmically against your palm. Other types of jingle bells are mounted on plastic or fabric and can be shaken by hand or attached to an ankle or wrist.

 *Tambourines* are a favorite of young children. They are circular frames of wood or plastic with a plastic or skin drumhead and small sets of jingles fastened around the frame. You can strike the head with your hand or finger, shake the tambourine to hear the jingles, or combine both actions.

**Figure 1–5   Continued**

*Finger cymbals* produce delightfully delicate sounds. Put one on a finger of each hand and bring them together to lightly chime the finger cymbals. You can also put one finger cymbal on your thumb and another on your middle finger of the same hand and strike them together.

*Cymbals* are usually made of brass and have handles or straps. Cymbals produce their best tone when they are struck while being moved in a vertical motion. Hold one cymbal slightly higher than the other, bring it down, and let it strike the lower one. You may want to practice playing cymbals and master the technique of producing a pleasant-sounding ring before you introduce cymbals to children. If your children can hear the lovely tone cymbals can make, they may be more inclined to respect them as a real musical instrument.

*Resonator bells* are played with a mallet and can provide children with experiences in pitch, melody, and harmony. Because resonator bells are tuned, children can experiment with an accurately pitched instrument while working out patterns and melodies.

*Orff instruments* were originally designed by German composer Carl Orff. Although these high-quality instruments are expensive, they are a wonderful addition to an early childhood environment. They produce beautiful, pure tones. The lowest pitched instrument, the metallophone, produces rich alto and bass tones. The bars are made of thick metal. The bars of the xylophone are made of hardwood. They are removable and can be taken apart and changed for different tonal patterns. The glockenspiel is the highest pitched instrument. The metal bars are also removable, and they produce a bright, soprano tone. Very young children may have difficulty playing the glockenspiel because of the small size, but 4- and 5-year-olds, as well as older children, will enjoy striking the bars and hearing the crisp, clear tones.

*Autoharps* can be valuable if you consider yourself to be a nonmusical teacher. You don't need special musical training to play an autoharp. It is a stringed instrument that can be played either by holding it flat on your lap or in an upright position. You strum the autoharp while pressing the buttons. Each button has a letter, or musical notation, that corresponds to the chords you are playing. Most music includes chord notation in the form of letters above the music bar. Follow the letter notation as you press the corresponding button while strumming the autoharp. Your children can learn to play the autoharp, too, so don't be afraid to let them explore all the chords, sounds, and sensory impressions the autoharp provides.

## Classical Music and Children

Musical experiences for young children must include classical music in addition to the music we usually associate with the early childhood classroom. Some children in your classroom may be growing up in homes where classical music is played and appreciated. These children are indeed fortunate. For those children who are growing up on a minimal musical diet of contemporary genres you may be the only resource for extending their musical experiences and the appreciation that comes from exposure to classical music. Research indicates that early association with classical music can increase children's enjoyment of music as an art form and increase children's aesthetic awareness (Cecil & Lauritzen, 1994).

E'mile Jaques-Dalcroze (1865–1950), a Swiss composer and harmony professor at the Geneva Conservatory at the turn of the century, thought of movement as a way of using the body as a "musical instrument" and believed that body movement was a counterpart to musical expression. He further believed that early musical intelligence could be encouraged by using one's body in conjunction with musical responsiveness. This understanding can be facilitated by drawing on the "universal language" of classical music: "Music is significant for us as human beings principally because it embodies movement of a specifically human type that goes to the roots of our being and takes shape in the inner gestures which embody our deepest and most intimate responses" (Jaques-Dalcroze, 1921, p. 129).

Classical music can be naturally infused into the early childhood classroom in a variety of ways, from playing Bach's *Preludes* during quiet activities to marching around the room to the "March of the Toys" from Herbert's *Babes in Toyland*.

Classical music comes in all forms, shapes, and sizes, and a few of the different styles available to you and your children are mentioned here. In addition to the symphony, there are sonatas, string quartets, concertos, concertinas, trios, and dances—and let's not forget opera. Opera has increased in popularity through the years, probably because the combination of music, movement, and speech are inseparably presented in ways that seem to touch our humanity. When opera is mentioned to students, they are often unexcited about studying opera because of lack of exposure or unpleasant experience. No one expects you to become an opera fan or that you introduce opera to your children in any formal kind of way. However, give yourself a gentle nudge and do not discount the idea of playing opera as quiet background music in your classroom. Children may not even notice that you have included a different type of music into your musical selections, but nevertheless you will have broadened their exposure

Children are usually responsive to musical instruments and love to experiment with different sounds and tone qualities.

to yet another classical form. Many years ago, after hearing selections from *Madame Butterfly* on several occasions during quiet time, a 5-year-old went up to the teacher and said that the lady's voice made her sleepy! What more could a kindergarten teacher ask for during quiet time?

Figure 1–6 lists some favorite instrumental classical music recordings that may be useful as you begin to build your own musical library, both for your personal enjoyment and for the listening pleasure of your children. These can be found on inexpensive compact discs, and the sound quality is exceptionally good. These are not listed in any particular priority, so when you approach the classical section of your local music store, select the titles that suggest your own sensitivity to the possibilities these recordings may hold for you.

Classical music must be played in early childhood classrooms right along with Raffi and Ella Jenkins. As McGirr tells us, "Too often, early childhood programs use only children's music, nursery rhymes, fingerplays and light, short humorous pieces, all played mainly on popular instruments. Young children are capable of much more sophisticated listening" (1995, p. 75). Exposure to classical music affords children unique opportunities to enjoy a whole complement of musical experiences and puts them in touch with a wide range of musical expression. Research indicates that early association with classical music can increase children's enjoyment of music as an art form and increase children's aesthetic awareness (Cecil & Lauritzen, 1994). Without

## Figure 1–6   Your Classical Music Collection: Suggested Recordings

**Wolfgang Amadeus Mozart.** *Symphony no. 39 in E-flat* and *Symphony no. 41 in C. no. 39 in E-flat,* the first of Mozart's greatest trilogy, is dated June 26, 1788. Within the space of only six weeks, Mozart composed his last three symphonies, and *no. 39* is the only one of the three to take full advantage of clarinets. It is composed of an "Adagio," "Allegro," "Andante," "Menuetto," and "Finale." *No. 41 in C* is dated August 10, 1788. It is believed that Mozart knew this was to be his last symphony. The last movement seems to express with absolute finality all that Mozart could wish to say through the medium of the full orchestra.

**Frederic Chopin.** *Sonata no. 3, op. 58.* This sonata is for those of us who love piano music. Robert Schumann wrote this about Chopin's *Sonata no. 3, op. 58:* "The idea of calling it a sonata is a caprice, if not a jest, for he has simply bound together four of his most reckless children" (Van Cliburn, 1992). However, George Sand said, "The self-sufficing coherence he achieved in this work marks him as a master who knew precisely what he was doing" (Van Cliburn, 1992). There is intense beauty and power in this piece that accumulates fantastic momentum and rushes to the crowning point with immense boldness and brilliance. The coda fulfills the work with a fiery conclusion!

**Ludwig van Beethoven.** *String Quartet no. 3 in D Major* and *String Quartet no. 4 in C Minor.* The string quartet has four parts so a composer has enough lines to fashion a full musical form; there is not much to spare for "padding." Beethoven was a long-term planner and follower-through of highly organized musical composition, and his string quartets, as his sketchbooks show, are filled with almost superhuman laboriousness. In the life work that came from four decades of compositional toil, he completed sixteen string quartets.

**Johann Sebastian Bach.** *Brandenburg Concertos nos. 1–6.* Bach was a composer of the Baroque period. At the head of an orchestra, he was a dominating figure and score reader. His hearing was so fine that he was able to detect even the slightest error in a large orchestra: "While conducting, he would sing, play his own part, keep the rhythm steady, and cue everybody in, the one with a nod, another by tapping with his feet, the third with a warning finger, holding everybody together, taking precautions everywhere and repairing any unsteadiness, full of rhythm in every part of his body." His vision was the greatest, his technique unparalleled, his harmonic sense frightening in its power, expression, and ingenuity. The *Brandenburg Concertos* are pronounced in the qualities of who Bach was as a person. They are filled with mysticism, exuberance, complexity, decoration, allegory, distortion, and exploitation of the grandiose (Schonberg, 1981). If you don't already own a recording of the *Brandenburg Concertos,* you must discover how all these qualities are represented in his music.

exposure to the great classical composers and their music, we cannot expect children to develop an appreciation for *all* music. Furthermore, without this opportunity, some children may not find out that classical music exists until they are young adults and find themselves in a college-level music appreciation class. We must encourage even the youngest children to listen to a variety of music, including classical, if we want them to develop musical appreciation in the broadest context.

*Music is your own experience, your thoughts,*
*your wisdom. If you don't live it, it won't come out your horn.*
*They teach you there's a boundary line to music.*
*But, man, there's no boundary line to art.*

—Charlie Parker

## REFERENCES

Boutte, G. (2000). Multiculturalism: Moral and educational implications. *Dimensions of Early Childhood, 28*(3), 9–16.

Cecil, N., & Lauritzen, P. (1994). *Literacy and the arts for the integrated classroom: Alternative ways of knowing.* New York, NY: Longman.

Chenfeld, M. (1978). *Teaching language arts creatively.* New York, NY: Harcourt Brace Jovanovich.

Copple, C., & Bredekamp, S. (Eds.). (2009). *Developmentally appropriate practice in early childhood programs* (Rev. ed.). Washington, DC: National Association for the Education of Young Children.

Deiner, P. L. (1983). *Resources for teaching young children with special needs.* New York, NY: Harcourt Brace Jovanovich.

Edwards, L. E., & Nabors, M. (1993). The creative arts process: What it is and what it is not. *Young Children, 48*(3), 77–81.

Gardner, H. (1973). *The arts and human development.* New York, NY: Wiley.

Gursky, D. (1991, November–December). The unschooled mind. *Teacher,* 38–44.

Harms, T., Clifford, R., & Cryer, D. (2005). *Early childhood environment rating scale* (Rev. ed.). New York, NY: Teachers College Press.

Hymes, J. L. (1981). *Teaching the child under six.* Columbus, OH: Merrill.

Jaques-Dalcroze, E. (1921). *Rhythm, music, and education.* New York, NY: Putnam.

Jenkins, E. (1995). Music is culture. *Scholastic Early Childhood Today, 9,* 40–42.

Jordan, S. (2001). *Lullabies around the world.* Sara Jordan Publishing, a division of Jordan Music Publications, Inc. Supported by the Government of Canada through the Canada Book Fund (CBF), an initiative of the Ontario Media Development Corporation.

McGirr, P. I. (1995). Verdi invades the kindergarten. *Childhood Education, 71,* 74–79.

Metz, E. (1989). Music and movement environments in preschool settings. In B. Andress (Ed.), *Promising practices in prekindergarten music* (pp. 89–96). Reston, VA: Music Educators National Conference.

Music Educators National Conference. (1994). *National standards for music education.* Reston, VA: Author.

National Association for Music Education. (1994). Reston, VA. www.menc.org/resources/view/performance-standards.

Puckett, M., & Diffily, D. (1999). *Teaching young children.* New York, NY: Harcourt Brace College.

Reninger, R. D. (2000). Ella Jenkins: The perennial music maker. *Teaching Music, 8*(1), 40–44.

Saul, J. D., & Saul, B. (2001). Multicultural activities throughout the year. *Multicultural Education, 8*(4), 38–40.

Schonberg, H. C. (1981). *The lives of the great composers* (Rev. ed.). New York, NY: Norton.

Seefeldt, C. (2005). *Social studies for the preschool/primary child* (7th ed.). Upper Saddle River, NJ: Pearson.

Van der Linde, C. H. (1999). The relationship between play and music in early childhood: Educational insights. *Genetic, Social, and General Psychology Monographs, 119,* 2–8.

Various artists. (1994). *Happy Chanukah Songs* [CD]. Toronto, ON, Canada: Madacy.

# CHAPTER TWO

# Music and Movement
# for Young Children

*We should consider every day lost in which
we have not danced at least once . . .*

Friedrich Nietzsche (1844–1900)

*There are many music and movement experiences that are appropriate for young children. Children move their bodies in expressive ways, they dance to the beat of the rhythms they hear, and they sing with spontaneity unmatched by even the most melodic adult voices. Music and movement activities fill the early childhood classroom with radiant happy faces and laughing, joyful children. This section explores music and movement for young children and introduces several aspects of music and movement, including dance, singing, playing instruments, dramatic movement, and action songs.*

## CHILDHOOD OBESITY AND PHYSICAL INACTIVITY

The American Heart Association (AHA) has a caption that should catch the eye of every early childhood education teacher: "CAUTION: CHILDREN NOT AT PLAY." The AHA reports on the amount of time that children spend running and playing, or rather not running and playing, and how often children sit in front of the television. We know from the research that about 25% to 30% of American school-aged children are overweight, which places them at risk for disease (e.g., Type II diabetes) and low self-esteem (National Institute Health Care Management [NIHCM] Foundation, 2004). We also know that 40% of 5- to 8-year-olds show at least one heart disease risk factor, including obesity, which has been associated with television viewing. "Children who watch the most television during childhood had the greatest increase in body fat over time" (Proctor et al., 2003). Several recent studies have reported successful school-based and family-based interventions to reduce obesity through less television use and increased activity (Epstein, Paluch, Gordy, & Dorn, 2000; Robinson, 2000; Robinson, 1999).

The preschool years have been identified as a crucial time to determine the causes of childhood obesity (Dietz, 1997). "Obesity" is defined as an excessively high amount of body fat in relation to lean body mass (National Research Council, 1989). The global rise of childhood obesity rates represents a critical public health problem. Early childhood educators must work with parents and families of preschool and early primary children to reduce the risk of obesity and the subsequent risk of adult chronic diseases (Proctor et al., 2003). The good news is that studies involving preschool-aged children have shown physical activity is protective of accelerated weight gain and inversely associated with change in body fatness (Klesges, Klesges, Eck, & Shelton, 1995; Moore, Nguyen, Rothman, Cupples, & Ellison, 1995). How are these studies being translated into action to prevent childhood obesity? The following sections discuss current programs designed to address this public health issue. The National Diabetes Education Program, The National Institutes of Health, and Kaiser Permanente have developed community tools and resources for children and families to lower their risk for obesity through healthier lifestyles. This research has shown that engaging in community-wide health education practices can impact healthy behaviors. The components of these programs can be modified by the early childhood educator in schools and communities (Moore, McGowan, Donato, Kollipara, & Roubideaux, 2009). The Centers for Disease Control and Prevention have explored the relationship between childhood obesity and school type by examining the National School Lunch Program and School Breakfast Program eligibility. This research project has specific recommendations for ideas to address childhood obesity (Li & Hooker, 2010).

## Head Start: I Am Moving, I Am Learning

In 2011 the Office of Head Start began nationwide training in I Am Moving, I Am Learning (IM/IL). This program is a proactive approach for addressing childhood obesity in Head Start children. The goals of IM/IL are to:

1. Increase the quantity of time spent in moderate to vigorous physical activities (MVPA) during the daily routine to meet national guidelines for physical activity
2. Improve the quality of structured movement activities intentionally facilitated by teachers and adults
3. Improve healthy food choices for children every day

IM/IL was created in response to regional and national trends toward childhood obesity. The project is designed to fit within the Head Start Performance Standards and the Head Start Child Outcomes Framework through enhancements, chosen by the individual Head Start program, to current teaching practices by providing more focused guidance on quality movement, gross and fine motor development, and child nutrition. Additionally, IM/IL goes beyond the classroom teaching practices to enhance the approach family service workers take with Head Start families in the area of movement and nutrition as well as in the approach Head Start health staff takes in working with children and their families. A comprehensive report of the most recent results of this study is available at the Office of Head Start website, www.hhs.gov.

So, what else must we do for our children? How can physical activity and nutrition change this pattern of obesity and encourage a healthy lifestyle for young children?

## Let's Move!

First Lady Michelle Obama is addressing this question through her Let's Move! obesity campaign program. "The physical and emotional health of an entire generation and the economic health and security of our nation is at stake," states Obama (Let's Move!, 2011).

The Let's Move! campaign will combat the epidemic of childhood obesity through a comprehensive approach that builds on effective strategies, and mobilizes public and private sector resources. Let's Move! engages every sector impacting the health of children to achieve the national goal, and provides schools, families, and communities simple tools to help children be more active, eat better, and get healthy.

To support Let's Move! and facilitate and coordinate partnerships with states, communities, and the nonprofit and for-profit private sectors, the nation's leading children's health foundations have come together to create a new independent foundation—the Partnership for a Healthier America—which will accelerate existing efforts addressing childhood obesity and facilitate new commitments toward the national goal of solving childhood obesity within a generation. Let's Move! is comprehensive, collaborative, and community-oriented and will include strategies to address the various factors that lead to childhood obesity. It will foster collaboration among the leaders in government, medicine and science, business, education, athletics, community organizations, and more. And it takes into account how life is really lived in communities across the country—encouraging, supporting, and pursuing solutions that are tailored to children and families facing a wide range of challenges and life circumstances. Already, the private sector is responding.

Mrs. Obama's campaign is being supported by the Wal-Mart Corporation. She said Wal-Mart's plans have "the potential to transform the marketplace and help Americans put healthier foods on their tables every day" (Jalonick & D'Innocenzio, 2011). Mrs. Obama lent star power to Wal-Mart Stores, Inc. executives as they announced the effort in Washington as part of her campaign against obesity. To start, the company plans to concentrate on products such as lunch meats, fruit juices, and salad dressings, which are high in sugar and sodium but that consumers don't realize they're consuming. They also plan to reduce sodium by 25% and cut added sugars in some of its store-based products by 2015, and to remove remaining industrially produced trans fats and develop a logo for products that meet its criteria for health.

Included in the Let's Move! campaign are helpful tips and step-by-step strategies for families, schools, and communities to help children be more active, eat better, and grow up healthy—essential components of the campaign. Seven of these strategies are as follows:

1. *Parents:* Parents and caregivers can set a great example for the whole family by creating a healthy environment at home. Making fruits and vegetables part of every meal, limiting treats, walking and playing, even shopping together—any combination of steps can add up to make a real difference and help build healthy habits for life.

2. *Schools:* Principals, teachers, and parents can help make schools healthier places to learn by providing quality nutrition, integrating physical activity during the school day, and teaching children about the importance of embracing a healthy active lifestyle.

3. *Community leaders:* Neighborhood organizations and faith-based groups are well positioned to initiate and coordinate activities to encourage healthy living and well-being. Trusted leaders in communities and congregations can empower families and communities to make better choices to improve the health of our nation's children.

4. *Elected officials:* Elected officials offer the unique ability to spur action and bring communities together in this movement. Mayors and municipal officials are encouraged to adopt a long-term, sustainable, and holistic approach to fighting childhood obesity. This movement recognizes that every city is different, and every town will require its own distinct approach to the issue.

5. *Chefs:* Chefs can have a tremendous impact on the health and well-being of children by adopting a school and working with teachers, parents, school nutrition professionals, and administrators to help educate kids about food and nutrition. By creating healthy dishes that taste good, chefs have a unique ability to deliver these messages in a fun and appealing way to the larger audience, particularly children.

6. *Kids:* There's one important goal to Let's Move! and that's to solve the problem of childhood obesity in a generation. Today's children deserve to grow up healthy and maintain a good weight when they reach adulthood. It's a big goal and all early childhood educators must do their part. When educators (and parents) teach children how to eat right and be active, children can be healthy and achieve their dreams as life-long healthy individuals.

7. *Health care providers:* Health care providers are poised to have a direct impact on the health of our children and make a real difference in solving the problem of childhood obesity. Each encounter is an opportunity to help families understand the importance of optimal nutrition and physical activity from the earliest moments of life until adulthood. Let's Move! is strengthened by individual efforts of all providers but even more when teams and partners work together with patients and families, in clinics, practices, homes, schools, and neighborhoods (U.S. Department of Agriculture, 2011).

The early childhood classroom teacher must integrate physical development and learning into the day's activities. In light of reduced physical education programs, classroom teachers need to familiarize themselves with the national standards in early physical education and plan activities to foster skill acquisition and link these to learning in other curriculum areas. Teachers can and must develop lessons and activities that support both the physical education curriculum and the early childhood curriculum at the same time. Teachers must talk to the school administrators to help them understand that reductions in recess time and physical education classes can be a contributor to the obesity crisis. Teachers must provide information and support to parents about the causes of obesity and prevention and intervention strategies. Unhealthy food, school vending machines, and the lack of physical activity in schools have been linked to obesity in children (Cline, Spradlin, & Pucker, 2005). Teachers must lobby for healthy food, healthy beverages, and lots of time—both indoors and outdoors—for robust physical activity. It is also important to model healthy habits in front of your children.

## Developmentally Appropriate Practice

The role of the early childhood teacher in physical education and health is to create positive and success-based environments in which children can develop fundamental motor skills through play-based learning activities. As specifically directed by Developmentally Appropriate Practice (DAP) when planning curriculum to achieve important goals in physical development, the following guidelines are recommended:

**Health and fitness.**   Teachers introduce children to healthy habits in eating and exercise and basic concepts of body function and physical health. Teachers provide snacks that are nutritious and sweets are never offered as incentive. Teachers also reinforce good hygiene habits.

**Gross motor development.**   Children have many opportunities to use large muscles in balancing, running, jumping, climbing, and other vigorous movements, both in play and in planned activities. Children play outdoors every day, even during the winter. Teachers encourage children to enjoy the pleasures of physical activity, as well as teaching children body and spatial awareness and movement skills (e.g., catching, jumping, balancing). Teaching of physical skills is sequential and designed to accommodate children's various skill levels and special needs. Boys and girls are encouraged equally and physical activities are integrated throughout the day (Copple & Bredekamp, 2009, p. 234).

## Early Childhood Environment Rating Scale

This valuable resource, introduced in Chapter 1, also provides important information on physical education. Specially, it addresses space and equipment for gross motor play and motor play. The ECERS-R (2005) recommends the following:

- Outdoor gross motor space has a variety of surfaces permitting different types of play (e.g., sand, black top, wood chips, grass).
- Outdoor area has some protection from the elements (e.g., shade in summer, wind break, good drainage).

- Space has convenient features (e.g., close to toilets, accessible storage for equipment; class has direct access to outdoors).
- Both stationary and portable gross motor equipment are used.
- Gross motor equipment stimulates skills on different levels (e.g., tricycles with and without pedals; different sizes of balls; both ramp and ladder access to climbing structures). (Harms, Clifford, & Cryer, 2005, pp. 18–20)

## BUILDING ON CHILDREN'S NATURAL MOVEMENTS

*Dancing*

Twirling, swirling,
Spinning with laughter;
Dancing makes me dizzy,
But only after!

—Linda Carol Edwards

It is important to remember that children need many opportunities to move—to walk, run, climb, bounce, and jump—not only to aid their muscular development, but also for the sake of pure enjoyment. At first, movements will be uncoordinated, but with plenty of opportunity to move and express themselves, the children will eventually gain control of their bodies, and their movements will become refined.

Children around the age of 2 years like to bounce up and down on a bed or a sofa. As they do this, it is not uncommon to hear them singing words to accompany their movement. For example, children might be heard singing "bouncy-bounce, bouncy-bounce," keeping time with their bouncing. Always provide some type of cushiony material, such as a small mattress or a gym pad, for this type of activity.

Have you ever noticed how many children run in complete abandon, waving their arms like birds? Have you ever watched and listened as youngsters keep perfect time while walking around the playground, dragging sticks behind them? Have you watched as they teeter back and forth from one foot to another, humming in rhythm to their teetering movements? An appropriate recording can be played, a song hummed or sung, or clapping provided to accompany these kinds of body movements. Join in with the children. Make it a game. Show your approval.

### National Association for Sport and Physical Education

In 1992, the National Association for Sport and Physical Education (NASPE) developed physical activity guidelines designed for the developmental needs of elementary-age children. In 2002, NASPE developed similar guidelines for preschoolers, birth to age 5. The guidelines recommend that 2-year-olds have at least 30 minutes of structured physical activity a day and from 1 hour to many hours a day of unstructured physical activity. NASPE's guidelines are the same for preschoolers with the addition that they receive a minimum of 60 minutes a day of structured physical activity. These recommendations are especially important for us who are in early childhood education. As teachers and caretakers, we must include movement as an intrinsic part of each day; movement must also take place in the classroom. Early childhood curricula guidelines (NAEYC) and physical education teachers (NASPE) sometimes stress different movement approaches. For early childhood professionals, movement tends to focus on

Children love to model actions in songs and games.

creative movement as a part of play within the curriculum. On the other hand, physical education teachers often stress movement in structured and prescribed ways. The importance of movement education, if presented through a developmentally appropriate curriculum, is ideal when we have a combination of the two. Early childhood teachers should incorporate both creative movement and structured movement combined with many open-ended experiences that encourage children to express movement in ways that are important to them. What does this means to those of us in early childhood education? It means that if movement experiences are fun then children are much more likely to want to keep moving throughout life.

Chenfeld's (1976) classic quotation, used by researchers and educators for years to describe the importance of movement, reminds us that "movement is as natural to learning as breathing is to living. We have to be taught not to move as we grow up in our inhibited, uptight society" (p. 261). Movement is synonymous with the growing child. Today, more than ever, we realize the great amount of learning that takes place through psychomotor activities. As indicated in Chapter 1, young children should be free to explore and experiment with their own movements in response to stimuli. It is important that they experience these natural body movements before they are asked to respond to those initiated by adults.

With careful guidance, movement exploration gives children an opportunity to become aware of their own abilities and what their bodies can do. Through these experiences, they often lose their self-consciousness and inhibitions. Many times, movement exploration leads to creative movements and dance. This process helps children discover new ways of using their bodies. As children's muscle coordination improves, they can begin to coordinate the rhythmic movements of their body with such stimuli as the beat of a drum, a rhythmic poem, a song, and the like.

We strongly believe that as children learn to control their body movements, they build feelings of satisfaction, self-worth, and confidence, which will grow and carry over into mastery of other areas. Undoubtedly, children will become less fearful of trying out other activities. Have you ever seen the expression on a child who has just found the "right combination" for skipping or who has just walked across the balance beam for the first time without falling off? Success in mastery of movements like these helps the child grow psychologically as well as physically. The primary goals of movement programs are to help young children become more aware of what their bodies can do and to help them develop the balance and coordination needed to control all parts of their bodies. Children should have no fear of failure with experiences in movement exploration. Teachers should be constantly aware of this point as they provide guidance in this area.

## THE ROLE OF MOVEMENT IN CREATIVITY

What is creativity? What are the most important issues to consider when we talk about creativity? There are two questions that provide a framework for studying the creative process. These questions can serve as discussion starters as we look at the role of movement in the creative process.

1. How do we define creativity?
2. What are the abilities involved in creative thinking?

There are many definitions of creativity ranging from the dictionary definition "characterized by originality; imaginative," to the Latin word *creare*, from "creo," which means "to produce, to create, make, make forth, beget, give origin to."

According to Torrance (1992), there are a number of abilities involved in creative thinking. Among these are:

- Fluency (the free-flow of associations related to ideas and thoughts)
- Flexibility (to explore various ways of approaching problems or solutions and looking at situations from many different perspectives)
- Originality (to have a new or novel idea or to produce something unique, to put a new stamp on something that already exists)
- Elaboration (to embellish or extend thoughts and ideas, to add detail or finishing touches)

Also according to Torrance, extensive research in the field of creativity indicates key personality traits of creative people that can be developed in young children. Figure 2–1 reflects Torrance's infinite wisdom.

## PLANNING FOR MOVEMENT ACTIVITIES

One of your primary responsibilities as a teacher of children is to establish a warm and safe environment of trust, freedom, and communication where positive and pleasurable music and movement experiences happen. Enjoyment of expression is the prime value of music and movement. We must be very careful that we don't demand perfection of form as children move through space or experiment with time and force. Our job is to create an atmosphere that welcomes this freedom.

How will you structure this atmosphere? How will music and movement thrive in your classroom? Involvement is more likely in an atmosphere in which children feel safe and are assured of the following conditions:

- It is safe to try.
- I can deal with events.
- My teacher encourages me to make the attempt.
- I am fulfilled for having done so.

When children find themselves in a safe, supportive, and encouraging environment, they are free to explore, experiment, and respond with unlimited creative expression.

**Figure 2–1   Creativity According to Torrance**

Creativity is digging deeper.

Creativity is looking twice.

Creativity is crossing out mistakes.

Creativity is talking/listening to a cat.

Creativity is getting in deep water.

Creativity is getting out from behind locked doors.

Creativity is plugging in the sun.

Creativity is wanting to know.

Creativity is having a ball.

Creativity is building sand castles.

Creativity is singing in your own way.

Creativity is shaking hands with the future.

*Source:* E. Torrance, cited in *Finding Creativity for Children*. Paper presented for the Leadership Accessing Symposium (ERIC Domain 348, 167) Reprinted by permission of the Torrance Center for Creativity and Talent Development, University of Georgia, Athens, GA.

Once you have established an environment in which children feel safe to try out new and different ways of expressing themselves, you may wonder how to begin. Good teachers always begin with a plan, and the following sections can be translated into lesson plans as you prepare to begin this journey with your children.

## Finding Your Own Space

Ensure that your children know that they have their own space and that their space belongs to them and only them. You can help your children identify their personal space by guiding them through an imagery process of finding their own imaginary space bubble.

1. Walk among the children, and point out all the space in the room. Show them the empty spaces between tables and chairs and wave your hand in the space between children. Ask the children to look up and see the space between them and the ceiling.
2. Have children find a space on the floor where they can stand, sit, or lie down without touching anyone else. Ask the children to move their hands and arms around, filling up as much space as they can.
3. Encourage children to move their legs and stretch them as far as they can, seeing how much space they can fill with just their legs.
4. Tell children to stand and move their arms through their own space, reaching as far as they can without moving their feet. Ask them to explore their own space with their feet and legs.
5. Ask your children to imagine that they are inside a big space bubble that is theirs alone. Tell them that no one else can come into their bubble or into their space unless they are invited. They can move inside their imaginary space bubble in many different ways. They can also carry their space bubble with them as they move around the room.

The following section, "Talks with Teachers," is one of five in this edition that focuses on viewing music and movement through the eyes of practicing classroom teachers. The first "talk" introduces you to Jane Schuler and the children in her first grade.

## TALKS WITH TEACHERS

Jane Schuler is an energetic and creative first-grade teacher at Marrington Elementary School in Goose Creek, South Carolina. Her degrees include a B.A. in Special and Elementary Education from Wintrop University and a M.Ed. degree in Early Childhood Education from the College of Charleston. She was also awarded a National Board of Professional Teacher Certificate and was most recently recognized as Teacher of the Year. Jane has been a first-grade teacher for over 20 years.

Jane and her children move to music every day.

Jane and her first graders have "special" music that they listen to during movement activities. Jane encourages the children to think about how they want to move on any particular day and select music from the CD collection that they would like to hear. When Jane first introduced this lesson, the children were slow to make the connection between certain rhythmic patterns and movement. However, it only took a couple of weeks for the children to become absorbed in the music and the movement that the music encouraged. It wasn't long before her children were asking Jane to bring in some new CDs so that they could figure out new and different ways of moving to new music. Jane provides the following examples that her children particularly enjoy:

### Classical Music and Movement Exploration

| | |
|---|---|
| **Walking** | Kabalevsky: "Pantomime" from *The Comedians* Prokofiev: "Departure" from *Winter Holiday* |
| **Marching** | Vaughan Williams: "March Past of the Kitchen Utensils" from *The Wasps* Grieg: "Norwegian Rustic March" from *Lyric Suite* |
| **Hopping** | Moussorgsky: "Ballet of the Unhatched Chicks" from *Pictures at an Exhibition* Bach: "Gigue" from *Suite No. 3* |
| **Swaying, Rocking** | Offenbach: "Barcarolle" from *The Tales of Hoffman* Saint-Saens: "The Swan" from *Carnival of the Animals* |
| **Sliding, Gliding** | Khachaturian: "Waltz" from *Masquerade Suite* Tschaikovsky: "Waltz" from *Sleeping Beauty* |

## Three Approaches to Movement Activities

Pica (2004) reviews three teaching methods—the direct approach, guided discovery, and exploration—and the role of each method for movement education programs for young children. Some movement activities are best learned through direct instruction.

### *The Direct Approach*

Direct instruction includes modeling, demonstrating, and imitating. It is through these modes that children learn to move in specific ways. "Emulating, repeating, copying, and responding to directions seem to be necessary ingredients of the early years" (Mosston & Ashworth, 1990, p. 45). For example, "Simon Says," "Follow the Leader," and "Where Is Thumbkin?" are all direct approach movement activities that most young children love. Fingerplays also fall in this same category.

"Simon Says" is a fun body-parts activity. Always play this game without the elimination process. When using "Simon Says" with very young children, slow down the tempo and model the actions. For older preschoolers, the game can be played faster and involve more body parts. "Simon" could make some of the following requests:

Touch your toes
Raise your arms
Reach for the sky
Place hands on hip
Touch your shoulders
Stand up tall
Touch your head
Touch your knees
Touch your mouth
Give yourself a hug!

Most toddlers love "Follow the Leader" and can clap, pat, raise their arms, and do other simple actions. Older children who have acquired the ability to walk on tiptoe can follow this motion. Once children are familiar with "Follow the Leader," you as the teacher might accompany yourself with a hand drum or tambourine as you gradually increase or decrease the tempo according to the locomotor and nonlocomotor skill levels of your children.

When performing "Where Is Thumbkin?" use the standard finger names: thumbkin, pointer, middle finger, ring finger, and pinky. As you ask the questions, the children respond with, "Here I am, here I am," "How are you?" and finally "Very well, thank you."

The direct approach is the least used method for early childhood settings. Although it is one way to help children learn to follow a series of directions, it does focus on skills rather than the process. The direct approach leaves very little room for creativity because all of the children are doing the same thing at the same time. And, they are doing exactly what the teacher is telling them to do!

### *Guided Discovery*

Guided discovery is a child-centered approach that encourages inventiveness and experimentation as children converge on the right answer. Guided discovery is most appropriate for older preschoolers and primary-grade children. For example, the teacher asks several questions that lead the children toward discovering how to do a forward role. Rather than demonstrating for the children, the teacher can ask the children to show an upside-down position or to show how they can lie with their tummy on the floor. The teacher then asks the children if they can roll forward and assume the same position. It is important to remember that when using the guided discovery approach, all of the children responses are "correct." Children have plenty of time to find a way to achieve the goal and the teachers can continue to ask questions and give suggestions until the desired outcome is achieved. It is equally important to remember that "guided discovery takes longer than the direct approach, many educators feel its benefits far outweigh the time factor" (Pica, 2004, p. 233).

### Movement Exploration

Developmentally appropriate practice encourages exploration for young children and should be the method most often used in early childhood settings. When children are given many open-ended possibilities for movement exploration, the results are a variety of responses. For example, if you ask children to move two parts of their bodies at the same time, some children might move their arms while others might move their arm and leg. This method encourages children to find their own way of responding. Children should be allowed to experiment with solving the problem without interference or demonstration by the teacher. Exploration requires time and patience, but on the other hand it encourages children to be creative with their ability to explore the world.

Exploration allows every child to participate and succeed at her or his level of development and ability. In addition to the self-confidence and poise continual success brings, this process promotes independence, helps develop patience with oneself and one's peers, and allows the acceptance of others' ideas. Perhaps most important for young children, exploration leads them to the discovery of the richness of possibilities involved in the field of human movement (Pica, 2004, p. 241).

## SINGING AS A SUPPORT TO MOVEMENT

It is well known that movement is essential to the healthy growth of young children. Music can provide an excellent medium for helping children acquire good listening skills that will gradually enhance their own creative responses. It is important to keep in mind that when children do actions to singing games and songs that require movement, they may not always sing the words. Adults should not be alarmed at this, as it is a normal developmental process. The more vigorous the activity, the less likely children will be able to sing the words. Teaching the words to a song first, before adding the movements, will help speed up the process of becoming adept at singing and moving simultaneously.

Singing games like "Ring Around the Rosie," "London Bridge Is Falling Down," "Looby Loo," "Hokey Pokey," "Jack in the Box," and "Jack Be Nimble" are ideal for initiating movements and bringing children together in a cooperative, happy experience.

Keep these things in mind when planning such activities:

1. Keep the session short.
2. Start with a familiar action song, such as "Clap, Clap, Clap Your Hands Together" or "Look and See."

Children love to move around while
playing their instruments.

3. Perform other body movements for a warm-up, such as touching different parts of
   the body, bending, stretching, and jumping in place.
4. If you are using a recording, the children may not join in with the singing. They
   may be too involved in doing the suggested actions and movements.
5. You may ask the children to model a certain action in the song or singing game.
   Or they may suggest particular movements themselves.
6. Teachers should join in the activity with enthusiasm. Children enjoy having the
   teacher take a turn in becoming a leader in a singing game.
7. If children do not want to become a part of the small group, do not force them.
   Often, they will want just to observe. It takes time to build trust between the teacher
   and child and between a child and the rest of the group.
8. At this age, children may find it difficult to learn and respond to the word *freeze*.
   A cue, such as holding up a hand or tapping twice on a drum, could be used
   instead. It is important for children to learn to stop an action or movement upon
   a designated cue from the teacher.

## MUSIC AS A SUPPORT TO MOVEMENT

Music should support movement. Children sometimes ask for musical accompaniment
as they move about. A sensitive adult can encourage a child's movements by clapping
or tapping on a drum or some similar instrument. When accompanying children's
movements, synchronize the accompaniment to the tempo of the movements. When
working with preschoolers, teachers need to accommodate the child's own rhythm
rather than have the child conform to the beat. This can be done by first watching and
listening to children as they clap, tap, walk, tiptoe, and the like, then providing accompaniment that matches the child's own body rhythm.

Traditional songs for young children are popular because they encourage movement. "Pat-A-Cake, Pat-A-Cake" encourages children and adults to play a movement
game together. "London Bridge" fosters cooperation and communication because
you can't fall down or "lock 'er up" by yourself. "The Farmer in the Dell" encourages

"Patty Cake" is an all-time favorite of children.

children to understand and focus on relationships as children take a wife, a dog, a cat, and a mouse.

## CHILDREN AND DANCE IN THE CLASSROOM

Isadora Duncan, one of the greatest dancers of the 20th century, is credited with having announced before a performance: "If I could *tell* you what I mean, there would be no point in dancing." Her powerful statement certainly exemplifies how young children approach the process of movement and dance.

As teachers, our prime concern should be to nurture, develop, and deepen children's abilities to respond affectively to the sounds, melodies, and rhythms generated by music. Music and movement represent ways of knowing as well as ways of expressing feeling, and they allow children to move beyond the common ways of experiencing their world and expressing what they know about it. Dancer Martha Graham once said, "The reality of the dance is its truth to our inner life; dance is the hidden language of the soul" (Brown, 1979, p. 50). She also said, "A dance is one instant of life—a vibratory piece of energy. A great piece of sculpture is never contained; it reaches out to affect the space around it. We exist in space—that is the energy of the world, and each of us is a recipient of that energy, if he so wills" (Mazo, 1991, p. 34).

With all of our understanding and acceptance of music, movement, and dance, it is of vital importance for the early childhood teacher to have both the willingness and sensibility to provide experiences in these ways of knowing for young children. To be better prepared to plan music, movement, and dance activities for your children, you should be aware of how young children explore these creative processes and how you can begin to stretch their horizons.

# NATIONAL STANDARDS FOR MOVEMENT AND DANCE

Young children learn by doing. Singing, playing instruments, moving to music, and creating music enable children to acquire skills and knowledge that can be developed in no other way. Because movement and music are basic expressions of human nature, every child should have access to a balanced, comprehensive, and sequential program of study in music and movement.

The Consortium of National Arts Education Associations, through a grant administered by the National Association for Music Education (MENC) (1994), developed standards that outline what every child should know and be able to do in the arts. Young children in the preschool years should engage in developmentally appropriate learning experiences designed to prepare them to achieve the standards for kindergarten and early primary. The following standards identify and demonstrate movement elements and skills in performing dance. These standards provide a framework for teachers who work with young children and should assist teachers in planning a movement curriculum that is developmentally appropriate.

### Identifying and Demonstrating Movement Elements and Skills in Performing Dance

Achievement Standard
- Students accurately demonstrate nonlocomotor/axial movements (such as bend, twist, stretch, swing).
- Students accurately demonstrate eight basic locomotor movements (such as walk, run, hop, jump, leap, gallop, slide, and skip), traveling forward, backward, sideward, diagonally, and turning.
- Students create shapes at low, middle, and high levels.
- Students demonstrate the ability to define and maintain personal space.
- Students demonstrate movements in straight and curved pathways.
- Students demonstrate accuracy in moving to a musical beat and responding to changes in tempo.
- Students demonstrate kinesthetic awareness, concentration, and focus in performing movement skills.
- Students attentively observe and accurately describe the action (such as skip, gallop) and movement elements (such as levels, directions) in a brief movement study.

*Source:* From National Standards for Arts Education Copyright © 1994 by Music Educators National Conference (MENC). Used by permission.

## Basic Dance Movements

When movement experiences and the sensations of moving are connected to the expressive and imaginative powers of the mover, we have dance. Dance involves a heightened kinesthetic awareness, a bodily intelligence, and a sharpened perception of movement as an aesthetic experience.

While dance may be an eloquent art form, it is nevertheless a form of expression that can be made easily accessible to young children. There is general agreement among practitioners, theorists, and writers dealing with the nature of dance as to what basic movements form an overall conceptual framework for dance and dance education

(Barrett, 1977; Dimondstein, 1971; Downey, 1995; Gensemer, 1985; Laban, 1948). All dance movements are a blending of three basic qualities: space, time, and force. Other factors that influence movement are flow, weight, body awareness, and relationships with others or objects. In addition, movement can occur through locomotion, nonlocomotion, representational responses, or a combination of two or more body movements. If all this sounds a bit complicated, relax. One of the most effective ways you can help children to develop the art of dance is to promote significant discussion about the meaning of these terms.

It is important to talk with children about the vocabulary of music and movement. Young children may not have the language skills or knowledge to use words like *time* in a musical context. They may relate time only to when they get up in the morning or to adults giving a clock significant meaning. Introduce music and dance vocabulary while your children are listening to music or exploring rhythm and beat so that the words are connected to their actual activity. Do not "lecture" children or teach them words and terminology out of context; instead, use accurate vocabulary unobtrusively as a means of describing what your children are experiencing.

The other thing you can do to expand your awareness of the language and the meaning of these words in a musical context is to respond to the creative movement process, not as a dance educator "giving" dance to children, but as a regular classroom teacher who is actively involved in sensing your own feelings for creative movement: "When children see adults working creatively, they understand this is something that people do in real life, something that gives enjoyment and satisfaction, and is not just a classroom exercise. In this way, children are able to move away from relying entirely on explanations and secondhand information, and have the chance to witness the behaviors and even the physical movements involved" (Dixon & Chalmers, 1990, pp. 16–17). Again, it is important to remember that we are focusing on the *process* of movement, not on the *product*.

Following are descriptions of common terms used in movement and dance.

### Space

The word *space* refers to the manner in which we use an area for movement. This can be either a "personal space" that no one else can enter or a more expansive area of "general space," which is everywhere else. Children need to be aware that once they are in a space, whether standing or sitting, that space becomes occupied. In movement and dance, the perception of space is viewed in relation to the body, the space of others, and the unoccupied place or general space.

You can help children define their personal space by asking them to extend their arms while turning around and around to make sure they can't touch anyone else. You might tap their imaginative powers by asking them to pretend that they are moving inside a very large bubble. Young children can carry their personal space with them as they move during locomotor activities. Leaping, jumping, skipping, and sliding are examples of locomotor activities that involve moving from one place to another.

Locomotor activities require a large, uncluttered space. You don't need a space as large as a gymnasium; a large open area in your classroom or even outdoors is more than adequate. It is important to remember that your children need to hear you and your suggestions during movement activities. In a large, oversized room, the children will have difficulty seeing and hearing you. If you find, however, that a large area is the only space available to you, you can easily solve the problem of the children not being able to hear you by using a percussion instrument (drum or tambourine) to signal to children that it is time for them to stop and listen. Movement invites squeals of delight, laughter, and many other appropriate "child sounds." A signal can provide structure and predictability to music and movement experiences, both of which are important in establishing and maintaining a secure and trusting environment in which your children feel safe to explore the process.

### Time

Time is a quality of tempo or rhythm. A movement can be slow or fast (time) and a succession of muscular relaxations and rests (rhythm). The speed of movement can change from faster to slower. A child's sense of tempo can be facilitated by a simple, percussion accompaniment that provides beats or a grouping of beats. In movement and dance, rhythm comes from two sources: either from music where children hear rhythm as it is produced through sound, or from dance, where children create rhythm from their movements. Moreover, the tempo of a movement can be a series of rhythmic changes involving a total kinesthetic response by which a child organizes and interprets tempo and rhythm through both internal and external stimuli—that is, what they hear in the music and the spontaneous feelings and emotions they feel in their bodies.

Time for young children is *not* "keeping time" or "being in time" with the music. Rather, it is an opportunity for children to be involved in exploration and improvisation of the qualities of tempo and rhythm. Dimondstein (1971) cautions us to not ask children to "dance by the numbers." Allow children to respond in ways that they can control their bodies and broaden the scope of their rhythmic expression.

### Force

The concept of force is also important in movement and dance. Children experience light, heavy, sudden, or sustained qualities of movement that require varying degrees of muscular tension. As children explore different qualities of force, they can experience the difference between pushing and pulling and between heaviness and lightness. They become aware of balance and the transference of body weight. Most important, perhaps, is that through an exploration of force, children may begin to understand the idea of being "centered," controlling their bodies from a place of balance from which energy is released and controlled.

Gensemer defines *force* as "the amount of tension or stress of a movement; the flow and control of energy" (1985, p. 39). For example, there are sustained movements expressed as smooth, easygoing flows of energy, such as lifting an imaginary, heavy object. There are swinging movements where one part of the body moves around another, such as swinging our arms in a circle over our heads. Percussion movement requires a sudden, quick, sharp release of energy, as when we shake a hand or a leg or our whole selves. Percussion movement can be facilitated by using instruments that produce sounds by hitting or beating. Children can discover the amount of force they use when beating a drum or hitting a triangle.

### Locomotor Activity

*Locomotor* refers to the quality of moving through space. Walking, running, jumping, hopping, skipping, leaping, sliding, and galloping are examples of locomotor movements. Nonlocomotor movements are stationary. Children move in ways that do not require them to move away from their area. Examples of nonlocomotor movement include stretching, bending, turning, twisting, swinging, and curling.

Throughout all of these expressive movement and dance encounters, children explore direction (straight, forward, backward, up, down), levels (high, low, or somewhere in between), relationships (above, below, over, under, through, around), and position of movement (horizontal, vertical, diagonal). Children also learn to organize the available space in relation to themselves and to objects and other individuals. As children experiment with and explore all of these different ways of creative movement, they are developing body control and confidence in the power and ability of their own bodies. Best of all, they are finding intrinsic pleasure in "being" the creator of movement and dance rather than "imitating" a prescribed, "follow me and do as I do" approach. The ideas presented in Figure 2–2 provide open-ended experiences for children. The activities are designed to allow freedom of expression, which will differ from child to child. As children become involved in these movement activities, they may begin to add drama in their own creative interpretation and imagination to their movements. For example, you might ask your children to move as if they were pushing a heavy wagon. Some of your children may have some knowledge of how to move a heavy wagon, while others may represent their understanding of wagons from what they have seen on television. As another example, you might ask children to pretend they are popping popcorn. How would they move as the kernels start to sizzle and then explode into fluffy, delicious popcorn? Whatever the case, when children express what they know about walking in the rain or how a jack-in-the-box actually pops forward, their interpretation must be honored. Most significantly, your children are moving their bodies in ways that represent what they know (or don't know) about the workings of their world.

Young children are beginners; they are just beginning to make discoveries about the vast repertoire of expression that comes through movement and dance. There will be plenty of time for them to take formal dance lessons in the next 20 or more years of formal "schooling" that lie ahead.

### Figure 2–2　Dramatizing Movement

- Move in a happy way.
- Move in an angry way.
- Move as if you were sad.
- See how gently (roughly) you can move.
- Dance like a rag doll.
- Pretend that you are a tree and that the wind is blowing you around.
- Gallop around the room like a horse.
- Hop around the room like a rabbit.
- Move as if you were carrying something very heavy.
- Swing and sway your body and arms like a monkey.
- Pretend you are swimming. How would your body, arms, and legs move?
- Pretend that you are a jack-in-the-box.
- Make yourself into a flat balloon, and slowly blow yourself up.
- Pretend that you are a puppet with strings and that someone else is making you move.
- How would you move if you were looking for something you have lost?
- Move as if you were walking in very deep snow, through a deep river, in hot sand, on cold ice.

# BASIC MATERIALS FOR MOVEMENT

The materials recommended in this section are the basic materials necessary for any movement program. Materials specific to age groups are integrated into Chapters 4 through 7. The use of materials and props can also encourage and stimulate children to express themselves through movement. Following are materials especially enjoyable to young children.

### Scarves

Give your children lightweight, colorful scarves, and encourage them to let each scarf flow up and down and all around as they move through space. Scarves can be magically transformed into capes for flying, wings for soaring, or umbrellas for dancing in the rain.

### Streamers

Children can use long streamers to make interesting, flowing designs as they move and sway in a group movement activity. When placed on the floor, streamers can define a space or become a bridge for little billy goats to tramp across.

### Hoops

You can place several hoops on the floor and let the children explore different ways of moving inside the hoop, in and out of the hoop, and outside the hoop. Encourage your children to experiment with putting some parts of their body inside the hoop and other body parts outside. For example, ask the children, "Can you put both feet in the hoop and let your hands walk around the outside of the hoop?" They also can use the hoops as they would a single jump rope to practice jumping skills.

### Beanbags

Play the beanbag game. Give each child a beanbag (have a variety of colors available). The leader (either the teacher or another child) suggests movements for the other children to follow: Put your beanbag on your head, and walk around the room without letting it fall off. Put the beanbag on your shoulder, your arm, your elbow, your foot. Put it on your back, and crawl around the room. Put it on the floor, and jump over it. Sit on your beanbag. Roll over your beanbag. Toss it into the air, and catch it with both hands. Combine the beanbag activities with the hoops or streamers.

### Parachutes

Parachutes with sewn-in fabric handles should *not* be used with young children. Children have a tendency to put their little wrists through the handles, and this makes it difficult for them to free themselves when the parachute is filled with air. If your parachute does have these sewn-in fabric handles, cut them off. When the force of an air-filled parachute gets too strong for children to hold on, they must be able to let go easily so that they are not pulled in any uncomfortable position. Encourage your children to move the parachute up and down. Help them move it in a circular pattern, or put a lightweight ball in the middle and let them bounce the ball around. You and your children (with the help of a few extra adults) can make a momentary tent out of your parachute. Viewed from underneath, the colors are beautiful. It is an

When you get a new parachute you must cut off the sewn-in handles.

easy process: Position your children and several adults at close intervals around the parachute. Raise it high in the air until it is full of air, run under it, and quickly sit on the edges. The parachute will balloon, and you and your children will delight in the magical quality it creates!

## FINGERPLAYS AND ACTION SONGS

Fingerplays and action songs are excellent ways to introduce young children to movement activities. Chapters 4 through 7 also include age-specific fingerplays and action songs.

The music and movement experiences in all of these activities can be changed and modified into developmentally appropriate practice for your children. Once you have had the personal experience of exploring the wonderful world of your own musical potential, you should also have a broader understanding of how you, as a professional, can bring similar yet age-appropriate activities to children. Your role as an early childhood teacher is to provide music and movement encounters that will bring satisfaction and enjoyment to your children. Mastery of pitch, rhythm, or melody is not the goal, and you certainly don't have to be a musical genius yourself. The goal is for young children to find pleasure and joy in the process of singing, moving, dancing, and playing instruments. Your job is to plan for these experiences, to be open and flexible in your planning, and to know the developmental levels of your children. You must search for new ideas and techniques. Even though young children love repetition, they will soon get tired of songs and fingerplays if you have only three or four in your repertoire. Finally, you must enjoy and find pleasure in the creative self-expression that flows naturally and spontaneously from the child's own wellspring of creative potential.

*Dancing with the feet is one thing, but dancing with the heart is another.*

—Author Unknown

## KEY IDEAS

1. School-based and family-based intervention can reduce obesity, especially when these interventions limit television watching and encourage increased physical activity.
2. The National Association for Sports and Physical Education (NASPE) provides specific physical activity guidelines that teachers can use when designing physical activities for children.
3. Children need a safe, supportive, and encouraging environment in which to explore, experiment with, and respond to movement activities.
4. Music should support movement.
5. The use of materials and props encourage children to express themselves through movement.

## SUMMARY

Music and movement activities provide children with expressive ways to dance to the rhythms they hear in their daily lives. Teachers must provide movement activities as an integral part of each day. It is through these experiences that children become more aware of their own physical abilities. In addition to facilitating movement experiences in the classroom teachers can also introduce different kinds of movement activities that promote new vocabulary words. Teachers and caregivers can also expand their own awareness of the movement process by being actively involved with the children.

## QUESTIONS TO CONSIDER

1. The early childhood years are a crucial time for determining the causes of childhood obesity. Contact the Food and Nutrition Information Center, www.nal.usda.gov/fnic/pubs_and_db.html, and outline the most common causes of childhood obesity in the early childhood years. How can you as a teacher provide ways that will combat the childhood obesity epidemic?
2. What is your preferred method for encouraging children to engage in movement activities in the classroom? Write a brief lesson plan outlining your ideas.
3. How can you incorporate the national standards for movement and dance into your curriculum?
4. What are some materials that are appropriate for movement education that are not listed in your textbook?

## REFERENCES

Barrett, K. (1977). Education dances. In B. Logsdon, M. Broer, R. McGee, M. Ammens, L. H. Alverson, & M. A. Robertson (Eds.), *Physical education for children: A focus on the teaching success* (pp. 328–333). Philadelphia, PA: Lea and Febiger.

Brown, J. M. (Ed.). (1979). *Graham 1937: The vision of modern dance*. Princeton, NJ: Princeton University Press.

Chenfeld, M. (1976). *Teaching language arts creatively*. New York, NY: Harcourt Brace Jovanovich.

Cline, K., Spradlin, T., & Pucker, J. (2005). Child obesity in Indiana: A growing public policy concern. *Education Policy, 3*(1), 5–15.

Copple, C., & Bredekamp, S. (Eds.). (2009). *Developmentally appropriate practice* (3rd ed.). Washington, DC: National Association for the Education of Young Children.

Dietz, W. H. (1997). Periods of risk in childhood for the development of adult obesity—what do we need to learn? *Nutrition, 127*: 1884S–1886S.

Dimondstein, G. (1971). *Children dance in the classroom*. New York, NY: Macmillan.

Dixon, G. T., & Chalmers, F. G. (1990). The expressive arts in education. *Childhood Education, 67*(1), 12–17.

Downey, V. (1995). Expressing ideas through gesture, time, and space. *Journal of Physical Education, Recreation, and Dance, 66*(9), 18.

Epstein, L., Paluch, R., Gordy, C., & Dorn, J. (2000). Decreasing sedentary behaviors in treating pediatric obesity. *Archives of Pediatric and Adolescent Medicine, 154,* 220–226.

Gensemer, R. E. (1985). Body movement and learning. In F. B. Tuttle, Jr. (Ed.), *Final arts in the curriculum* (p. 39). Washington, DC: National Education Association.

Harms, T., Clifford, R., & Cryer, D. (2005). *Early childhood environment rating scale* (Rev. ed.). New York, NY: Teachers College Press.

Jalonick, M., & D'Innocenzio, A. (2011). Associated Press.

Klesges, R. C., Klesges, L. M., Eck, L. H., & Shelton, M. L. (1995). A longitudinal analysis of accelerated weight gain in preschool children. *Pediatrics, 95,* 126–130.

Laban, R. (1948). *Modern education dance.* London, England: MacDonald and Evans.

Li, J., & Hooker, N. H. (2010). Childhood obesity and schools: Evidence from the national survey of children's health. *Journal of School Health, 80*(2).

Mazo, J. (1991). Martha remembered. *Dance, 65*(7), 34.

Moore, K. R., McGowan, M. K., Donato, K. A., Kollipara, S., & Roubideaux, Y. (2009). Community resources for promoting youth nutrition and physical activity. *American Journal of Health Education, 40*(5), 298–303.

Moore, L. L., Nguyen, U. D. T., Rothman, K. J., Cupples, L. A., & Ellison, C. A. (1995). Preschool physical activity level and change in body fatness in young children. *American Journal of Epidemiology, 142,* 982–988.

Mosston, M., & Ashworth, S. (1990). *The spectrum of teaching styles: From command to discovery.* White Plains, NY: Longman.

National Association for Music Education (MENC). (1994). www.menc.org/resources/view/performance-standards.

National Association for Sport and Physical Education (NASPE) Outcomes Committee. (1992). *The physically educated person.* Reston, VA: National Association for Sport and Physical Education. Retrieved from http://www.aahperd.org/naspe/template.ctm?template=ns_active.html

National Institute Health Care Management (NIHCM) Foundation. (2004). *Obesity in young children: Impact and intervention.* Research Brief. Washington, DC: NIHCM.

National Research Council. (1989). *Diet and health implications for reducing chronic disease risk.* Washington, DC: National Academy Press.

Obama, M. (2011). Let's move! Retrieved from http://www.letsmove.gov

Pica, R. (2004). *Experience in movement: Birth to age 8.* Cliffton Park, NY: Thomson-Delmar.

Proctor, M., Moore, L., Gao, D., Cupples, L., Bradlee, M., Hood, M., & Ellison, R. (2003). Television viewing and change in body fat from preschool to early adolescence: The Framingham Children's Study. *International Journal of Obesity, 27,* 827–833.

Robinson, R. (1999). Reducing children's television viewing to prevent obesity. *JAMA, 282*: 1561–1567.

Robinson, R. (2000). Can a school-based intervention to reduce television use decrease adiposity in children grades 3 and 4? *Evidence-Based Nursing, 3*(43).

Torrance, E. (1992). Cited in R. Hill, *Finding creativity for children.* Paper prepared for the Leadership Accessing Symposium, Lafayette, IN. (ERIC Document 348, 169).

U.S. Department of Agriculture. (2011). Let's move! Retrieved from http://www.letsmove.gov

### Resources

Administration for Children and Families. (2010). Efforts to meet children's physical *Activity and Nutritional Needs: Findings from the I Am Moving, I Am Learning Implementation Evaluation,* by M. K. Fox, K. Hallgren, K. Boller, & A. Turner. Washington, DC: U.S. Department of Health and Human Services. www.acf.hhs.gov/programs/opre/hs/eval_move_learn/reports/implement_moving_learning/implement_moving_learning.pdf

# CHAPTER THREE

# Music and Movement for Children with Special Needs

*It's not that easy being green,*
*When green is all there is to be* * . . .*

*Kermit the Frog*

---

*14 words from "It's Not That Easy Being Green" reprinted by permission of The Joe Raposo Music Group.

*Very few of the children in our classrooms are "green," but just like Kermit, they all have combinations of abilities and strengths. There may be a tendency to view children with special needs in comparison to typically developing children. As we all know, there is really no "normal" child. It is clear to all teachers who have taught for any length of time that all children have special needs.*

*Those of us who work with all children ensure that music and movement are a vital core of the activities that occupy each day. Their interests and abilities should be the basis for developing curricula for all children. When we listen to our students, we learn that each child brings a set of unique characteristics to the learning environment. When we remember to think first of the child, separate from his or her peers and of the differences and likenesses among all children, we can more effectively develop lessons and activities that meet the needs of all children. The key to working with any child is to know his or her areas of strength and build upon them, as a part of the total educational pattern. Learning for children should be a holistic process—they are not compartmentalized.*

## SUPPORTIVE ENVIRONMENTS FOR CHILDREN WITH SPECIAL NEEDS

The Individuals with Disabilities Education Act (IDEA) requires that every student with disabilities be educated in the least restrictive environment (LRE). Specifically, the law stipulates that:

> To the maximum extent appropriate, children with disabilities, including children in public or private institutions or other care facilities, [will be] educated with children who are not disabled, and that special classes, separate schooling or other removal of children with disabilities from the regular educational environment [may occur] only when the nature or severity of the disability is such that education in regular classes with the use of supplementary aids and services cannot be achieved satisfactorily. (Public Law 105-17, 1997: 105th Congress. 20 U.S.C., Sec.1412[a][5]).

In the least restrictive environment (LRE), educational services are delivered in settings that best meet the needs of the child and are closest to the typical general education setting. In other words, the least restrictive environment must provide for each child's unique needs to be effectively served. The LRE is the setting that is closest to a regular school program (Heward, 2006).

Many authorities (Cook, Klein, & Tessier, 2008; Gould & Sullivan, 2005; Miche, 2002; Pica, 2004) write about children with special needs. They stress the importance of a least restrictive environment for providing the best opportunities for learning. Certainly, this should be the goal for all children. We take the position that anyone responsible for the well-being of children is presumed to have a solid and thorough knowledge of human growth and development and to build upon that knowledge.

A least restrictive environment is achieved first by realistically assessing one's own skills, attitudes, and abilities, as well as one's breadth of knowledge regarding children with special needs. If there are gaps in information, excellent textbooks and articles in professional journals enrich understanding. Observing children, talking to others whose daily work involves children with special needs, or working on a one-to-one basis with a child who needs extra attention will quickly build one's confidence and capacity to recognize special abilities or disabilities (Cook et al., 2008).

Inclusive early childhood education meets the needs of all young children.

### Early Childhood Environment Rating Scale Revised (ECERS-R)

Now is a good time to revisit the ECERS-R (Harms, Clifford, & Cryer, 2005). This guide to creating appropriate environments for young children is especially useful when addressing the needs of children with special needs. The following list identifies the indicators that establish provisions for children with disabilities:

- Staff follows through with activities and interactions recommended by other professionals (Ex. medical doctors, educators) to help children meet identified goals.
- Modifications are made in environment (such as a ramp) to allow the children to attend, or a therapist who visits the program to work with the children, program, and schedule so that children can participate in many activities with others.
- Parents are involved in sharing information with staff, setting goals, and giving feedback about how the program is working.
- Most of the professional intervention is carried out within the regular activities of the classroom.
- Children with disabilities are integrated into the group and participate in most activities.
- The staff contributes to individual assessment and intervention plans (p. 66).

A least restrictive environment infers a variety of instructional styles. Some children will show a preference for a particular sensory modality; some learn at a slower pace than others; some are more easily distracted; some respond more readily to visual cues and some to action cues. We need to expand our repertoire, learn as much as possible about the nature of special needs, and then adapt our techniques to the individual child (Rosenberg, Westling, & McLeskey, 2008).

A least restrictive environment also provides a broad variety of materials and manipulatives, carefully selected for an advantageous "fit" between child and media. In this multimedia world of DVDs, CDs, digital music players, WiFi, the Internet, instruments, musical toys, puppets, and satellite television and radio, the primary task is one of screening and selecting the best in music for children with special needs.

We must look with a critical eye at the work and play space of the child with special needs. What elements facilitate and enhance learning? Which elements inhibit and frustrate? Is there a cacophony of sound, glaring color, or distractions? Is the environment one in which participation and appreciation of music will flourish? Will music provide a socializing factor and develop individual skills regardless of limiting conditions? Do you see "least restrictive environment" in a new light?

## ROLE OF THE TEACHER

As a music and movement resource, this text cannot develop fully the range of exceptionality exhibited by the children one might encounter in a classroom, child care center, nursery school, or other child care environment. In most situations, the number of such children is small. Typically, a teacher might ask, "What activities are appropriate for all the children who are my responsibility?" or "What modifications or adaptations are useful for children with special needs?" Usually the major modification needed is slower pacing in a more structured setting. Careful observation of children with special needs and their behavior pattern is a given. How might an adult's creative abilities be used with this particular child to use music and movement in the daily routine? There are aspects of music and movement that any child can enjoy and learn. The current trend of placing the exceptional child with typically developing children in general education classrooms and social groups, called *inclusion,* should ensure that these children will derive the benefits of music in a natural setting. Music and movement offer the potential for growth that recognizes no differences in abilities (Gould & Sullivan, 2005). Now, read Diane Cudahy's story of working with a child with a hearing impairment.

### TALKS WITH TEACHERS

Diane Cudahy is an associate professor in the School of Education at the College of Charleston. She is also the Director of the Teachers Fellows Program, which recruits academically strong high school students who want to become public school teachers. She holds a BS in Kindergarten and Primary Education from the College of New Jersey and a PhD from the University of Tennessee with a concentration in cultural studies in education. Before moving to the college level, she taught in the public schools in New Jersey, Michigan, and Tennessee.

Diane tells a wonderful story about her second year of teaching at schools in Linden, New Jersey. She taught children with special needs. Diane writes:

Ben, a delightful seven-year-old with a hearing impairment, was fascinated by the old upright piano in the classroom. He loved to play the keys but unfortunately could not hear the full sounds of the piano. We asked the people in the maintenance department to remove the top wooden cover of the old piano and replace it with clear Plexiglas. We then removed the bottom 'front' of the piano and left it open. When Ben wanted to play the piano, he could see the hammers striking the strings. When he would sit on the floor close the piano, he would reach up and play the keys with one hand while placing his other hand on the lower strings. This enabled him to feel the vibrations of the strings. As a result, Ben could see the hammers striking the upper strings and feel the vibrations in the lower strings.

Diane's ingenuity and thoughtful process enabled Ben to enjoy the piano and to participate with his peers during music time.

The basic areas of singing, rhythms, informal use of instruments, and music listening experiences are a part of the music education of all children. For the child with special needs, different techniques might be applied, but whatever the method, working on a one-to-one basis or in small groups is strongly recommended. Determine what works, then adapt and refine.

Children in a music setting show the following responses:

- Sheer fun and enjoyment
- Attentive listening
- Increased attention span
- Participation with others
- Relaxed demeanor
- A cooperative spirit
- Nonverbal exchanges such as smiling, foot tapping, finger snapping, clapping, keeping time, swaying, and rocking
- More fluent language and speech clarity

The needs of the exceptional child are not unlike those of the typically developing child. They include a need for:

- Security
- Self-respect and gratification
- Love and attention
- Movement
- Positive interpersonal relationships
- A sense of belonging, worth, and acceptance
- A feeling of accomplishment and contribution

Music and movement can play a major part in satisfying these needs. However, specific uses of music and movement must be determined for individual children.

Particularly with children with special needs, teachers must be patient, realistic about the rate of progress, and supportive, providing reliable feedback to reinforce self-concepts and successful efforts. Recognize that there are more similarities than differences between children with special challenges and those without and that all conditions have a range of severity. Plan your musical and movement activities accordingly. Let your daily encounters with the children reflect your understanding. Continue to build your professional knowledge background regarding special needs. Figure 3–1 outlines some music and movement ideas for children with disabilities.

## General Suggestions for Children With Special Needs

Teachers who work with children with special needs should include the following musical and movement activities in their programs:

- Songs of identification: names, families, pets
- Favorite songs: "Happy Birthday," "Good Morning," television jingles, rhymes, family favorites
- Action songs involving specific body parts and motions: clapping, hopping, and nodding

**Figure 3–1    Music and Movement for Children with Disabilities**

Music and movement experiences are as important to children with disabilities as they are to all the other children in your classroom. You must make modifications in your activities to help these children express themselves as freely as they can, while deriving all the benefits the musical experience provides. The following general guidelines will help you begin to plan music and movement activities for children with disabilities:

- Provide helmets as safety devices for children with limited balancing skills.
- Give hand signals as well as verbal signals, and face children each time you make a suggestion.
- Encourage children in wheelchairs to use facial expressions to represent how they feel as they move themselves or are pushed by you or others in the group.
- Provide tactile clues for children with visual disabilities and visual clues for children with hearing disabilities.
- Allow children with limited finger movements to use other body parts when mimicking fingerplays.
- Provide carpet squares so children will have an awareness of boundaries in the general space.
- Pair children who are visually impaired with other children who can provide personal, verbal clues.
- When you are unsure about how to plan music and movement experiences for children with disabilities, seek the advice of the specialist in your school or district.

- Humorous songs or those with surprises
- Special-day songs on holidays
- Songs that can incorporate rhythm instruments such as drums and bells
- Songs using balls, puppets, and scarves
- Songs with a definite rhythm
- Songs that require the following of directions
- Name exercises in songs

## Good Teaching Techniques

Teachers should use the following effective techniques:

- Use many different approaches with a variety of media; vary level and pace.
- Use small segments.
- Build familiarity, give experience.
- Provide a choice of activities.
- Offer levels of difficulty.
- Recognize differences in attention span.
- Avoid overstimulation, lengthy activity.
- Remember to build in balance of activities.
- Inform, avoid surprises.
- Build success.

Remember, children will show the way!

# MUSIC AND MOVEMENT FOR CHILDREN WITH SPECIAL NEEDS

Most authorities consider children with special needs to include those with physical, intellectual, or learning disabilities; those with visual and hearing impairments; those with speech and language disorders; those who are classified as gifted; and those with behavior and emotional disorders. Deiner (1983) added the culturally distinct.

## Learning Disabilities

Learning disabilities (LD) refer to disabilities in children with a variety of learning differences, including dyslexia, auditory and visual processing, attention disorders, and memory problems. Educators often disagree on the definition of learning disabilities. However, these disabilities often lead to academic underachievement and problems with communication and the social skills necessary for life. Because learning disabilities are not as easy to recognize as hearing or visual disabilities, the children can often be mislabeled. Common misdiagnoses include hyperactivity, immaturity, or emotional disturbance. Teachers and caregivers should always consult with parents, therapists, and physicians when planning music and movement activities for children with learning disabilities. Also, children with these disabilities need to be with teachers who are knowledgeable and sensitive to the children's needs and who understand the importance of family involvement (S. Gurganus, personal communication, March, 2006).

*Attention deficit disorder* (ADD) comes in two forms, with and without hyperactivity. Children with *attention deficit hyperactivity disorder* (ADHD) cannot sit or participate in musical activities for long with the rest of the group. They often wander off in the room on their own or spend time clowning around in front of the other children. One of the ways teachers can help them to focus during music and movement activities is to assign them to a particular location and to praise them for staying on task. Children with ADD, however, are able to hyperfocus. In other words, they can concentrate on one task and tune out everything else if they find the task appealing. For these children, it is best to deliver music and movement activities on an individual basis. Teachers can provide headphones for the children to listen to music or introduce them to computer animation with musical accompaniment as a way of helping them to attend to music and movement activities.

## Children with Speech and Language Impairments

A child with a *speech impairment* needs singing—its phrasing, rhythm, and emphasis. Music sharpens the ear and aids the development of focus and listening skills (Miche, 2002).

Nearly two thirds of the children who are speech impaired suffer from articulation defects. When they speak or sing, sounds are distorted, substituted, or omitted, the most common being the *d, l, r,* and *s.* Songs that incorporate these sounds in a kind of speech game are useful.

Sing, sing,
Say your name.
Sing, sing, sing,
All the same.
La, la, la,

Sing, sing, sing.
La, la, la,
Ring, ring, ring.
La, la, la,
Ding, dong, ding.
La, la, la,
Sing, sing, sing.
Sally, Sally, Sally,
Sing your name.
Sally, Sally, Sally,
Say your name.
Ring around the rosies,
Sing your name.
Ring around the rosies,
Play the game.

Select songs of reasonable length and difficulty. Teach a song in phrases. Have the children listen and then repeat each phrase. Because articulation and listening are most important, be a good model in speaking and singing.

Cleft-palate speech, delayed speech, and stuttering are other impairments in which music may alleviate distress through relaxation of the muscles and vocal chords. Often severe stutterers can sing without stuttering and yet stutter when speaking.

Many of the traditional, simple songs of early childhood offer excellent memory and speech training opportunities. The repetition, lively movement, and humor of such rhymes as "Three Blind Mice," "Row, Row, Row Your Boat," "Baa, Baa, Black Sheep," "This Old Man," "Pop Goes the Weasel," "Old MacDonald Had a Farm," "Ten Little Indians," "One, Two, Buckle My Shoe," and "Shoo, Fly" make these songs particularly good for nonverbal children. In fact, adults working with children with speech disabilities might deliberately select songs that promote strong language and speech development. Even television commercials, jingles, and popular songs are appealing. Watch a group of young children enjoying and participating in "Sesame Street." Even the youngest quickly learns the sprightly tunes, which encourage speech production. Use pictures to illustrate the songs, or experiment with choral verse in which children participate as one. Tape the child's voice as he or she speaks and sings and then play the tape back for him or her to encourage speech production.

## INTELLECTUAL DIFFERENCES AND MUSIC AND MOVEMENT

The child who is identified as a slow learner or as gifted, who is perceptually challenged, or who has severe intellectual disabilities can profit from musical and movement activities. Early identification of these special differences can facilitate planning appropriate programs for each child. Guidance and support from adults provide the contact, security, and encouragement necessary for these and all children. Music has a unique value; it develops self-confidence and opens up channels of communication.

Authorities agree that music experiences should begin at the earliest possible age; some say even before birth! Teachers and parents should seek every opportunity to provide stimulating musical experiences. The child then learns to value music by anticipating enthusiasm and excitement, thus growing musically as well as socially.

Encouraging exploration of space helps children find exciting new ways to move.

Old favorites such as "I'm a Little Teapot," "Humpty Dumpty," "Hickory, Dickory, Dock," "Sing a Song of Sixpence," "Little Miss Muffet," and "Little Bo-Peep" can be introduced with colorful illustrations and movements to facilitate learning. For the very young learner with mental challenges, music and movement can strengthen memory and concentration, thus promoting achievement.

Drums, resonator bells, cymbals, zithers, and Autoharps® can be used. Music with short phrases and repeated tones is suggested. Keep selections brief, varying the length with age and ability of the group. Wrist bells, wood blocks, and triangles can be used to develop eye-hand coordination. Strong melody appeals, but mixing rhythm instruments and singing are not advised for these children.

The rate of development in the child with intellectual and developmental disabilities, such as Down syndrome, is uneven. Background is acquired at a slower pace, and musical and movement experiences need to be repeated more often and in many different ways. Never be discouraged while working with children with intellectual or developmental disabilities. Responses may be hidden.

The child with intellectual and developmental disabilities will have a shorter attention span. Singing, playing instruments, and moving to music are enjoyed. Rote learning of songs, repetition, melody, and a sequential presentation are usually successful. Visual aids and devices for manipulation are useful and add to understanding and enjoyment. Try both instrumental and vocal media.

Rocking the body to music, clapping, and brisk marching can be demonstrated and enjoyed. A song such as "Row, Row, Row Your Boat" is appealing. "Jack Be Nimble" can be chanted and acted out. Short phrases, familiar topics, a strong rhythm, and repetition are most successful. Many authorities suggest that singing be the focal point for these children. Give them ample opportunity to sing, and emphasize enjoyment. CD's, digital music players, and piano have all found a place in the lives of children with intellectual or developmental disabilities. The same music may not soothe all individuals. Some children will respond favorably, others adversely. The reactions of each child are unique.

Creativity, ingenuity, understanding, and patience, coupled with a wide variety of musical activities, can enrich the lives of both adult caregivers and children with learning differences as they work together.

### Autism Spectrum Disorder

Children with autism manifest delays in social skills and language. Some children with autism spectrum disorder also have cognitive delays. In fact, children with autism may have delayed language development, social interaction difficulties, and a need for regular routines and rigid structure. These children may be very sensitive to sound, light, and touch.

Children with autism may also benefit from the qualities of music and movement. Such children appear to be oblivious and unaware of surroundings; music may break through this barrier. Often such a child will rock to music, sing or hum, or follow along with the singer. Usually children with autism require a one-to-one learning situation, and progress is slow. There is some evidence that children with autism tend to prefer just a few types of music, which are simple and repetitive in nature. One-syllable verbal instructions, one-gesture signs, moving and speaking in synchrony with the child, and adapting a rhythm to that of the child may increase attention and learning.

When teachers use music and movement with children with autism, they must observe the children's sensitivity to sounds and volume of the music and adjust it to a comfortable level for them. Children with autism spectrum disorder also need a quiet place where they can go to be alone, especially when they become overwhelmed by classroom activity. Music and movement may be a catalyst to help these children participate in group activities. Much remains to be investigated in understanding this physiological disorder with genetic inheritance as a major factor. We believe that music and movement can add an important dimension to the lives of children with autism.

## CHILDREN WHO ARE PHYSICALLY CHALLENGED

Children who are physically challenged are the fastest growing population of children receiving special education services (Heward, 2006). There are many known and unknown causes of physical disabilities. These disabilities include neurological or musculoskeletal impairments such as cerebral palsy, spina bifida, multiple sclerosis, poliomyelitis, and arthritis. Children with such limitations must cope with a restriction of mobility. In these cases the attitude of the teacher is crucial in promoting achievement. It is important that the teacher or other adults in the classroom have a clear understanding of the type of the impairment and the physiological effects movement can have on these children. For example, children with spina bifida, cerebral palsy, or arthritis must be given rest periods so that they don't experience pain.

It is very important that teachers remember to plan music activities for all children, including children with special needs.

Following are several activities to use with children who are physically challenged. Gurganus (2007) suggests that children be given streamers to wave while their classmates are marching, using fingerplays to assist children who experience muscle-control problems, and experiment with larger motor movements. Teachers should always encourage children who are physically challenged to participate at whichever level they are comfortable. For example, if children cannot hold rhythm instruments or streamers, the teacher can attach these around the child's wrists or ankles. Children in wheelchairs need large areas in which to move to music, and their classmates can take turns dancing with wheelchair-bound children. Krebs (1990) recommends cane or crutch tapping as a substitute for hand clapping or foot stomping.

Singing offers relaxation and eases tension. Rhythms, too, can be enjoyed if the child can manage lightweight, simple instruments such as sticks, bells, sand blocks, tambourines, or drums. Sometimes body rhythms such as nodding, swaying, moving the upper body, and tapping fingers and hands are possible. Some physical therapists employ mat exercises with music. Simple fingerplays set to music offer opportunities for musical appreciation and enrichment and the release of pent-up feelings. Coordination and control will often improve and muscles strengthen through use of rhythms.

It is productive for the adult working with a child who is physically challenged to consult with other individuals involved: the therapist, the physician, and certainly the parent. Adaptations in programs in the music environment may be helpful. Keep in mind that children with multiple handicaps may withdraw into themselves and operate within a small radius. They may have problems with laterality and directionality; concepts such as *up, down, over, under,* and *around* may confuse them (Heward, 2006). Music can be used quite successfully to help children master these concepts. Those with multiple challenges may take part peripherally, and security soon builds because there is no right or wrong in music and no competition.

## Cerebral Palsy, Muscular Dystrophy, Spina Bifida, Arthritis, Epilepsy, and Neurological Challenges

A relatively large group of children suffer from *cerebral palsy*. In cerebral palsy, damage to the central nervous system affects one side of the body or the entire body. Speech and language are sometimes impaired. The adult caregiver must respond to the needs of each child and adapt the music participation level correspondingly.

*Muscular dystrophy* may present other problems as muscles slowly deteriorate. Singing and movement through rhythmic activities should be encouraged. *Spina bifida, arthritis,* and *epilepsy* may be slight or advanced in young children. Problems with gross motor activities, locomotion, and control may limit participation. A child with arthritis, in particular, may have difficulty using rhythm instruments or being involved in simple dances. Movement is beneficial, but check for signs of pain or discomfort in the child. It is important to provide ample time for rest and relaxation for children with these challenging conditions. Remember the therapeutic quality of music and its power to soothe and relax.

For children with limited mobility or loss of mobility in limbs or extremities, some adaptations can be made in music activities and simple musical instruments to enable children to experience the joy of music and the well-being that results from participation.

Children with *neurological challenges* are often described on the basis of their actions, and their special needs can be confused with many others. Behaviors are nearly always exaggerated, extreme, and persistent, particularly in these aspects:

- Rigidity (wanting everything to be as always, for example, the same song or the same key and tempo; disturbed and disoriented by change)
- Hyperactivity (irritable attention; paying too much attention to everything; unable to distinguish between important and less important)
- Emotional liability (exhibiting inappropriate and extreme expressions, laughter)

Those working with the neurologically challenged report that such children often respond strongly to music. For many, music is the first medium that holds their attention.

## Children with Visual Impairments

The Education of All Handicapped Children Act (PL 94-142) offers this definition of when children are considered to have visual impairments: Even when the impairment is corrected, it adversely affects their learning. Many children with visual disabilities also have learning disabilities, developmental delays, and attention disorders (Miche, 2002).

Children with *visual impairment*, including those who read and write in Braille and those who are able to read enlarged print, can particularly profit from music and movement activities because they may not be able to participate in other art forms. Through music and movement these children may venture into new activities and explore a larger world. Young children with visual impairments require little in the way of special adaptation to music and movement activities; auditory and primary learning styles can be employed. Auditory memory can be enhanced through music. Concrete experiences and tactile aids should be provided, especially exploration of the rhythm instrument and opportunities to touch and to play other instruments. Do not forget CD and digital music players and the many resources found online.

Many children with visual impairments enjoy keyboard instruments as well as rhythm instruments. Popular music stars such as Ray Charles and Stevie Wonder are excellent role models for children who are visually disabled.

Teachers can use a number of methods when working with children with visual impairments. For example, children with visual impairments should sit near the teacher

Provide children with a rich variety of tactile and manipulative experiences.

so the children can see more easily. The teacher can hold hands with the child or pair the child with a partner who places his or her hands on the shoulders of the child with visual problems. This closeness between the teacher and the child or between a child with visual impairments and a partner can help alleviate some of the fear and apprehension the visually impaired child might experience. Teachers must be sensitive to this fear and design movement activities that begin with stationary movements, such as bending or swaying. Once the children are comfortable moving in one spot, you can gradually extend the movement experiences to safe, ambulatory motions, such as crawling or rolling, since these keep the child in contact with the floor. Children with visual impairments *can* learn how to hop and gallop or perform more complicated movements, but you may have to guide them as they learn how to do these movements. Teachers should also use verbal cues and very clear directions when encouraging music and movement activities for the child with visual impairments. For example, when a teacher says "everyone turns around and around," the child with visual impairments can participate along with all the other children. Music and movement can encourage children with visual challenges to participate in something they can do well. In addition, music and movement provide social interaction that may not be available to these children in other areas of their lives.

## Children with Hearing Impairments

Children with hearing impairments need exposure to music and movement activities that help promote flexibility, relaxation, and hearing activity. They profit from sitting close to the adult, to modification of sound volume, and to the use of visual stimuli. The social stimulation of music and movement and the sense of belonging to the group can be invaluable.

Children with hearing impairments can participate in rhythmic activities, dancing, and keyboard experiences. Autoharps® can provide an unusual experience; have the children touch the vibrating strings and put their ears against the instrument to "hear" the music. Headsets can be used to amplify the music to develop concepts of loud and soft, near and far, and high and low. Playing musical instruments also increases muscle strength and joint motion and develops coordination.

The challenge of supporting a child's use of a hearing aid is an important one.

Noneducators tend to assume that children with hearing impairments cannot experience music or movement. This is not true. The majority of children with hearing impairments are not totally deaf. Instead, children have varying degrees of hearing loss (S. Gurganus, personal communication, March, 2006). Children with hearing impairments need music and movement education just as much as a child with typical hearing. The development of rhythm and movement is critical to the development of the "whole child." Activities that have great promise for children with hearing impairments include tapping, clapping, and playing rhythm instruments, especially the ones that make a loud sound such as cymbals and drums. Maracas have tactile appeal, and children can feel the vibrations as they shake these instruments. Many children with hearing impairments can hear good-quality, low-pitched drums. As they listen to these low pitches, they can also notice the feel of the vibrating drumhead. When children with hearing impairments place a hand on the speakers of a music player, they can feel the vibrations of a deep-bass pulsation through their hands. Teachers can hold hands and dance with hearing-impaired children while helping the children match rhythm to movement. This is especially helpful for children with balance problems.

Children with hearing impairments can be helped to learn nursery rhymes by emphasizing the tactile sense—placing their fingers on the lid of the piano to feel vibrations or sitting on the floor near large speakers or drums. Gurganus (2007) recommends placing a CD player on the floor and turning the bass to the maximum volume. Invite children with hearing impairments to take off both shoes so that the vibrations of the bass can be felt through the feet. This enables them to feel the beat of the music so that they can move their bodies, arms, and heads to the rhythm of the musical beat. The children's own experiences when feeling rhythm and beat through vibrations is more important and meaningful than teacher-assisted instruction.

Much repetition is necessary for children with hearing impairments to feel the rhythm. Strong rhythmic actions such as marches, hopping, and skipping can make music a personal experience for them. These actions also improve body coordination and speech rhythm. When we consider the degree of the impairment, we can see why music is not always emphasized. Clear speech is of paramount importance to children with hearing impairments; thus involvement in music can be extremely beneficial. Songs, chants, choral speaking, and poetry put into rousing songs all offer avenues of expression and possibilities for speech and language development.

Teachers who have children with hearing impairments in their classroom should learn sign language. In addition to learning signs that the child with hearing impairments understands, the teacher should practice communication skills through exaggerated facial expressions and pantomime.

The music classroom can serve as an excellent vehicle for the integration for children with hearing impairments; it includes enjoyment and education for everyone.

Children of all cultures engage in solitary play.

## GIFTED AND/OR TALENTED

*Gifted* children will usually want to extend music activities, to experiment with a variety of instruments, to develop CD and digital music collections, to enjoy hearing musicians, to learn about the lives of the performers, and to emulate the stars of the day. Often gifted children can be precocious with melody or composition. However, the musically talented child should enjoy the regular activities suited to any young child. Outside the school setting, children gifted musically may be deeply involved in performance and practice. We need to avoid exploiting or displaying such a child.

Enrichment activities should be appropriately complex to challenge and stimulate. Quality should be stressed as well as individual initiative. Here is an instance in which the teachers/caregivers might well learn from the child as they share music experience, appreciate new selections, and explore new modes. We are not all musicians, but we can all learn from one another.

Most important, parents and other adults need to be aware of resources and enrichment opportunities within the community that will expand the musical interests of the gifted child. Teachers can recommend that families investigate area libraries, theater and dance groups for children, and civic groups. But remember to consider the child first, the talent second.

Music has a critical role in the education of children with special needs; it can build group spirit and cohesion; it can extend memory; it can offer a much-needed place in the spotlight; it can rehabilitate the spirit; it can provide a beginning, an introduction into the world of all children, and a first opportunity to be like others.

*We cannot separate the care and education of children.*

—Dew Faerie

## KEY IDEAS

1. Think about the statement that "everyone is differently able."
2. Children with special needs differ from typically developing children only in degree of condition.
3. Like typically developing children, children with special needs possess varying ranges of musical talent and movement ability.
4. Music, because it is nonverbal, may be an entrée to participation in everyday activity for children with special needs.
5. Music develops self-confidence and opens up expanded language development and channels of communication.
6. Music provides a way for children with special needs to belong to a group and make a positive contribution to it.
7. Music can be a great enabler. It cuts across all barriers, including time, age, race, and status.
8. People with disabilities are not unable.

## SUMMARY

The goals of music and movement for children with special needs are much the same as those for all other children. Emotional and aesthetic benefits are paramount. Auditory, visual, and kinesthetic skills are stressed, as is *quality* of musical and movement experiences. Because music and movement are nonthreatening and nonpunitive mediums, they can open avenues for communication, thus enabling the child with special needs to feel included in all classroom activities. Each child responds in a unique way to music and movement. Children grow in special ways and adapt to their individual need for the benefits and joys of music and movement.

## QUESTIONS TO CONSIDER

1. Due to the increasing numbers of children with special needs in our schools, add to your collection at least 10 songs appropriate to a typical group setting. Illustrate activities for each song.
2. Select three songs. Describe how each could be adapted to meet the needs of special learners.
3. Explore the community in which you live. What resources are available for children with special needs? Cite instances where music and movement are unifying influences.
4. Cite examples of music and movement as a great enabler.
5. What examples can you give of individuals in public life who have overcome limiting physical conditions?
6. Participate in the activities of the Special Olympics in your area or research this organization on the Web. How does this event contribute to community well-being?

## REFERENCES

Cook, R., Klein, M., & Tessier, A. (2008). *Adapting early childhood curricula for children in inclusive settings* (7th ed.). Upper Saddle River, NJ: Pearson.

Deiner, P. L. (1983). *Resources for teaching young children with special needs*. New York, NY: Harcourt Brace Jovanovich.

Gould, P., & Sullivan, J. (2005). *The inclusive early childhood classroom; Easy ways to adapt learning centers for all*. Upper Saddle River, NJ: Pearson.

Gurganus, S. (2007). *Math instruction for students with learning problems*. Boston, MA: Allyn & Bacon.

Harms, T., Clifford, R., & Cryer, D. (2005). *Early childhood environment rating scale* (Rev. ed.). New York, NY: Teachers College Press.

Heward, W. (2006). *Exceptional children: An introduction to special education* (8th ed.). Upper Saddle River, NJ: Pearson.

Krebs, P. L. (1990). Rhythms and dance. In J. P. Winnick (Ed.), *Adapted physical education and sport* (pp. 379–389). Champaign, IL: Human Kinetics.

Miche, M. (2002). *Weaving music into young minds*. Albany, NY: Delmar.

Pica, R. (2004). *Experiences in movement birth to age 8* (3rd ed.). Clifton Park, NY: Thomson/Delmar Learning.

Rosenberg, M., Westling, D., & McLeskey, J. (2008). *Special education for today's teachers: An introduction*. Upper Saddle River, NJ: Pearson.

## CHAPTER FOUR

# Music and Movement
# for Infants and Toddlers

*What's best about music is not to be
found in the notes . . .*

Gustav Mahler

*Today, music permeates children's lives through more avenues than ever before. Music in the early years contributes to healthy development for all children.*

*The child's whole world is filled with sound and music. It is everywhere. Children all over the world have an ability to make and respond to music. They like to explore its many possibilities, like to create it, and are highly motivated by its fascinating sounds and rhythms.*

*Children's musical growth is similar to the rest of their development. As children grow, they are constantly gathering all sorts of sounds and movement impressions. Children who have ample opportunities to experiment with sound and movement will acquire a rich background for later musical growth and understanding.*

## INFANCY AND MUSIC

From the moment of birth and even before, children adapt to the sounds within their environment, relating them to their own abilities to create and explore the rhythms and tonal patterns of sound. It has been determined that in the fifth month of pregnancy, the fetus responds to sounds of all kinds. It is not unusual to hear a mother-to-be announce that her unborn baby is much more active when she strums and plays a guitar or Auto-harp® held close to her body.

The unborn baby's sense of hearing is activated when music is played at the same time each day. Being careful to adjust the volume, some expectant mothers place the headphones of a portable music device on their stomachs and play classical music to the fetus. As cited by Shetler (1985), "Infants who received systematic prenatal stimulation exhibit remarkable attention behaviors, accurately imitate sounds made by adults and appear to structure vocalization much earlier than infants who did not have prenatal musical stimulation" (p. 27).

Soon after birth, infants begin to use their resources for exploring the world around them. They search for the sound when voices are heard. From the fourth week, babies

Young children enjoy acting out the song "Sometimes I Am Tall".

can detect who is near them by the timbre (characteristic quality) of the voice. Around 3 months of age, they are often awakened or comforted by the sound of the parent's or caregiver's voice. Typically, babies will turn their eyes and head in the direction from which the sound is coming. Even though they cannot grasp the object, babies will become excited, wiggle, and smile at the sound of a bell attached to a familiar toy.

At approximately 4 months, babies may use their feet or hands to strike a favorite toy that produces a pleasant sound when it is struck. At first, this action is reflexive and accidental in nature, but if the sound is interesting, pleasing, or perhaps amusing, infants will tend to repeat the action time and again. At around 4 months, they also enjoy the sound of their own laughter and repeat it.

There are two basic stages of music making during the child's first year and a half. The first stage is approximately from birth to 3 or 4 months. Crying is the baby's first sound. "A baby's cry can vary in pitch, volume, and rhythm, showing rudimentary musical patterns" (Miche, 2002, p. 77). Babies will coo, gurgle, squeal, and babble during this stage. During the first year, babies will experiment in making sounds that are pleasing.

The second stage of music extends from approximately 4 months to 18 months (Brewer, 2004). Babbling will increase. Often the vocalizations of babies will be motivated by hearing their parents sing or talk to them. Between 6 and 9 months of age, musical babbling, defined as making speech sounds on various pitches, begins and often is produced when the baby moves to music. It is frequently produced when someone sings to the infant.

From 6 to 9 months, as babies continue to grow and experiment with their voices, their sounds often take on the form of singing. At this stage of a baby's development, they are in almost constant motion and will frequently make sounds to accompany their play and movement. These sounds are often produced as babies interact with objects in their play. Around 11 months of age, jabbering begins, and by 18 months, a child is speaking and ready to sing. In their own way, babies constantly communicate with those around them. Very rarely are these beginnings of musical sound and bodily movement absent from the young child.

## INFANCY AND MOVEMENT

As we all know, infants spend more time sleeping than anything else. However, movement experiences are crucial for infants, probably more than any other age group. Current research reveals that today's infants are spending almost 60 hours a week sitting in things, such as car seats, baby swings, and high chairs. Recent brain research (Gabbard, 1998) provides insight into the importance of movement for infants: "Early movement experiences are beneficial to optimal brain development" (p. 54). Gabbard reveals that movement experiences for infants are essential to neural stimulation (use it or lose it). The optimal time for motor skill development is from the prenatal period to around age 5 (Robert, 2001). It is not always necessary to have movement programs for infants. Infants like to be held, and they like one-on-one time with adults. Basic verbal and visual interactions between infants and adults and floor time that allow infants to move on their own in their own space are appropriate activities for promoting basic motor skill development.

As all educators know, children's early learning experiences are based on sensorimotor activities. Infants and toddlers learn best when they can explore and discover, observe and imitate, and move about in their environment. As children look, hear, touch, taste, and smell, they are gathering information through their senses. The development of motor skills can be broken down into two categories: gross motor skills (using large muscles such arm, legs, and trunk) and fine motor skills (using muscles like those in the hands and fingers). Assist infants and toddlers in their abilities to become more coordinated and to have greater control over their bodies. An important part of sensorimotor development occurs when an infant or toddler is cuddled, tickled, rocked, and held. These intimate interactions between adult and child have a profound effect on cognitive, affective, and sensorimotor development. As Albarecht and Miller (2001) note:

> Children gain coordination of fine and gross motor skills by repeating the patterns of those skills over and over again, strengthening the communication and coordination between neurons. Babies who do not have experiences on the floor, moving their bodies, reaching and batting at objects, picking up many different objects, etc., may not receive enough stimulating experiences to increase synaptic coordination and communication. (p. 255)

## Movement Learning Activities for Infants

Infants love the tried-and-true classical game of "peek-a-boo." Places your hands over your face and say, "Where's Mommy (or Teacher, Helper, Friend, etc.)?" As you move your hands away from your face, you laugh, and the baby laughs with you. You could extend this game to hiding your whole body. For example, hide behind the chair and ask, "Where's Mommy?" Infants love this social interaction. Infants also love to dance. Cradle the infant in your arms and dance through the day. You can dance between changes, you can dance your way to feeding time, and you can dance for the pure joy of moving with an infant. Simple games such as "This Little Piggy Went to Market" help infants develop bodily awareness, which is where movement education truly begins.

*This Little Piggy*

This little piggy went to market.
This little piggy stayed home.
This little piggy had roast beef.
This little piggy had none.
This little piggy cried "wee-wee-wee"
all the way home.

Music educators recommend finding time every day to sing and play with babies.

Point to each toe in turn, starting with the big toe, and on the last line tickle underneath the baby's foot.

Don't forget to give the infant plenty of things to kick and throw. Soft stuffed animals or small pillows give an infant something to touch, kick, and throw. Invent games to encourage as many cross-lateral experiences as you can to keep your infant moving, laughing, and exploring.

Fingerplays such as "Slowly, Slowly, Very Slowly" are also excellent movement activities for infants.

*Slowly, Slowly, Very Slowly*

Slowly, slowly, very slowly
Creeps the garden snail.
Slowly, slowly, very slowly
Up the wooden rail.
Quickly, quickly, very quickly
Runs the little mouse.
Quickly, quickly, very quickly
'Round about the house.

Use hands to mime the actions suggested by the words, or play with the baby as a tickling game.

*'Round and 'Round the Garden*

'Round and 'round the garden
(Run your index finger around the baby's palm)
Went the teddy bear,
One step,
Two steps,
(Jump your finger up the baby's arm)
Tickly under there.
(Tickle the baby under the arm)
'Round and 'round the haystack,
Went the little mouse,
One step,
Two steps,
In his little house.

*Pat-a-Cake*

Pat-a-cake, pat-a-cake,
Baker's man,
Bake me a cake
As fast as you can.
Pat it and prick it
And mark it with a B,
And put it in the oven
For Baby and me.

*To Market, To Market*

To market, to market,
To buy a fat pig;
Home again, home again,
Jiggety jig.
To market, to market,
To buy a fat hog,

Home again, home again,
Joggety jog.

(Say this verse while giving the baby a knee ride)
Stephanie Johnston's toddlers love singing and acting out the following songs.

*Jump! Jump! (To the tune of: BINGO)*

There was a class that had a girl and Mary was her name-O
Jump, jump Mary
Jump, jump Mary
Jump, jump Mary
We're glad you're here today!
We conclude using the whole class...we're the "Seashell Class".
There was a school that had a class and the Seashells were their name-O
Jump, jump Seashells
Jump, jump Seashells
Jump, jump Seashells
We're glad you're here today!

Stephanie introduces this song the first week of school and reports that it is a wonderful community builder and provides her a way to assess who can jump.

*A Ram-Sam-Sam (traditional Moroccan folk song)*

A ram-sam-sam (alternate hammering fists together)
A ram-sam-sam (alternate hammering fists together)
A gooley, gooley, gooley (rolling fists)
And a ram-sam-sam (alternate hammering fists together).
A raffy (raise your arms above your head)
A raffy (raise your arms above your head)
A gooley, gooley, gooley (rolling fists)
And a ram-sam-sam (alternate hammering fists together).

**Where, Oh Where**

American Traditional Game

1. Where, oh where is dear lit-tle Mar-Y? Where, oh Where is
dear lit-tle Mar-Y? Where, oh Where is dear lit-tle Mar-Y?
Way down yon-der in the paw-paw patch.

This is a crazy, nonsense action rhyme that the children absolutely love. Even the shyest of children will participate!

"Where, Oh Where" is another traditional game/song that helps build classroom community by encouraging children to recognize each others' names.

## AUDITORY STIMULATION OF INFANTS

Between birth and 1 year, most infants begin to refine their ability to listen to different sounds in their environment. It is during the early years that infants need to hear a variety of sounds and learn to focus their attention on them. It is essential for parents and caregivers to provide very young children with many listening experiences in which the children can actively participate. Music experiences are invaluable as children learn listening skills. Very young children will often combine listening with active participation as they move their bodies to the music. The next section suggests ways to increase auditory stimulation.

### Birth to 1 Year

A well-developed sense of hearing is important to all future learning. Parents and others caring for infants should provide sound-stimulation toys and experiences that will promote auditory development. One such toy is a weighted apple that will reproduce a series of "ting-a-ling" sounds when it is shaken or struck. When an infant is a few weeks old, the parent can shake the musical toy so it can be heard. Later, when the infant is being changed or is lying awake in bed, the musical toy should be placed close enough so that the infant can produce the same sound by striking the toy. The infant will probably continue to repeat this behavior because it is pleasing. Parents should be close by to enjoy and guide this experience with their child. Between 3 and 6 months, the infant will respond to sound stimulation or speech by vocalizing. Around 5 months, infants will react and vocalize to their own names.

Babies learn very early how to shake toys to make noises.

**Figure 4–1    Promoting Auditory Development, Birth to 6 Months**

1. Talk, hum, chant, or sing to the baby when you diaper, bathe, dress, and feed the baby. Poems and nursery rhymes are good choices.
2. Soothe and calm a restless infant by singing or playing a quiet song like "Hush Little Baby" or "Sleep Baby Sleep." Hold the baby in your arms. Sing or hum the song softly, and use a gentle rocking motion.
3. If the baby seems upset or unhappy, sing a livelier tune to catch the baby's attention. Then change to a quieter, soothing lullaby type of song to quiet the child. To make a baby more attentive, begin by singing a soothing lullaby and then change to a more active and rhythmic one.
4. Let the baby hear the ticking of a clock, as long as the ticking sound is not harsh. As infants and toddlers grow older, they are fascinated by the different sounds of clocks.
5. When talking to the baby, vary the tone of your voice. A baby likes to hear sounds that keep changing. Use inflection in your voice.
6. Occasionally play selections from a good-quality music system.

Those caring for infants younger than 6 months will find the suggestions in Figure 4–1 helpful in promoting auditory development.

Babies need singing models so they can learn to sing, just as they need good speaking models to imitate for talking. When they hear others sing, they discover that there is another way of expressing themselves that is different from talking. When adults and older children sing to them at close range, babies can see the shape and movement of the lips as the sounds are produced. Forrai (1996) reminds us that "music greatly influences the development of young children, especially with regard to their speech, movement, social, and emotional development" (p. 18).

One of the best ways parents and caregivers can model singing is to sing about what is going on. Make up little musical phrases. It doesn't matter what notes you sing; make up the tune and rhythm spontaneously to fit the words. After a few attempts, you will be surprised at how easy it is to make up these little musical episodes.

Songs and rhythms that actively involve babies tend to be their favorites—and parents and caregivers like them, too. Babies will generally smile and squeal with delight when someone helps them clap their hands or move their legs up and down to a favorite nursery rhyme or lilting, rhythmic tune. A baby's face will light up as she opens and closes the lid of a music box; she will delight in being in control of starting and stopping those beautiful sounds.

The staff of the Parent-Infant-Toddler Program at the Child Development Center at Kent State University has used music and auditory discrimination extensively. Soon after the program was implemented, staff members quickly became aware that they had underestimated the enjoyment and importance to the children of the role of auditory discrimination and stimulation. They observed that infants showed continuous preferences for the auditory play materials. Some of these materials included Ticking Clock (Fisher-Price), Happy Apple (Childcraft), musical instruments (such as bells and drums), pots, pans, spoons, toys that squeak, and action-response toys (for example, a push-pull musical cylinder). They also observed the immediate impact of the sound of a recording playing in the classroom. When a staff member would begin playing a recording, virtually all of the infants in the 3- to 11-month class would stop interacting and turn toward the sound of the music.

**Figure 4–2   Promoting Auditory Development, 6 to 12 Months**

1. Talk, hum, and sing to the baby. Talk about toys, and play games like pat-a-cake and peek-a-boo. Infants enjoy songs even more if their names are mentioned.
2. Attach a mobile near the baby's crib. Many mobiles revolve and have music boxes that play delightful nursery-rhyme tunes. Other mobiles contain objects that make different sounds when struck with the hand or foot.
3. Tie a bell to the baby's bootie or shoestring. Older infants like to shake a bell.
4. Provide lightweight, colorful rattles that produce different sounds. Choose rattles with pleasing, musical sounds. Many rattles are just noisemakers.
5. Shake a set of keys.
6. At times, hold the telephone receiver up to the baby's ear so the voice on the other end can be heard. Babies are usually fascinated by this.
7. Clap your hands. Go from loud clapping to soft clapping. Take hold of the baby's hands. Clap them together. Sing in time to the clapping.
8. When reading books containing pictures of animals or other objects that make sounds, try to imitate the sounds with your voice.
9. Give the baby a pan and lid or a pan and a wooden spoon. Some babies prefer these sound makers over musical toys.
10. Hold the baby in your arms, and dance to music. Change your movements according to the tempo and mood of the music.

Those caring for infants older than 6 months will find the additional suggestions in Figure 4–2 helpful in promoting auditory development.

## THE IMPORTANCE OF LULLABIES FOR INFANTS

Since response to sound is one of the most highly developed abilities in the newborn infant, children need to be musically nurtured from birth. Staincliffe Maternity Hospital in England soothes new infants by playing recorded music of such composers as Brahms, Handel, and Mozart. The effect on the infants works wonders, hospital attendants say. In some hospitals, a program of lullaby music is piped into rooms where mothers are feeding their babies.

Lullabies from the greatest composers and spontaneous melodies sung and hummed by loving caregivers have brought comfort and sleep to countless babies. For generations, people throughout the world have sung lullabies to their babies as they cuddled them in their arms and gently rocked them to sleep. Modern research is only beginning to discover the full importance of lullabies. Hearing soft, rhythmic songs brings a sense of calmness and security to the sensitive infant. In addition to soothing an infant, rocking and singing help the infant become accustomed to the "feelings" of sound motion. Without this type of gentle introduction to music, many infants will continue to react with a startle to sudden movement and loud sounds and noises.

Another benefit of singing lullabies is the communication that occurs between the caregiver and the baby. An infant often seems to respond directly to the singer by cooing and babbling, thus encouraging the development of speech and singing. See Figure 4–3 for more ideas on singing lullabies to infants.

**Figure 4–3   Suggestions for Singing Lullabies to Infants**

1. Build a repertoire of favorite lullabies. If possible, memorize them. This is important, as many of today's young parents have no memories of being lullabied and are not familiar with the most beautiful lullabies from around the world. There are excellent lullaby books on the market. There is also a wide variety of good lullaby compact discs (CDs) available. *Note:* CDs should be used only as accompaniment or as an aid when learning new songs. The parent's or teacher's voice should always be present.
2. Some infants prefer one lullaby over another; however, don't limit your singing to only music labeled *lullabies.* Try singing contemporary songs and show tunes. Infants often enjoy variety and a change of pace.
3. As you securely hold and gently rock an infant, smile warmly and look directly into the infant's face and eyes. This kind of "bonding" brings contentment and security to the infant.

In today's technological world, people are accustomed to hearing music produced by top professionals. It's understandable that when comparing themselves to professionals, some people feel inadequate in making music on their own. It is not unusual for parents and teachers to become unduly concerned about the quality of their singing voices. Some will not attempt to sing to or with children. It is more important that adults sing to babies than that they sing well. Authorities like Lind and Hardgrove (1978) remind us,

It is not the quality of the voice that matters, it is the connection. . . . It is not the on-key, smooth mechanical perfection that brings joy to infants as well as adults. The joy comes in the rendition, and the example of this intimate parent-to-infant message encourages the child to sing. (p. 10)

Some of our favorite lullabies can be found on a great website, http://lullabies.adoption .com/. Here, you will find all the lyrics to old favorites such as "All Through the Night," "Brahms' Lullaby," "Day Is Done," "Toora, Loora, Loora," and "All the Pretty Horses."

**ROCK-A-BYE BABY**

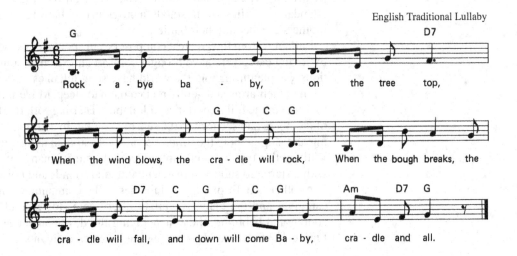

English Traditional Lullaby

# LULLABIES FROM AROUND THE WORLD

Since lullabies are usually soft and slow, they create a soothing mood that infants find calming. There are many well-known lullabies from around the world, and four are included here. Take the time to make up your own melodies for these lullabies or memorize them as a soft-spoken chant. As I stated earlier, babies really don't care if you can sing on key. The most important part of singing lullabies to infants is the one-on-one intimacy that they convey. The first lullaby, "Sleep My Baby" was introduced to me by my friend and colleague Dr. E. Olaiya Aina, who was born in Nigeria.

*Sleep My Baby*

Sleep, my baby, near to me
Lu-lu, lu-lu, lu-lu
Close your velvet eyes
Far away in their nest
Baby birds flutter down to rest
High in the trees far from harm
Tiny monkey sleeps
Deep in his mother's arms
Sleep, my baby, near to me
Lu-lu, lu-lu, lu-lu
Close your velvet eyes

(E. O. Aina, personal communication, July, 2005)

The next lullaby, "Bamboo Flute," was introduced to me by Dave Smith, a former graduate assistant. He spent a semester abroad teaching Chinese children who were English language learners.

*Bamboo Flute*

From the bamboo mother makes a flute,
Bamboo flute for baby small,
Held in little hands,
Pressed to rosy lips,
Lilting melodies rise and fall
Lu, lu, lu, lu, melodies rise and fall
Lu, lu, lu, lu, sleepy heads nod and fall

The next lullaby comes from the Chippewa Nation. This was a favorite of mine when I was teaching public school in North Carolina. There are at least three Native American Nations represented in the area of the state where I taught, and I've known this Chippewa lullaby for as long as I can remember.

*Chippewa Lullaby*

Pine tree gently sigh
Sing a lullaby
For my baby
Little brook let flow
Murmur soft and low
For my baby
Breezes come and sing
Let the cradle swing
For my baby

The delightful lullaby "El Coquí" from Puerto Rico provides a soothing transition to nap time. The words and music follow.

**El Coquí**
(The Frog)

Puerto Rican

El co-quí sings a lul-la-by soft-ly.    I can hear el co-quí all night long;    Though I fall fast a-sleep when it's bed-time,    In my dream comes his sweet lit-tle song: Co-quí, Co-quí, Co-quí, quí, quí, quí! Co-quí, Co-quí, Co-quí, quí, quí, quí!

## Additional Learning Activities for Infants

Infants are attentive to musical sounds and games in their environment and move gradually from receiving to participating. Parents and infant caregivers can do much to nurture the attention and response infants give to music. Honig (2001) recommends that parents and caregivers find time every day to sing with babies during routine activities: "Sing about what you are doing—diapering, rocking, settling the baby on a play mat" (p. 24). Using music in this manner will attract attention and help build positive emotional bonds.

The following activities have been used successfully in the Parent-Infant-Toddler Program at Kent State University. These are examples of even more things you can do with infants and toddlers in your own classroom.

### Fancy Footwork

***Participants***
A 3- to 8-month-old infant and an adult

***Materials***
Velcro strip ankle bells

***Explanation***
Gently shake the ankle bells in front of your baby to focus the baby's attention. Allow time for examining. Now place the bells on your baby's ankles. Observe how your baby responds. If the baby becomes frustrated, remove the bells. Perhaps your baby simply wants to see or touch them at first.

### Purpose

This activity is one way of offering leg exercise to your baby in preparation for creeping and crawling. It offers opportunities to flex and extend the legs. It is also an action-response activity: "When I move my legs, the bells ring!"

### Variation

Take a stuffed animal, hang a few bells on it, and tie it with heavy string to the crib rails so that it hangs just above baby's feet. This tempting toy is out of hands' reach, so feet become the next best thing to make the sound. Baby may kick vigorously. The bell sound will be a motivating factor in getting the baby to stretch and kick.

---

## TALKS WITH TEACHERS

Alice Sterling Honig, Ph.D., is a professor emerita of Child Development at Syracuse University. Dr. Honig describes strategies for implementing movement and music with infants and toddlers.

Seat babies on the floor in infant seats and in a cozy circle surrounding you. Slowly pound out the cheerful rhythms of the nursery rhymes in a chanting voice as you emphasize each syllable. Babies bounce their bottoms in time with the rhythm of your sing-song voice. Take a baby on your lap and do the song that moves from the slow, rocking motion of the farmer's horse that plods along, to the trotting horse that moves with a bit more vigor, to the final verse where the racing horse goes "gallop, gallop, gallop." Baby may bounce his tush and request "More!" just to get you to start all over again singing that song with increasing vigor of lap-rocking movements as the song goes on. If there is a piano in the infant room, seat a baby on your lap and play simple, familiar melodies, such as "Happy birthday to you" or "Row, row, row your boat, gently down the stream" with one hand while snuggling baby on your lap safely with your other hand. Babies experience genuine pleasure in hearing a favorite song and in being given your individual nurturing attention combined with loving touch. Babies learn early on and first-hand how wonderful playing a musical instrument can be.

Sing lullabies lavishly in low hypnotic tones, as accompaniments to caressing back rubs at naptimes. Babies are soothed by lullabies. Sing lullabies from different lands and languages. Babies drift into sleep hearing the repetitive, comforting note progressions of lullabies from different lands. Sing the verses over and over. The more you repeat the same verses, the more babies will grow familiar both with tunes and with words. You are increasing brain integration of emotional pleasure plus language learning.

Stretch toddler attention span and memory by singing couplet songs that tell a simple story. "Mr. Froggy went a-courting and he did ride um hum, um hum" is an excellent couplet song, with every two lines rhyming. Toddlers listen with interest as Mr. Froggy woos Ms. Mousie, get her Uncle Rat's consent to the marriage, and the wedding preparations move forward, as in the couplet: "Then in came two little ants, um hum, um hum; then in came two little ants, and they did lead the wedding dance." Sing the same songs over and over so that the melodies become dear and familiar to the toddlers, who nod their heads, clap, bounce, and even call out words and rhymes they remember from time to time. Keep the rhythmic beat, but go slow in singing long songs, so that toddlers can try to keep up with the words and tunes.

Play simple rhythms on a musical instrument, whether piano, tambourine, or drum. Prepare a basket with musical instruments for toddlers to choose. Provide toddlers with wrist bells, small drums, triangles and other safe instruments so that they can practice keeping time to the beat of a favorite melody as they try to sing with you. Repeat the same songs over and over. Give toddlers a chance to coordinate all those muscles, including tongue, lips, fingers, wrists, to accompany each song. As you create patterns of musical beats, toddlers are practicing sequences of movements. You are enhancing their memories as well as their ability to feel the sequences in their rhythmic waving of arms and tapping out of beats. Because language phrases consist of rhythmic sequences of sounds, your music session with instruments boost toddler ability to coordinate body parts in ways that can support their early language learning. Encourage toddlers to fill in the blanks in familiar rhyming songs. As you sing "Twinkle, twinkle little? . . . ," pause, and wait for the toddlers to fill in the word "star."

*Source:* Honig, A. S. (1995). Singing with infants and toddlers. *Young Children, 50*(5), 72–78. Honig, A. S. (2005). The language of lullabies. *Young Children, 60*(5), 30–36.

Toddlers can use instruments to produce sounds, and they can use their voice to sing songs.

### Mirrors with Infants

*Participants*
A 6- to 8-month-old infant and an adult

*Materials*
Hand mirror

*Explanation*
Place the baby comfortably on your lap, and have the baby look into a hand mirror to see the reflection. "Look, here's _____. Where's_____?" Have the baby point to the image in the mirror. The question and response may be sung. Do this at various times, and you will notice that babies will begin to recognize themselves. About a year from now, they will play act in front of a mirror, striking poses and making faces.

    In time, you can add to this activity by pointing to parts of the body and naming them after you're sure that the baby recognizes the total as him- or herself. Parts of the body may be sung as you point to them.

*Caution*
It takes two to play this game. If the mirror is breakable, do not leave it unattended.

### Touch and Name

Parents are encouraged to try a "Touch and Sing" adaptation as they play the game with baby.

*Participants*
A 6- to 12-month-old baby and an adult

### Explanation

Touch different parts of your baby's body, and name them. For example, "This is_____'s nose. Here is _____'s foot. Where is _____'s arm? Here it is. Here is your arm!" Now, touch your own body parts, and do the same thing. "Here is Mommy's nose." If others are close by, touch their noses; for example, "Here is Daddy's nose."

### Purpose

To develop in babies an awareness of themselves and their body image and to help babies understand the difference between themselves and others. In addition, the activity shows connections between objects or actions and words, including names and pronouns. Even though it will be a while before babies use these words, they will learn (through this type of experience) to recognize words and their meanings.

### Variation

Once the child begins, through practice, to learn the names of some of the parts of the body, try turning the game around. Ask, "Where is _____'s arm? Where is Mommy's arm?"

---

## Give and Take

### Participants

A 9- to 12-month-old baby and an adult. Some babies will continue to enjoy this game or a variation of it after their first year.

### Materials

A block, small ball, or some other object like a rattle or small musical toy that can be easily held in the baby's hand.

### Explanation

Having developed the ability to grasp, most babies now are learning to let go. This is an example of a game that many babies initiate independently. Be enthusiastic as you play the game. Give the object to the baby and say, "Here's the ball" (or whatever the object is). Then put your hand out as if to receive it back. When the baby places the object in your hand, take it and say, "Thank you." If the baby imitates your "thank you," respond, "You're welcome."

The responses may be sung. Continue this give and take for as long as the baby enjoys it.

### Purpose

To give babies practice in letting go and using their hand muscles in a controlled way. This activity also serves as a form of social interchange. It is a good way to teach the use of appropriate language to accompany social interchange.

---

# NATIONAL STANDARDS FOR INFANTS AND TODDLERS

The national standards for music and movement education for toddlers are general in nature. We are including the standards here so that you can review them before developing activities to encourage music and movement development in toddlers.

Toddlers and very young children experience music by hearing it, by feeling it, and by experimenting with pitch and timbre in their vocalizations. Children should experience music daily while receiving caring, physical contact. Adults can encourage the musical development of toddlers by:

1. Singing and chanting to them, using songs and rhymes representing a variety of meters and tonalities
2. Imitating sounds
3. Exposing them to a wide variety of vocal, body, instrumental, and environmental sounds
4. Providing exposure to selected live and recorded music
5. Rocking, patting, touching, and moving with the children to the beat, rhythm patterns, and melodic direction of music they hear
6. Providing safe toys that make musical sounds the children can control[*]

## Developmentally Appropriate Practice

Copple and Bredekamp (2009) remind us that security, exploration, and identity formation are all important developmental factors in relationships and learning throughout the first three years of life. However, each dominates a different period. Security is the prime motivation for the young infant. Responsive adults help young infants to feel comfortable and to be focused as they develop a sense of trust in the adult's ability to understand them, keep them safe and secure, and make predictability possible. Although toddlers are naturally still very involved in exploration, this period of development is dominated by the work of forming an identity. As a toddler comes to understand his own experiences and becomes aware of the experiences of others being separate from his, he is solidifying his sense of self. Infants and toddlers need security most of all. They thrive on the warmth and caring that come from close relationships. Having someone special who responds quickly to their cues helps young children build a base of security that will support their exploration, learning, and identity formation. (pp. 54–57) Your role as a teacher is to provide a trustful environment for every child in your care. Now, let's take a look at the National Association for Sport and Physical Education standards. You will use these standards as you continue to design lessons for the children in your care.

## National Standards for Physical Education

The National Standards for physical activity provide guidelines for the age categories of infants, toddlers, and preschoolers.

### For infants

**Guideline 1.** Infants should interact with caregivers in daily physical activities that are dedicated to exploring movement and the environment.

---

[*]From *National Standards for Arts Education*. Copyright © 1994 by Music Educators National Conference (MENC). Used by permission. The complete National Arts Standards and additional materials relating to the Standards are available from MENC—National Association for Music Education, 1806 Robert Fulton Drive, Reston, VA 20191; www.menc.org.

**Guideline 2.** Caregivers should place infants in settings that encourage and stimulate movement experiences and active play for short periods of time several times a day.

**Guideline 3.** Infants' physical activity should promote skill development in movement.

**Guideline 4.** Infants should be placed in an environment that meets or exceeds recommended safety standards for performing large-muscle activities.

**Guideline 5.** Those in charge of infants' well-being are responsible for understanding the importance of physical activity and should promote movement skills by providing opportunities for structured and unstructured physical activity. (National Association for Sport and Physical Education, 2011. A complete statement of physical activity guidelines is available at www.aahperd.org.)

### For toddlers

**Guideline 1.** Toddlers should engage in a total of at least 30 minutes of structured physical activity each day.

**Guideline 2.** Toddlers should engage in at least 60 minutes—and up to several hours—per day of unstructured physical activity and should not be sedentary for more than 60 minutes at a time, except when sleeping.

**Guideline 3.** Toddlers should be given ample opportunities to develop movement skills that will serve as the building blocks for future motor skillfulness and physical activity.

Capture toddlers' attention by playing pat-a-cake.

**Guideline 4.** Toddlers should have access to indoor and outdoor areas that meet or exceed recommended safety standards for performing large-muscle activities.

**Guideline 5.** Those in charge of toddlers' well-being are responsible for understanding the importance of physical activity and promoting movement skills by providing opportunities for structured and unstructured physical activity and movement experiences. (National Association for Sport and Physical Education: Moving into the Future, National Standards for Physical Education, 2nd edition.)

The following sections provide specific ideas for incorporating developmentally appropriate practice based on the National Standards into the curriculum for infants and toddlers. These ideas include, nursery rhymes, chanting, rhythm, movement, and songs and instruments.

## NEW OPPORTUNITIES FOR TODDLERS

As children continue to grow and to become more interested in their world, music can offer new opportunities for moving, listening, creating, singing, and playing instruments. Besides imparting to children the enjoyment and pleasure of music activities, adult guides can also teach children skills and competencies by choosing *appropriate* activities. The selection of activities should be based on what can reasonably be expected of children at certain stages of their development. Teachers, such as music and physical education teachers, need to work closely to plan music experiences that are suitable for young children of different ages. A child's environment can have a profound impact on the very young. Parents and teachers who want to instill a love of music within young children must lay the groundwork during a child's earliest years.

### Creating the Environment

Teachers who make music a natural and ever-present part of the classroom environment teach children to be curious about music and to listen to many styles of music. Teachers should encourage the development of aural and vocal music skills throughout the early years when the child is developing expressive language skills (Scott, 1989). Fox (1991) notes, "Reinforcement and valuing of music by significant others most probably indicates to children the importance of music and its role in our lives" (p. 45). It is vital that the selection of music activities and experiences be based on sound principles of child growth and development.

Wide variations exist in children's maturation and experience. Figure 4–4 offers an overview of the characteristics of 2-year-olds, which should prove helpful to caregivers who wish to provide musical experiences that are appropriate for young children.

**Figure 4–4   Selected Characteristics of 2-Year-Olds**

- Enjoy listening to certain sounds, such as the fluttering of the tongue, and enjoy imitating them
- Answer questions like "What does the cow say?" by making the appropriate sound
- Can point to or put hands on body parts on request
- Rock or sway hips to a familiar tune, although not necessarily in time with the music
- Like to play peek-a-boo and hiding games
- Continue to reproduce sounds or combinations of sounds to explain wants and needs (for example, may half-sing, half-say, "Bye-bye," when they want to go for a ride in the car)
- Generally enjoy being held and sung to
- May "mouth" the words of a song or whisper them while others sing
- May choose to join a group socially but not to sing
- Will often refrain from singing any of the words to songs like "Twinkle, Twinkle, Little Star" because they are concentrating so intently on doing the actions

## NURSERY RHYMES

Adults who love poetry and music will find themselves reciting poetry and nursery rhymes and singing those unforgettable nursery songs to the very young. Children's interest in a world of sound can be enhanced through different qualities of tone, varying pitches, and rhythmic movements. Adults working with young children should share with them the many delightful Mother Goose rhymes and the chants of early childhood.

### Using Nursery Rhymes with Toddlers

It is quite natural for toddlers to move their bodies to the rhythm of nursery rhymes and chants. Howle (1989) reminds us that rocking frequently accompanies singing experiences, and lullabies are certainly no exception. She suggests that sensory stimuli, such as touching, rubbing, smiling, warmth, and cuddling, aid in mental development while promoting a loving relationship between parent and child. These early music experiences prepare the child for later development in music, speech, and movement. Additional benefits include the development of communication skills. Young children respond directly to the adult who is singing, and this attention can prompt the adult to begin talking to the child. This encourages speech development, listening skills, and the ability to hear rhyming words (Howle, 1989). As children grow older, the appeal of rhymes seems to increase. Young children care little about the origin and meaning of nursery rhymes; their value lies in their delightful rhythms, repetition, good humor, nonsensical words, and imagination. Children receive much pleasure from listening to and attempting, in their own inimitable ways, to repeat the chants and rhymes while moving their bodies to the interesting rhythmic patterns.

It is desirable to say and sing these rhymes over and over again and to include the family in this sharing process. If children are provided with these experiences, they will soon spontaneously participate in these fun episodes. This activity establishes a good foundation for children's lifetime reading and musical tastes.

The nursery rhymes in Figure 4–5 are considered classics in children's literature beloved by generations of young children. If you are unfamiliar with any of these rhymes, now is a good time to learn them, especially if you plan to work with very young children.

**Figure 4–5   Nursery Rhymes**

*Five Little Pigs*

This little piggy went to market;
This little piggy stayed at home;
This little piggy had roast beef;
And this little pig had none;
This little pig said, "Wee, wee, wee!"
All the way home.
[One line for each of the child's toes]

*To Market, To Market*

To market, to market, to buy a fat pig,
Home again, home again, jiggity jig;
To market, to market, to buy a fat hog,
Home again, home again, jiggity jog;
To market, to market, to buy a plum bun,
Home again, home again, market is done.

*Baa, Baa, Black Sheep*

Baa, baa black sheep
Have you any wool?
Yes, sir, yes, sir, three bags full.
One for my master, one for the dame,
One for the little boy that lives in the lane.

*Humpty Dumpty*

Humpty Dumpty sat on a wall,
Humpty Dumpty had a great fall;
All the king's horses and all the king's men
Couldn't put Humpty together again.

*Little Jack Horner*

Little Jack Horner
Sat in a corner,

Eating his Christmas pie.
He put in his thumb
And pulled out a plum
And said, "What a good boy am I!"

*Pussy Cat, Pussy Cat*

Pussy cat, pussy cat, where have you been?
I've been to London to visit the queen.
Pussy cat, pussy cat, what did you do there?
I frightened a little mouse under the chair.

*Jack and Jill*

Jack and Jill went up the hill
To fetch a pail of water;
Jack fell down and broke his crown,
And Jill came tumbling after.

*Roses Are Red*

Roses are red,
Violets are blue;
Sugar is sweet,
And so are you!

*One Potato*

One potato, two potato,
Three potato, four;
Five potato, six potato
Seven potato, more.

*Rain, Rain, Go Away*

Rain, rain, go away,
Come again another day,
Little Johnny wants to play.

## CHANTING

Children love the sound of their own voices. Parents and teachers should encourage young children to improvise and should themselves serve as models. Buchoff (1994) recommends that parents and teachers model chants for children by reading them aloud dramatically and with enthusiasm many times. Buchoff also suggests that teachers snap their fingers while chanting to emphasize the rhythm of the chants and to encourage children to listen for the beat. Bring the chant to life by modifying the volume and pace of the chant to fit the message or mood. Present the chant in full form, complete from beginning to end, and avoid dividing the chants into lines or phrases. Remember that chanting should be for fun and pleasure. It is inappropriate to expect very young children to memorize chants. The goal must be to give children the opportunity to share the joy of rhyming words and language play.

Rhythm instruments are a lot of fun.

## The Link Between Speech and Rhythm

Some authorities call the half-speaking, half-singing sounds children make as they go about their play "chanting." Whether children are pounding with a hammer, pushing a toy, or running with a balloon, one can hear melodic fragments. Anderson and Lapp (1996) describe a chant as any group of words that is recited with a lively beat. Through chanting, all children speak together in unison. They learn the importance of clear and expressive pronunciation as their voices combine to make the message of the chant come alive.

Children often half-speak, half-sing names of people, animals, and the like, using the tones of the minor third:

Songs or little melodies using the pentatonic scale often make use of the minor third. The scale has five tones to an octave. Found in the diatonic scale, the five-tone scale is do, re, mi, sol, la. The scale can originate in any tone. It is often found in songs children make up themselves:

To develop further the tie-in between speaking and singing, it is advisable to sing requests and the like to children:

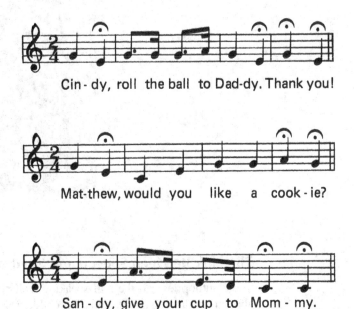

Observe that the minor third chants just introduced comprise a two-note pattern. This is a very natural and easy way to improvise a little tune to sing to a child. I want to stress the importance and value of making up these short, fun melodies, in which one sings about the everyday things the child or people around the child are doing. Babies and toddlers who have had such rich and plentiful experiences, who have been talked to, played with, and sung to, will be able to join in quite accurately with words and "snatches" of melodies of familiar songs, chants, or nursery rhymes when they are starting to talk.

The chants in Figure 4–6 are fun for very young children because the actions are easy to imitate and the words and rhythms are repetitive.

Too often, teachers and caregivers have narrow ideas about what constitutes music when they work with young children. They need to listen to children and observe them carefully. Children can respond to music that is brought to them. It is up to parents and

**Figure 4–6　Spoken Chants**

### Clap Your Hands

Clap your hands just like me,
Clap as slowly as can be.
Now clap fast and you will see,
What great fun clapping can be.

[Add your own verses, and let the children make up their own verses using different body parts. For example: "Snap your fingers," "Tap your toes," and "Blink your eyes."]

### I Have Hands

I have hands that clap, clap, clap.
I have feet that tap, tap, tap.
I have eyes to see you too,
Peter Talbert, I see you.

[Point to the child named, and continue the chant until all the children have heard their names.]

teachers to provide meaningful music experiences for these active, persistent music makers. Songs from all cultures and countries offer a wonderful source for teachers and parents alike.

## MUSIC FROM AROUND THE WORLD

One legendary woman has worked with children from all over the world and has written songs in many languages, including Spanish, Chinese, Hebrew, Korean, Maori, and Swahili. Ella Jenkins has brought a treasury of songs to children of the world. She has appeared on several television programs, including *The Today Show, Showbiz Today, Barney and Friends, Mister Rogers' Neighborhood*, and *Sesame Street*. She is the quintessential authority on multicultural music for children. She has received the American Society of Composers, Authors and Publishers (ASCAP) Foundation Lifetime Achievement Award in the area of children's music. In fact, she was the first woman to receive an ASCAP Lifetime Achievement Award. Her albums and videotapes have received the Parents' Choice Award, and her album *Sharing Cultures with Ella Jenkins* was nominated for a Grammy Award.

The lovely chant, "Hola, hola, hola," is one that 1- and 2-year-olds will giggle about as they listen to their teacher singing or chanting it. You never know what is going to tickle the funny bone of a 2-year-old, but in this case you'll soon notice that "Hola, hola, hola" engages all children in the group.

Anna Hatchett earned a Master of Arts in Teaching from the College of Charleston. She spent a summer in Spain on an exchange program where she lived with a family while tutoring their three young children. Although her tutoring required that she speak only English with the children, she also made up songs for the children that they all sang in Spanish. Anna wrote the following chant for a lively group of 2-year-olds with whom she had been playing while she was in Spain.

Try it with your group and see how many giggles you get out of your toddlers.

Hola, hola, hola,
Como estás?
Muy bien, gracias.
(Hello, hello, hello,
How are you?
Very well, thank you.)

Ella Jenkins's classic album *You'll Sing a Song and I'll Sing a Song* introduces many of her songs and chants. This recording and many others are available through Jenkins's website, www.ellajenkins.com. In the meantime, teachers and children whose first language is English can chant this old favorite:

*Peas Porridge*
Peas porridge hot
Peas porridge cold
Peas porridge in the pot
Nine days old!

Teachers can also make up chants based on themes, children's interests, the weather, and other relevant subject matter. Teachers should begin with simple chants in the children's native language to help them get used to the rhyme and rhythm before introducing chants in other languages.

## ELEMENTS OF MUSICAL BEGINNINGS

All growth, musical or otherwise, is an active process. For optimal musical development to occur, children must be actively involved in making music from their birth. Some learning does take place through watching and listening to others, but the best learning takes place through trying for oneself. Before you begin thinking about

Children can sing "Hola, hola, hola" as a greeting in Spanish.

ways to plan and implement music experiences for young children, it is important to understand the basic stages of early musical development. The following description of musical development for 2-year-olds includes suggested music and movement activities for young children.

## Two-Year-Olds

The 2-year-old enjoys rocking, swaying, moving up and down, clapping games, fingerplays, and action songs. For example, "Sometimes I Am Tall" encourages young children to reach up high and bend down low. Here are the words and directions:

*Sometimes I Am Tall*

Sometimes I am tall.
[Stand at full height]
Sometimes I am small.
[Bend down close to the floor]
Sometimes I am very, very tall.
[Stretch on tiptoe]
Sometimes I am very, very small.
[Bend down as close to the floor as possible]
Sometimes tall, sometimes small.
(Stretch high and bend low)
See how I am now.
[Stand normally]

### *Fingerplays*

A favorite fingerplay of 2-year-olds is the traditional "Eency Weency Spider." Children should be allowed to make their own spider any way they want to make it. Too many times, well-meaning teachers show just how to make a "proper" spider and distract children from the fun of the fingerplay. All spiders created from children's fingers are correct and perfect! Other favorites are also listed here for you and your children's enjoyment.

*Eency Weency Spider*

The eency weency spider climbed up the waterspout.
[Children transform their fingers into their own climbing spider]
Down came the rain and washed the spider out.
[Wiggle fingers in downward motion]
Out came the sun and dried up all the rain.
[Arms in circle over head]
And the eency weency spider climbed up the spout again.
[Fingers repeat climbing motion]

*Two Little Blackbirds*

Two little blackbirds sitting on a hill. (Index finger on each hand fluttering motion)
One named Jack, and one named Jill. (Raise one hand, then the other)
Fly away Jack, fly away Jill. (Right hand flies behind back, then left)
No little blackbirds sitting on the hill.
Come back Jack, come back Jill. (Right hand returns to front, then left)
Two little blackbirds sitting on a hill. (Both hands back to original position)

*Two Little Feet*

Two little feet go tap, tap, tap. (Suit actions to words)
Two little hands go clap, clap, clap.
A quiet little leap up from my chair.
Two little arms reach high in the air.
Two little feet go jump, jump, jump.
Two little fists go thump, thump, thump.
One little body goes round, round, round,
And one little child sits quietly down.

*Open-Shut Them*

Open, shut them,
Open, shut them, (Open and close hands making a fist)
Let your hands go clap. (Clap hands together)
Open, shut them,
Open, shut them,
Put them in your lap. (Put hands in lap)
Creep them, crawl them,
Creep them, crawl them,
Right up to your chin. (Fingers creep toward chin)
Open up your little mouth,
But do not let them in. (Quickly put hands behind back)

*My Wiggles*

I wiggle my fingers, (Suit actions to words)
I wiggle my toes.
I wiggle my shoulders,
I wiggle my nose.
Now the wiggles are out of me,
And I'm just as still as I can be.

### Movement

Two-year-olds also enjoy experimenting with imitating rhymes and rhythms and responding to music through body movements. "Teddy Bear, Teddy Bear, Turn Around" is a wonderful prelude to nap time.

*Teddy Bear, Teddy Bear*

Teddy Bear, Teddy Bear, turn around,
Teddy Bear, Teddy Bear, touch the ground.
Teddy Bear, Teddy Bear, tie your shoe,
Teddy Bear, Teddy Bear, that will do!
Teddy Bear, Teddy Bear, go upstairs,
Teddy Bear, Teddy Bear, say your prayers.
Teddy Bear, Teddy Bear, turn off the light,
Teddy Bear, Teddy Bear, say "Good night!"

### Simple Songs and Instruments

Two-year-olds can learn short, simple songs and enjoy experimenting with instruments and sounds. Rhythm sticks are wooden sticks with both a smooth surface and a ribbed surface. They are small enough in diameter to fit nicely into the hands of 2-year-olds. Children hold one stick in each hand and strike them together or scrape one stick over the ribbed surface of the other. Rhythm sticks can be used to strike other objects, such as the floor, sleeping mats, and other things in the classroom. Two-year-olds love to

"Teddy Bear, Teddy Bear" is a wonderful song for helping active children calm down.

"march" around the room, striking their rhythm sticks. Teachers can use a tambourine to help keep the beat.

Children at this age can respond to songs with simple patterns. The lyrics and music for some beloved songs are provided as follows.

### Walk, Walk, Walk to School

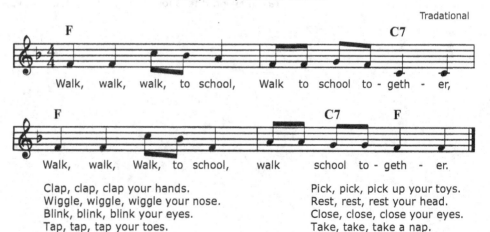

Clap, clap, clap your hands.
Wiggle, wiggle, wiggle your nose.
Blink, blink, blink your eyes.
Tap, tap, tap your toes.

Pick, pick, pick up your toys.
Rest, rest, rest your head.
Close, close, close your eyes.
Take, take, take a nap.

**Bluebird, Bluebird**

American Singing Game

1. Blue – bird, Blue – bird,    thro' my  win – dow,    Blue – bird, Blue – bird,

thro' my  win – dow,    Blue – bird, blue – bird,    thro' my  win – dow,

Oh,    John – ny, aren't you    tired ?___    Take  a  lit – tle friend  and

tap  him  on    the  shoul – der,    Take  a  lit – tle  friend  and

tap  him  on    the  shoul – der,    Take  a  lit – tle  friend  and

tap  him  on  the  shoul – der,    Oh,  John – ny, aren't you    tired ?___

## If You're Happy

American Singing Game

If you're hap-py and you know it, clap your hands,

If you're hap-py and you know it clap your hands,

If you're hap-py and you know it, then your face will sure-ly show it, If you're

hap-py and you know it clap your hands.

2. If you're happy and you know it, tap your toe.
3. If you're happy and you know it, nod your head.
4. If you're happy and you know it, do all three.

The traditional pattern song "Put Your Finger on Your Nose" is very appropriate for 2-year-olds because it repeats the same phrases over and over and introduces only two different movements. For teachers who want to sing, rather than chant, this little verse, the melody to "If You're Happy and You Know It" is a perfect fit.

*Put Your Finger on Your Nose*

Put your finger on your nose, then your toes.
Put your finger on your nose, then your toes.
Put your finger on your nose. Put your finger on your nose.
Put your finger on your nose, then your toes.

### Exploring Space

Young children are eager to explore space as they move forward and backward, up and down. They also enjoy moving low to the floor and walking on tiptoe. The "imaginary space bubble" described in Chapter 1 is a good activity to help children define their own personal space. They can move inside their imaginary space bubble in many different ways. They can also carry their space bubble with them as they move around the room. It is important to remember, however, that 2-year-olds are still egocentric in that their thinking does not take into account the viewpoint of others. Because of this special trait, they may move in and out of other children's bubbles. When this happens, be gentle, and remember that the whole idea is to have fun while learning new patterns of movement and new ways to explore the space in the classroom.

Adults in the classroom provide many experiences and opportunities to extend children's language and musical abilities. We introduce children to nursery rhymes and fingerplays, encourage children to sing songs and listen to recordings, and facilitate children's play of movement games and action songs. Always be aware of the role you play in providing musical experiences that match your children's developmental needs.

*A jazz musician is a juggler who uses harmonies instead of oranges.*

—Benny Green

## SELECTIVE SKILLS FOR CHILDREN BIRTH TO 36 MONTHS

A reference list of selected skills for children from birth to 36 months is shown in Figure 4–7. It describes cognitive and expressive language and gives parents and caregivers approximate ranges during which young children will begin to respond to sound and music.

**Figure 4–7    Selected Skills Reference List for Children Birth to 36 Months**

| Cognitive | 1. Responds to voice birth–2½ months |
| | 2. Awakens or quiets to mother's voice 3–6 months |
| | 3. Localizes sound with eyes 3½–5 months |
| | 4. Shows interest in sounds of objects 5½–8 months |
| | 5. Plays peek-boo 6–10 months |
| | 6. Moves to rhythms 11–12 months |
| | 7. Enjoys nursery rhymes, nonsense rhymes, fingerplays, poetry 18–30 months |
| **Expressive Language** | 1. Cry varies in pitch, length, and volume to indicate needs like hunger and pain 1–5 months |
| | 2. Coos open vowels (*aah*), diphthongs (*oy* as in *boy*) 2–7 months |
| | 3. Reacts to music by cooing 5–6 months |
| | 4. Babbles to people 5½–6½ months |
| | 5. Attempts to sing sounds to music 13–16 months |
| | 6. Attempts to sing with words 18–23 months |
| | 7. Recites a few nursery rhyme 30–36 months |

*Source:* Selected from *Hawaii Early Learning Profile (HELP)*® Activity Guide by the Enrichment Project for Handicapped Infants, by Setsu Furano, Katherine A. O'Reilly, Carol M. Hosaka, Takoyo T. Inatsuka, Toney L. Allman, and Barbara Zeisloft. Available from VORT® Corporation, Palo Alto, CA 94306.

## KEY IDEAS

1. Children's musical growth is similar to the rest of their development.
2. In homes where musical expression is encouraged, children's responses to music are better and of a higher quality as they grow older than the responses of children from other homes.
3. Music making should begin in infancy.
4. Movement experiences are more important for infants than any other age group.
5. Movement experiences in an intimate setting between an infant and adult are basic to healthy cognitive, affective, and motor development.
6. Babies usually favor songs and rhythms that actively involve them.

## SUMMARY

Music and movement is basic for all people, from infancy through adulthood. Those caring for the very young can provide a good beginning for music enjoyment and appreciation by singing and sharing music, such as lullabies, chants, and rhymes. Begin to explore music with children when they are infants; share the variety and richness of our musical heritage. In addition to nurturing through food and love, add the nurturing quality of music. Infancy is a good time for beginning with simple activities and music experiences. When you, as a caregiver, become involved, so will the very young child in terms of alertness, awareness, and enjoyment.

## QUESTIONS TO CONSIDER

1. Begin an informal 2-week log of an infant you observe. Record short, precise details of the infant's activities. Are any of the activities influenced by music or rhythm?
2. Visit a preschool setting. How is music used as a learning experience or as an activity integrated throughout the day?
3. Try at least four of the activities suggested in this chapter. Record your observations and how you modified the activities to suit your purpose or the infant's reactions.

## RECORDINGS

*Mother Goose Time Musical Recordings* Musical recordings created with babies in mind. http://www.amazon.com or Tower Records at http://www.towerrecords.com or www.unc.edu/-sllamber/pathfinder/music.html.

*Music for Little People* A sing-along for toddlers. www.musicforlittlepeople.com/

## SONG COLLECTIONS

*Preschool/elementary (Ages 3–8)* Compiled by John M. Feierabend. Favorite American folk songs filled with magic, wonder, and make-believe.

*Piggyback songs for infants and toddlers.* A wonderful collection of more than 100 fingerplays and songs, www.amazon.com, Jean Warren Marion H. Ekberg Books.

# REFERENCES

Albarecht, K., & Miller, L. G. (2001). *Infant and toddler development*. Beltsville, MD: Gryphon House.

Anderson, P. S., & Lapp, D. (1996). *Language skills in elementary education*. New York, NY: Macmillan.

Brewer, J. (2004). *Introduction to early childhood education: Preschool through primary grades* (5th ed.). Boston, MA: Allyn & Bacon.

Buchoff, R. (1994). Joyful voices: Facilitating language growth through the rhythmic response to chants. *Young Children, 49*, 26–30.

Copple, C., & Bredekamp, S. (Ed.) (2009). *Developmentally appropriate practice in early childhood programs* (3rd ed.). Washington, DC: National Association for the Education of Young Children.

Forrai, K. (1996). The influence of music on the development of young children: Music research with children between 6 and 40 months. *Early Childhood Connections, Journal of Music and Movement-Based Learning, 2*(4), 14–18.

Fox, D. B. (1991). Music, development, and the young child. *Music Educators Journal, 77*(5), 42–46.

Gabbard, C. (1998). Windows of opportunity for early brain and motor development. *Journal of Physical Education, Recreation, and Dance, 69*, 54–55, 61.

Honig, A. S. (2001). Building relationships through music. *Scholastic Early Childhood Today, 15*(4), 24–25.

Howle, M. J. (1989). Twinkle, twinkle, little star: It's more than just a nursery song. *Children Today, 18*(4), 18–22.

Lind, J., & Hardgrove, C. (1978). Lullabies. *Children Today*, 10.

Miche, M. (2002). *Weaving music into young minds*. Albany, NY: Delmar/Thomson Learning.

Music Educators National Conference. (1994). *National standards for music education*. Reston, VA: Author.

National Association for Sport and Physical Education. (2011). *Moving into the future: National standards for physical education* (2nd ed.). Reston, VA: American Alliance for Health, Physical Education, Recreation and Dance.

Robert, D. L. (2001). Successful preschool movement programs. *Teaching Elementary Physical Education, 12*, 30–33.

Scott, C. R. (1989). How children grow—musically. *Music Educators Journal, 76*(2), 28–31.

Shetler, D. J. (1985, March). Prenatal music experiences. *Music Educators Journal*, 27.

# CHAPTER FIVE

# Music and Movement
# for 3-Year-Olds

*Music is a more potent instrument than any other for education . . .*

*Plato*

*Music and movement activities for young children must include a variety of opportunities to explore music and movement through singing, dancing, listening, and playing instruments. Dancing, as a form of movement, is addressed throughout this chapter because to a 3-year-old, movement is dancing! These activities must also include experiences through which children can verbalize and visualize musical ideas.*

*Early childhood educators know that play is the primary means through which children grow, and appropriate music and movement experiences for young children should always occur in child-initiated, child-directed, teacher-supported play environments. The teacher's role is to provide a stimulating environment and to facilitate children's involvement with music and movement activities. Young children also need time to share and make music with others in small groups.*

## CHARACTERISTICS OF 3-YEAR-OLDS

Where live music with a marked rhythm is being played, most 3-year-old children will be seen bouncing up and down, swaying and twirling their bodies to the music. When working with children of this delightful age, we find that sound and movement are almost inseparable. Because children are so sensitive to sound and movement, we will present and discuss some of the activities they might enjoy if given the opportunity; at the same time, we will indicate how conceptual development can take place with these activities. Knowledge of the characteristics of 3-year-olds helps us plan meaningful experiences for them. Selected characteristics are listed in Figure 5-1.

## THREE-YEAR-OLDS' RESPONSE TO SOUND AND MOVEMENT

Music often elicits a particular response from 3-year-olds. They can be seen swaying or stepping in time to an appropriate rhythm. One has only to watch young children as a band plays a lively march or dance to observe their response to music. If they are

**Figure 5–1   Selected Characteristics of 3-Year-Olds**

- Are very active and like music to which they can respond
- Like music having marked rhythm, such as band music, nursery rhymes, or catchy TV jingles
- May gallop like a pony
- Often clap hands or tap hips to rhythm when hearing music
- Attempt to dance to music by bending knees in a bouncing motion, turning circles, swinging arms, and nodding the head
- Are able to sing phrases of songs
- Can lie or sit down quietly and listen for longer periods of time
- Enjoy making sounds to accompany play
- Like imaginative, dramatic play
- Begin to show interest in listening to and playing real musical instruments like drums, rhythm sticks, and tambourines

in a setting in which they can move, most of them will invariably begin to clap their hands and move their feet in time to the music. Their faces will light up with pleasure and delight.

Three-year-olds enjoy banging. Any percussion instrument can instantly become a rhythm instrument. Tambourines are lightweight and can be carried and tapped by children as they move around the room. Teachers can use tambourines to encourage children to change from a slow movement to a fast movement (Strickland, 2001). Select music to which children can listen and play along. Be sure to include different styles of music, such as jazz; country-western; classical; gospel; contemporary sounds such as reggae, hip-hop, and rap; and lively multicultural music. Children should have the opportunity to play their instruments along with many different kinds of music. Through these experiences 3-year-olds learn the feeling of rhythm, learn how to establish a beat, are exposed to music from different cultures, and have fun (Smith, 2000).

Music making at this age is usually an individual activity. During a play period, for example, Sara may use a wooden spoon to tap on a pan; Andrew might push his fire truck across the floor as he makes an authentic siren sound with his voice; LaQuisha might stand on tiptoe to reach and play the white keys on the piano. On occasion, children will form a musical group of their own and play their sound-producing instruments together. It is from these spontaneous activities that we should take our cues in helping children enjoy these playful, musical experiences.

Music for young children facilitates discovering sounds both inside and outside the home and school. As teachers, we need to observe young children closely, particularly in their play, and learn more about the many ways in which they deal with sound and movement. Children at this age are always on the move and involved in sound-making experimentation.

Singing and moving come naturally to children.

## Developing Listening Skills

As children grow and develop, one of the most important things we can do is help them build good listening skills. Children have little motivation on their own to listen carefully unless parents and teachers encourage it. This does not imply that we must impose drill-like, structured procedures to accomplish this purpose. We need to assist children in helping them make sense out of the myriad kinds of sounds in their environment. As Carleton (2000) reminds us,

> Listening is necessary to hear same and different letters of our alphabet, words, sounds in our environment, and musical pitches. There will be a lifetime of sounds our children will need to identify. The sooner we encourage listening skills, the more opportunities children will have to develop them. (p. 54)

## Music and Movement in Context

For children to make sense and meaning of the sounds they hear, sounds need to be put in context. Teachers can do this quite easily by helping children relate sounds closely to everyday objects and events. It is easier to do this for children around the age of 3, since children at this age are becoming more mobile and have increased ability to talk about the things they are doing. Children need to acquire language so they can talk and think about sound. With the help of understanding adults, conversations about sound can be initiated through a variety of ways. For example, the adult might say to the child, "Listen, do you hear the siren? Is that the fire truck?" (Use your own judgment when talking about any type of siren to young children. Emphasize this sound to make children feel safe rather than afraid.) Here are some other examples you might use: "Listen to that barking dog. He sounds like he is very happy!" "That's the doorbell ringing! I wonder who's at the door. Do you have any idea?" "I hear the telephone ringing. Do you hear it, too?" "Hmmm, do you smell the popcorn? Listen and see if you can hear it popping."

One of our challenges as teachers is to provide quality music and listening experiences with respect to the collective needs of all children. Because children's intuitive responses to music and listening activities may vary, be sure to remember that all responses have value. It would be a boring classroom indeed if all the children responded the same way at the same time.

# PLANNING MUSIC AND MOVEMENT ACTIVITIES FOR 3-YEAR-OLDS

Giving children both opportunities and encouragement with music and movement experiences can lead to a lifetime of enjoyment. It is extremely important that children be given a variety of experiences. Some of these may be through listening, others through exploration of what their bodies can do, such as singing, dancing, and playing instruments. At various ages and stages, children will discover new and different ways in which music can enrich their lives.

Since most children naturally love to sing, allow them to pursue this activity as much as possible. Don't limit singing to nursery rhymes. Present some songs you love or songs you learned as a child. Children really don't care where the songs came from, they just love hearing new and interesting lyrics and melodies. The benefits of singing are many. As you have read in previous chapters, singing improves vocabulary and language skills. Singing is an excellent tool for facilitating auditory memory in addition to introducing children to the often new dynamic of group singing.

During this age, movement activities should be given high priority. Andress (1989) notes that "in the area of movement, research supports the long-held belief that preschool children move at a faster overall tempo than adults and that effective teaching in terms of beat coordination involves matching the tempo of the child" (p. 30). This finding is often forgotten. At least four essential elements should always be included in music activities for young children: singing, listening, playing instruments, and moving (Smith, 2000). These are the core activities in music and movement development. The following "Talks with Teachers" presents one teacher's success story with music and movement with 3-year-olds.

Remember that when you plan music and movement experiences for young children, it is imperative to keep in mind their growth and development patterns. Too often, children are asked to engage in activities that are beyond their abilities. As you continue to think about the importance of children's developmental patterns and stages of growth, you should consider the Music Educators National Conference standards for music education. In addition to the MENC music standards, you must also review, consider, and address the standards on Sport and Physical Education for preschoolers. The following sections review these standards and provide guidelines to guide in planning music activities for young children.

## TALKS WITH TEACHERS

Phyllis Gates is the Master Teacher of 3-year-olds at the N. E. Miles Early Childhood Development Center (ECDC) at the College of Charleston. She received her Master of Arts in Teaching in Early Childhood Education from the College and taught in the public schools for 2 years before coming to the ECDC. Phyllis and her children love to experiment with musical instruments. Here she describes how the children were inspired to create their own musical instruments after reading *What Instrument Is This?* by Rosmarie Hausherr.

Photos and descriptions of different instruments and the sound each makes are presented. First, the children play a guessing game by responding to my descriptions of individual instruments. Amazingly, the children can identify most of the instruments just by hearing a description. Next, we listened to several different recordings featuring these instruments, and the children played another guessing game in which they identified the name of the instrument by the sound it made. At this point, the children wanted to make their own instruments. We used the book series *Musical Instruments* from the Heinemann Library to decide what we wanted our instruments to look like. For the next couple of days, we gathered household objects. Over the course of a couple of weeks, the children created several musical instruments. They used their own colors and designs to make their instruments original works of art. Before we knew it, we had a complete orchestra! The children spontaneously created a marching band and ended up performing a concert for the whole school. Here's a photograph of several of the children playing and singing with their handmade instruments.

Homemade instruments come to life in the classroom.

## NATIONAL STANDARDS FOR MUSIC EDUCATION

Three-year-olds need an environment that includes a variety of sound sources, selected recorded music, and opportunities for free improvised singing, moving (dancing!), and the building of a repertoire of songs. An exploratory approach using a wide range of appropriate materials provides a rich base from which conceptual understanding can evolve in later years. A variety of individual musical experiences is important for children at this age, with little emphasis on activities that require children to perform together as a unit.

The Music Educators National Conference (MENC) established standards (1994) that reflect the organization's beliefs concerning the musical learning of young children. These standards provide a framework for teachers who work with young children and should assist teachers in planning a music curriculum that is developmentally appropriate. The national standards for 3-year-olds are more general in nature than those for older children. Younger children should be exposed to a variety of sound sources and recorded music. They should be given opportunities to freely improvise songs and to build a selected repertoire. Children at this age should have a variety of individual musical experiences, with little or no emphasis on activities that require them to perform.

In a position statement, the MENC reports that effective music teaching in the preschool classroom should:

1. Support the child's total development—physical, affective/emotional, social, and cognitive
2. Recognize the wide range of normal development in preschoolers and the need to differentiate their instruction
3. Facilitate learning through active interaction with adults and other children, as well as with music materials
4. Consist of learning activities and materials that are real, concrete, and relevant to the lives of young children

5. Provide opportunities for children to choose from among a variety of music activities, materials, and equipment of varying degrees of difficulty
6. Allow children time to explore music through active involvement*

All of the activities and experiences presented in this edition are built on these standards and can be adapted to individual children, different classroom settings, and the regular classroom teacher's ability to explore these ideas with young children.

### Singing and Musical Awareness

Researchers have found that during the preschool and primary years, children demonstrate positive attitudes toward many kinds of music (Wilcox, 1999). Feierabend (1999) says, "We see a very large difference in the singing capacity and musical awareness between children five years old and younger who have been exposed to music and those who have not" (p. 19). Current research makes it clear that children use music as meaningful communication in their earliest years of development. Parents and teachers must be involved in early music experiences with children and must continue to offer opportunities for shared music making in their homes and classrooms (Fox, 2000).

## MOVING INTO THE FUTURE: NATIONAL STANDARDS FOR PHYSICAL EDUCATION

It is important to use the physical education national standards to develop physically educated children who have the knowledge, skills and confidence to enjoy a lifetime of healthy physical activity. Guidelines for preschoolers from the National Association for Sport and Physical Education (2011) include the following:

**Guideline 1.** Preschoolers should accumulate at least 60 minutes of structured physical activity each day.

**Guideline 2.** Preschoolers should engage in at least 60 minutes—and up to several hours—of unstructured physical activity each day, and should not be sedentary for more than 60 minutes at a time, except when sleeping.

**Guideline 3.** Preschoolers should be encouraged to develop competence in fundamental motor skills that will serve as the building blocks for future motor skillfulness and physical activity.

**Guideline 4.** Preschoolers should have access to indoor and outdoor areas that meet or exceed recommended safety standards for performing large-muscle activities.

---

*From *National Standards for Arts Education*. Copyright © 1994 by Music Educators National Conference (MENC). Used by permission. The complete National Arts Standards and additional materials relating to the Standards are available from MENC—National Association for Music Education, 1806 Robert Fulton Drive, Reston, VA 20191.

**Guideline 5.** Caregivers and parents in charge of preschoolers' health and well-being are responsible for understanding the importance of physical activity and for promoting movement skills by providing opportunities for structured and unstructured physical activity.*

As a way of getting started, you might want to practice writing a lesson plan. This can be a daunting task, especially if you are working with a master teacher. It's not as complicated as you might think. A mock lesson plan is included here to help you get started.

## Designing Lesson Plans

While there is no universal rule for designing lesson plans, keep these few general guidelines in mind when you begin writing. The basic components of a lesson plan are:

1. Objectives
2. Assessing Prior Knowledge
3. Procedures
4. Guided Practice
5. Closure
6. Materials and Equipment
7. Assessment

Here are some tips for writing lesson plans.

1. *Objectives.* These should be based on the national or state standard you are addressing. A good way to turn a standard into an objective is to look for the action verbs within a standard and turn those descriptors into verbs that can be directly observed and assessed. For example, Content Standard 1 for music education K–4 reads: "Student will sing alone and with others, a varied repertoire of music." Use the verb "to sing" as the key to your objective. "The children will sing expressively (such as with happiness or sadness), with appropriate dynamics (such as loud and soft), phrasing (pausing at the end of a phrase), and interpretation (to figure out the meaning of the words in the song)." Refer to Bloom's Taxonomy of Action Verbs to make sure your objective is observable and measurable. Writing an objective as "The children will learn a song" is not easily observed without formal assessment.
2. *Assessing Prior Knowledge.* You want to assess the children's knowledge of songs and their ability to sing a varied repertoire of music through discussions, expressions, and asking children to classify, describe, or explain different aspects of different songs and/or music.
3. *Procedures.* Always include an *Introduction* because it helps ease the children into the lesson, providing a transition between their prior knowledge and/or experience and what you will teach them. The Introduction may be brief but should include (A) making the children aware of the purpose of the lesson, (B) relating the lesson to previous learning, and (C) relating the lesson to the children's experience. Your actual procedures involve the steps you will follow during your lesson. Concrete or "hands-on" activities should always be the dominant part of the lesson to promote

*Reprinted from ACTIVE START: A STATEMENT OF PHYSICAL ACTIVITY GUIDELINES FOR CHILDREN FROM BIRTH TO AGE 5, with permission from the National Association for Sport and Physical Education (NASPE), 1900 Association Drive, Reston, VA 20191, www.NASPEinfo.org <http://www.naspeinfo.org/>.

more meaningful learning. In this section, it is critical that you specify ways you will actually teach (i.e., demonstration, modeling, explanation) the concepts. It is also useful to have a numbered list to which you can refer if you get "lost in the moment."

4. *Guided Practice.* During guided practice the children are given an opportunity to practice and apply the skills you have presented during the lesson. This means you will observe children engaged in the activity. Teachers intervene and provide support and guidance as needed. Different activities will require different levels of interaction or support. For example, you might place a recording of the songs you are introducing in one of the learning centers and give the children an opportunity to sing while they play or listen using headphones. You will observe and ask questions about their enjoyment of the songs or ask them to describe what they heard and how it made them feel.

5. *Closure.* It is important to summarize the lesson for the children to solidify learning and understanding or to provide closure since the lesson was presented in steps. It is important to pull it all together at the end so the children understand on a conscious level what they have learned and why. This enables them to later apply their knowledge in different contexts. Make specific notations in your lesson plan about how you will wrap up the lesson and prepare the children for the next activity or event. Young children are happier in a classroom characterized by routine and predictability. In other words, they want to know when they have finished a task (lesson) and what will happen next.

6. *Materials and Equipment.* Make a detailed list of everything you will need to teach the lesson. You will use this list prior to the lesson to make sure you have not forgotten anything important, such as prerecorded music.

7. *Assessment.* A standards-driven curriculum focuses much attention on assessment. As early childhood educators we must remember that assessment procedures must be designed to provide children with opportunities to demonstrate their capabilities in a fair manner and in an authentic setting. Ideally, teachers can measure children's achievements through a combination of authentic assessment strategies, including observation and anecdotal records. Recording the results of a child's music experiences, the child's growth and musical expression, the skills mastered, and the child's attitude toward leaning and interaction with other children can provide the teacher with a profile of the child's progress. It can also help the teacher guide children to further growth. Assessing young children's involvement with music, songs, and movement must be a broadly defined process conducted with sensitivity and respect.

The Talks With Teachers feature in this chapter shared the story of Phyllis Gates and her children exploring musical instruments. Consider using her story to practice writing a lesson plan based on how Phyllis and her children experimented with and made musical instruments.

## GENERAL GUIDELINES FOR SELECTING MUSIC AND MOVEMENT ACTIVITIES

The following general guidelines will help you select music and movement activities for 3-year-olds.

- Large group experiences in music should be kept to a minimum. Give individual children and small groups plenty of time and space to sing, move, make sounds, and listen to music.

- The effective use of music promotes body movements, such as jumping, running, and hopping. Children of this age will respond at their own body tempo.
- Much of children's singing at this age is spontaneous and self-initiated and appears as they engage in play. Provide opportunities for spontaneous play activities, particularly of the motor kind.
- At appropriate times, you can enrich children's play activities and movements with your own spontaneous singing of musical phrases and short songs.
- Children have a tendency to choose their own pitch range. It is not important to match your pitch to those of children, but it is important to remember that children will pitch their singing voices according to their own needs or developmental level.
- New music material should be introduced slowly. Children like to sing familiar songs. They love humorous songs.
- Not all children will join in singing or dancing activities at the same time or at the same pace. Some children may prefer to listen without joining in. Other children may only sing or dance to parts of a song—maybe a phrase that has caught their attention. Other children enjoy just listening to favorite songs over and over before they feel comfortable participating in group activities.
- At this age, children like to experiment with instruments but should not be expected to keep "time" with the music. Introduce individual instruments one at a time so that children can become acquainted with each instrument's distinctive sound, its shape, and its name. Carleton (2000) recommends that the young child's classroom "contain four or five rhythm percussion instruments, a small keyboard, CD players with headset(s) and a variety of recorded songs and instrumental music. Instruments and recorded music can be rotated on a monthly basis for maximum learning" (p. 56).

Drums and xylophones provide variation in sound to encourage rhythmic experimentation.

## Songs to Use with 3-Year-Olds

Three-year-olds can sing along with familiar songs and can establish and maintain a regular beat. For example, the 3-year-olds at the N. E. Miles Early Childhood Development Center at the College of Charleston (www.cofc.edu/~child/staff.html) recently learned "Tony Chestnut" and delighted themselves in the movements, familiar phrases, and regular beat that "Tony Chestnut" provides.

Three-year-olds also enjoy singing songs with repetitive words and often talk and sing during their daily activities. Two all-time favorites of children this age are "Row, Row, Row Your Boat" and "Old MacDonald Had a Farm." Three-year-olds can successfully make the rowing movements and sing at the same time and have been known to roll on the floor giggling when singing "E–I–E–I–O."

Three-year-olds often suggest new words for songs or add additional verses. They are also interested in rhythm instruments and enjoy playing with adults who provide simple rhythmic patterns to imitate. For example, "People on the Bus" includes the frequent use of rhythmic speech with a simple pattern that is easy to imitate.

Children can create their own motions to represent the words. They can also make up new verses such as "The children in the room move forward and back."

Of course, 3-year-olds can learn simple fingerplays. They can also clap in different tempos and at different levels when imitating an adult. "Clap, Clap, Clap Your Hands" is a simple fingerplay with just enough variety in the words to keep a 3-year-old interested.

### TONY CHESTNUT

Traditional

Arranged by LINDA EDWARDS

To - ny Chest - nut knows I love you, To - ny knows,

To - ny knows, To - ny Chest - nut knows I love you,

That's what To - ny knows.

(Children point to body parts as they follow the motions of an adult.)

| Toe | knee | chest | head | nose | eye | hug | point |
|-----|------|-------|------|------|-----|-----|-------|
| To- | ny | Chest- | nut | knows | I | love | you. |

## ROW, ROW, ROW YOUR BOAT

Traditional

Arranged by LINDA EDWARDS

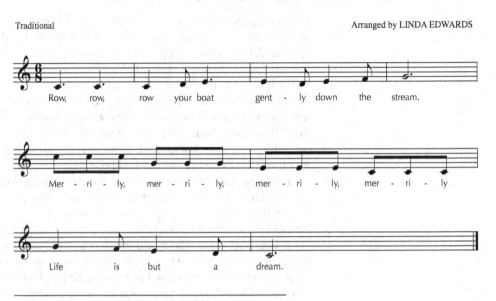

Row, row, row your boat gent - ly down the stream.

Mer - ri - ly, mer - ri - ly, mer - ri - ly, mer - ri - ly

Life is but a dream.

"Row, Row, Row Your Boat" can also be sung as a three-part round but singing rounds is inappropriate for very young children. Stick to the melody and have fun rowing!

## OLD MACDONALD HAD A FARM

Traditional

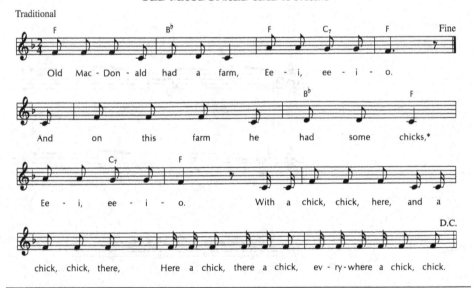

Old Mac - Don - ald had a farm, Ee - i, ee - i - o.

And on this farm he had some chicks,*

Ee - i, ee - i - o. With a chick, chick, here, and a

chick, chick, there, Here a chick, there a chick, ev - ry-where a chick, chick.

Most children like to sing the traditional song "Old MacDonald Had a Farm." It is usually one of the first ones they memorize. They are "tickled" and excited as they hear their own voices produce the animal sounds in strict adherence to the interesting rhythmic pattern ("with a chick, chick, here, and a chick, chick, there," etc.). Throughout the years, this song has been adapted for many purposes. One of the ways it has been used is to help children learn their short and long vowel sounds. It is an enjoyable way for them to memorize the sounds. Once they learn it in the song, the children can easily recall a sound by associating it with the animal. The vowels are substituted for the animal sounds. For example:

**Short Vowel Version**

(Sing the following to the tune of
  "Old MacDonald")
Old MacDonald had a farm, Ee-i, ee-i-o.
And on this farm he had a cat, Ee-i, ee-i-o
With an ă - ă here, And an ă - ă there, Here an, ă
  There an ă,
  Every where an ă - ă.
Old MacDonald had a cat, Ee-i, ee-i-o.
Other verses: a hen—ĕ
             a pig— ĭ
             an ox— ŏ
             a duck— ŭ

**Long Vowel Version**

(Sing the song as above, but substitute animals having the
  long vowel sounds)
For example: a tapir—ā
             a sheep—ē
             some mice—ī
             a goat—ō
             a mule—ū
*Note:* Zoo animals could be used instead of farm animals

## THE PEOPLE ON THE BUS

American Traditional

Arranged by LINDA EDWARDS

The peo-ple on the bus go up and down, up and down,

up and down, The peo-ple on the bus go

up and down, All round the town.

The wipers on the bus go swish, swish, swish.
The wheels on the bus go round and round.
The horn on the bus goes beep, beep, beep.

"The Bus" from SINGING ON OUR WAY of OUR SINGING WORLD SERIES, p. 153. Copyright © 1959, 1957, 1949. Adapted by permission of Pearson Education, Inc. All rights reserved.

## CLAPPING SONG

Traditional

Clap, clap, clap your hands, clap your hands to - geth - er.

Children's abilities to learn the actions and words of fingerplay vary with age and experience. Music that promotes body movements will encourage children to engage in spontaneous and self-initiated play activities. It is important to remember that children of this age need many opportunities to sing, move, and dance.

## Listening to Recorded Music

Children of this age enjoy listening to recorded music and responding to or imitating the motions of others. Teachers should build their own libraries of recorded music, including classical, folk, jazz, gospel, country-western, and other popular genres. College students should be encouraged to begin building their music libraries while still in school. Recorded music makes great gifts for birthdays and holidays. Most school librarians will have copies of the *Schwann Spectrum* catalog of compact discs (CDs) for reference. Listings in this catalog include available commercial recordings of musical selections by composer. You might consider organizing your musical library according to composer, country, or genre (classical, rock, pop, folk) and labeling these on the CD cases. Follow these general guidelines when purchasing and organizing CDs:

- Choose a recording by a well-known and well-respected performing ensemble, conductor, or solo artist.
- Be sure the recording was properly engineered from an excellent master source and was well crafted.
- Purchase a recording that falls within your budget.

Music that promotes body movement will encourage children to engage in spontaneous and self-initiated play activities.

It is important to remember that children of this age need many opportunities to sing, move, and dance.

## MUSIC FROM AROUND THE WORLD

As part of the "Music in Cultural Context" series in *Music Educators Journal*, Campbell (1995) interviewed Mellonee Burnim on her views of African American music. Burnim talked about African American religious music, particularly spirituals and gospel songs:

> Gospel music is a celebration and an affirmation of life. It is through the performance of gospel music that African Americans can identify with their cultural and historical past. Gospel music functions in ways similar to the Negro spiritual that was created during the period of slavery; in fact, it is an extension of the spiritual. (p. 42)

Early childhood teachers know that young children learn best through play and that activities involving movement of various body parts and a lot of action usually get their attention. In keeping with the African American tradition of gospel and spirituals, two songs that are appropriate both to the tradition and to the developmental stage of 3-year-olds are "This Little Light of Mine" and "There's a Little Wheel." As Burnim reminds us, "When one sings gospel music, one sings it completely and totally, immersed in body and in spirit" (Campbell, 1995, p. 46). When young children sing these songs, they can truly be immersed in both body and the spirit of singing.

*The truest expression of a people is in its dance and music.*

—Agnes de Mille

## THIS LITTLE LIGHT OF MINE

Spiritual

This lit-tle light of mine, I'm gon-na let it shine.

This lit-tle light of mine, I'm gon-na let it shine.

This lit-tle light of mine, I'm gon-na let it shine, let it

shine, let it shine, let it shine.

This big world of ours, I'm gonna help it shine,
This big world of ours, I'm gonna help it shine,
This big world of ours, I'm gonna help it shine,
Help it shine, help it shine, help it shine.

## THERE'S A LITTLE WHEEL

Spiritual

Arranged by K. BAYLESS

1. There's a lit-tle wheel a-turn-ing in my heart, There's a

lit-tle wheel a turn-ing in my heart. In my heart,_____ in my

heart,_____ There's a lit-tle wheel a-turn-ing in my heart.

Other verses that may be added to "There's a Little Wheel a-Turning":

2. Oh, I feel so very happy in my heart,
3. There's a little drum a-beating in my heart,
4. There's a little harp a-strumming in my heart,

5. There's a little bell a-ringing in my heart,
6. There's a little bit of kindness in my heart,
7. There's a little song a-singing in my heart,

## KEY IDEAS

1. For 3-year-olds, music making and dancing is often an individual activity.
2. Children learn by listening and experimenting.

3. Caregivers should capitalize on the child's environment and responses as cues.

## SUMMARY

Observation and participation will provide the teacher with ample direction for music making with 3-year-olds. Observation means seeing, asking questions, listening, and looking—wherever young children are. Participation means playing, singing, chanting, and moving with young children. Spontaneity and creativity should mark much of the activity at this age level. The environment should be uncomplicated and uncluttered to promote freedom of expression. Above all, keep in mind that for "threes," music is predominantly individual. Music is for enjoyment and delight; music is for sharing.

## QUESTIONS TO CONSIDER

1. Select four or five unusual objects that could be used to build good listening habits. Describe an activity with each.
2. Find and record several catchy, action-oriented rhythms appropriate for 3-year-olds. How might your recording enhance listening skills?

3. Interview the mother of a 3-year-old, and determine how the home environment is used to develop the child's perceptual awareness.
4. Visit a child care center. Select three songs from this chapter to present to the children. Summarize the results.

## SONG COLLECTIONS

*100 Songs for Kids.* (1998). Mommy and Me Enterprises. All rights reserved. Mommy and Me Enterprises © MADACY Entertainment Group, Inc. P.O. Box 1445, St. Laurent, Quebec, Canada H4L421. Mommy and

Me™ name and logo are trademarks of Mommy and Me Enterprises. Licensed by The Rainmaker Group. Woodland Hills, CA 91364.

## REFERENCES

Andress, B. (1989). Music for every stage. *Music Educators Journal, 76*(2), 22–27.

Campbell, P. S. (1995). Mellonee Burnim on African American music. *Music Educators Journal, 82*(1), 41–48.

Carleton, E. B. (2000). Learning through music: The support of brain research. *Childcare Information Exchange, 133*, 53–56.

Feierabend, J. M. (1999). Make music, America! At MENC's national conference. *Teaching Music, 7*(3), 19–27.

Fox, D. B. (2000). Music and the baby's brain: Early experiences. *Music Educators Journal, 87*(2), 23–27.

Music Educators National Conference. (1994). *National standards for music education.* Reston, VA: Author.

National Association for Sport and Physical Education. (2011). *Moving into the future: National standards for physical education* (2nd ed.). Reston, VA: American Alliance for Health, Physical Education, Recreation and Dance.

Smith, C. (2000). For the love of music—and children. *Childcare Information Exchange, 133*, 45–60.

Strickland, E. (2001). Move to the music. *Scholastic Early Childhood Today, 15*(4), 36–37.

Wilcox, E. (1999). Straight talk about music and brain research. *Teaching Music, 7*(3), 29–33.

# CHAPTER SIX

# Music and Movement
# for 4-Year-Olds

*Knowledge is tied to action. It is through
children's exploration and discovery among their actions
that the first structures of mind are formed . . .*

Jean Piaget

*Around 4 years of age, children are beginning to take a real interest in music and movement of all kinds. As physical development progresses from large to small muscle control, the random movements during the infant stage progress to the point at which the child gains control over specific parts of the body and refines their use. Early childhood developmental specialists describe movement in terms of locomotor skills, manipulative development, and cognitive development. Locomotor skills include movements such as walking, running, jumping, hopping, galloping, and skipping. Manipulative development includes movements such as reaching, grasping, releasing, throwing, catching, and striking. "In the cognitive realm, movement activities can help preschoolers learn body parts and understand abstract, spatial concepts such as up and down, backward, forward, and sideways, and over and under" (Paglin, 2000, p. 28).*

*Movement is fun for young children, and movement for movement's sake is significant. Children learn to use their bodies and move with confidence. They feel more self-assured and enjoy themselves while developing a physical awareness that enhances their ability to explore on their own.*

*Laban's (1963) classic theory on young children and movement includes two areas of awareness that young children develop through movement. Laban suggests that children develop body awareness and space awareness. Laban is generally considered the father of movement education and his system of analyzing movement through the elements of time, weight, space, and flow have significantly added to our understanding of how children develop motor skills.*

## STAGES OF DEVELOPMENT

Early childhood developmental specialists often describe movement in terms of locomotor and nonlocomotor skills. Locomotor skills, often referred to as travel skills, transport the body from one point to another. Nonlocomotor skills are movements that children can perform while staying in the same place. Nonlocomotor skills include bending, stretching, twisting, and turning the body. It is important to keep in mind that stages of development overlap and each child will develop movement skills along a continuum, mastering these abilities at different ages.

Additional ideas for locomotor skill development include moving in space at different *levels*. The following different levels are presented in a hierarchy from easy to difficult.

| **Low Level** | **Middle Level** | **High Level** |
|---|---|---|
| Long body roll | Knee walk | Giant steps |
| Belly crawl | Squat walk | Pogo stick jumps |
| Hip walking | Frog jump | Run under streamers |
| Seal walk (using arms, legs dragging like a seal) | Walk on knees and elbows | March using high knees |
| Sitting and moving forward and backward | Four-legged walk (use arms and legs) | Run and jump, leap |
| | | Run and freeze |

In addition to encouraging children to move at different *levels*, teachers can use the following locomotor activities to broaden children's experiences and vocabulary:

- *Crawling.* Crawling involves lying on the stomach and using the elbows and hips to move. Children can pretend to be worms, snakes, or salamanders as they crawl across the room.
- *Creeping.* When children creep, they use their hands and feet to move across the room. They can creep like a dog, spider, or duck. Four-year-olds are excellent creepers.
- *Jumping.* Children can jump when they take off from one foot or both feet. Encourage children to jump in different ways. For example, they can jump with their feet together, or apart, land on one foot, pretend they are bouncing balls, or jump as if they are jumping for joy.
- *Galloping.* A gallop is a combination of a walk and a run. Children leap with one foot, while the other one catches up. Teachers can provide rhythmic galloping sounds, using rhythm sticks or hand clapping.
- *Hopping.* Four-year-olds can hop as if they are a pogo stick. They can also hop in and out of a hoop that has been placed on the floor.
- *Sliding.* Teachers should demonstrate sliding so that the children are not confused about this particular movement. Children can slide forward, backward, and side to side.

Ideas for nonlocomotor skill development include:

- *Stretching.* Make your body as tall as you can as you reach for the ceiling. Lie on the floor on your back and stretch your feet and legs high into space. Lie on your

Children can play circle games to experiment with moving in space at different levels.

stomach and stretch your head back, kick your feet in the air, and stretch your arms out to the side.

- *Bending.* Bend forward and touch your knees (toes, legs). Bend over and move like a rag doll. Stretch up high to get cookies off the counter. Bend down and pick some flowers from the garden.
- *Shaking.* Shake like you are freezing. Shake like a bowl full of jelly. Shake like a tree being blown by the wind.

As you may recall from Chapter 2, Pica (2004) suggests three different approaches for early childhood teachers when planning music and movement activities for young children. The direct approach is teacher directed and taught through demonstration, modeling, and imitation. For example, hand clapping can be demonstrated and imitated by young children who have not been introduced to clapping. The guided discovery method allows children to experiment while a teacher guides them through a process. For example, the children are asked to move like a rabbit, hopping and leaping. Or a teacher might ask children questions such as "How do rabbits move?" The third approach, exploration, encourages children to respond to open-ended suggestions that can produce a variety of responses. For example, if children are asked to pretend to grow from a seed into a tall tree, numerous combinations of movement are possible. When combined with music, more experimentation is encouraged and more possibilities are available to children.

At 4 years of age, children are almost continually in motion: walking, jumping, running, rocking, swinging, galloping, stomping, and tapping. In many instances, these movements can be channeled into the dramatization of action songs or simple, musical episodes or stories. The selected characteristics of 4-year-olds, shown in Figure 6–1, will be helpful when selecting and planning appropriate music activities for this age group.

**Figure 6–1    Selected Characteristics of 4-Year-Olds**

- Like to gallop, jump, walk, or run in time to music
- Are much more fluent with language, like to talk and chatter, want adults to listen and to give their undivided attention
- Have more interest in detail and direction (for example, can usually find a favorite book or CD from a shelf upon request)
- Enjoy simple versions of imaginative, dramatic play
- Enjoy singing games and rhythm instruments (they still need to explore, experiment, and manipulate instruments)
- Are beginning to dramatize songs
- Spontaneously make up their own songs, often with repetitive words and tunes that resemble familiar ones

**Consider the following when planning musical activities for a child this age:**
- Encourage informal singing throughout the day.
- Continue to improvise short action songs based on what the child is doing.
- Provide plenty of opportunities for the child to dramatize songs and to "act out" song-stories.
- Provide simple props like scarves, puppets, and instruments for the child to use with musical activities.
- Introduce humorous, active songs, which hold high appeal.
- Continue to introduce rhythm and melody instruments to enhance musical activities.
- Provide increased opportunities for movement with music, such as performing locomotor movements (walking, running, jumping), nonlocomotor movements (swinging, pushing, bending), and clapping or tapping the beat of a steady rhythm.
- Encourage children to move and dance to music using their own creative ideas.

# NATIONAL STANDARDS FOR MUSIC EDUCATION FOR 4-YEAR-OLDS

The standards in this section are intended for 4-year-old children. It is important to remember that the skills of young children develop along a continuum, and developmentally appropriate activities can be used with younger children (Music Educators National Conference, 1994).

## Four-Year-Old National Standards

### *Content Standards: Singing and Playing Instruments*

Young children enjoy singing and playing instruments. Four-year-olds are able to differentiate between their singing and speaking voices. They are also able to express themselves by playing instruments. The following standards identify the type of singing and instruments that are most suitable for 4-year-olds.

- Children use their voices as they speak, chant, and sing.
- Children sing a variety of simple songs in various keys, meters, and genres, alone and in groups, becoming increasingly accurate in rhythm and pitch.
- Children experiment with a variety of instruments and other sound sources.
- Children play simple melodies and accompaniments on instruments.

### *Content Standards: Creating Music*

Four-year-olds are quite capable of creating sound patterns with their bodies, their voices, and instruments. They often create simple melodies while at play. They also create musical sounds to express an idea. The following standards focus on a child's ability to create music.

- Children improvise songs to accompany their play activities.
- Children improvise instrumental accompaniments to songs, recorded selections, stories, and poems.
- Children create short pieces of music, using voices, instruments, and other sound sources.

Teachers do not have to be musically talented to enjoy singing with children.

Children respond through movement to music of various tempos, meters, dynamics, modes, genres, and styles to express what they hear and feel in works of music.

- Children invent and use original graphic or symbolic systems to represent vocal and instrumental sounds and musical ideas.

### Content Standards: Responding to Music

Four-year-olds are able to recognize musical phrases and show an awareness of simple cadences. They can identify the speed of music (fast/slow, getting faster/slower) and can describe the volume of music in their own words. The following standards focus on responding to music.

- Children identify the sources of a wide variety of sounds.
- Children respond through movement to music of various tempos, meters, dynamics, modes, genres, and styles to express what they hear and feel in works of music.
- Children participate freely in music activities.

### Content Standards: Understanding Music

Four-year-olds will listen attentively to a selected repertoire of music. They are also capable of using musical terms and concepts to express thoughts about music. They are good at practicing basic audience and performance etiquette. This last set of standards addresses understanding music.

- Children use their own vocabulary and standard music vocabulary to describe voices, instruments, music notation, and music of various genres, styles, and periods from diverse cultures.
- Children sing, play instruments, move, or verbalize to demonstrate awareness of the elements of music and changes in their usage.
- Children demonstrate an awareness of music as a part of daily life.[*]

*From *National Standards for Arts Education*. Copyright © 1994 by Music Educators National Conference (MENC). Used by permission. The complete National Arts Standards and additional materials relating to the Standards are available from MENC—National Association for Music Education, 1806 Robert Fulton Drive, Reston, VA 20191.

## TALKS WITH TEACHERS

Deanna Satzger is the Master Teacher for the 4-year-old class at the N. E. Miles Early Childhood Development Center at the College of Charleston. She has worked in a variety of preschool settings, including one in New York City that served a large number of United Nations families. Deanna received her Master of Arts in Teaching in Early Childhood Education from the College of Charleston and is certified in elementary and early childhood education.

Deanna and her 4-year-olds plan for many multi-sensory musical experiences. Deanna writes:

Listening to Sergei Prokofiev's classic *Peter and the Wolf* is a favorite in my class and the basis for many multi-sensory musical experiences. We begin our exploration of this piece through dance. The lights are dimmed so that the children can concentrate more fully on the sound and feeling of the music. They are encouraged to be the characters; be the music, as they move freely about the room. Throughout the year the children hear and dance to a variety of music including orchestral pieces, so expressing themselves in this manner is something they are familiar and comfortable with. We also use *Peter and the Wolf* in the traditional way, as a means for introducing the children to instruments of the orchestra. We play matching games with pictures of the instruments and the characters in the story. Playing clips of instruments outside of the context of *Peter and the Wolf* and letting the children match sound to the instrument picture helps to reinforce their understanding.

Another activity we do is drawing the music. Each child is provided a piece of notebook-sized laminating film and markers and asked to draw what they hear as the orchestra plays. Some children draw lines, sharp and squiggly. Others represent their understanding with mock and conventional musical notes or pictures of the instruments they hear. Now it is time to bring their renderings of the music to life. Each child has a chance to project her/his music on the wall for all to see using the overhead projector. (Our projector is often available for the children to use to experiment with light and shadow as a center in the classroom.) Using simple cut-out characters, the children manipulate Peter and the rest of the cast over the music they have drawn as the recording is played. The children find it very satisfying to put on this show for their classmates.

Deanna and the other teachers at the N.E. Miles Early Childhood Development Center are constantly "documenting" the children's work. Documentation allows children to revisit their personal contributions to learning and provides insights for the teachers about how children learn and think. Recently I sat down with Candace Jaruszewicz, PhD, Director of the N. E. Miles Early Childhood Development Center, for an interview on how she and the teachers use "visual documentation" at the center. The following section is a summary of my interview with Dr. Jaruszewicz.

Visual Documentation at the N.E. Miles Early Childhood Development Center, on the campus of the College of Charleston (C. Jaruszewicz, personal communication, February 14, 2011)

1. *What is documentation?* Most people associate "visual documentation" with the emergent curriculum used in Reggio Emilia Italian preschools and the Project Approach (Katz & Chard, 1997). Teachers use media to create displays that "tell the story" of children's work over extended periods of time. Displays typically include photographs and images, artifacts, children's transcribed comments or conversations, and written reflective teacher narratives. The Reggio documentations were originally created on large, flat panels, using cut/paste methods, but the advent and availability of digital media has considerably expanded format options to include interactive online and/or software applications such as PowerPoint, PhotoStory, wikis/blogs, etc.
2. *What about it interested you?* Early in my teaching career as an art educator, displaying students' work was an expected part of my job. I realized that while simple labels were

*(continued)*

(Continued)

useful, including more detailed descriptive information about the work represented in the displays was very helpful to classroom teachers, families, and my superiors! I also found that over time, I was becoming much more reflective about what I was choosing to write and that doing documentation was helping me make sense of my work. As my professional career shifted towards early childhood education and I was introduced to the Reggio Emilia approach in the mid 1990s, the descriptions and examples of visual documentation were an "aha" moment for me, as they provided a "name" for what I had been exploring on my own, and a clearly articulated framework for thinking about it.

3. *How is it connected to Reggio?* The *100 Languages of Children* (Edwards, Gandini, & Forman, 1994) provided the first detailed explanation and description of visual documentation as a key element of the emergent curriculum used in the Reggio Emilia municipal preschools. Thousands of people around the world have also visited the *100 Languages* traveling documentation exhibits of Reggio children's project work.

4. *What are the benefits for children?* When teachers thoughtfully and accurately represent children's work at multiple periods of time over the course of a long-term project, children benefit from the ability to "revisit" earlier stages in their thinking process, which promotes higher level thinking, metacognition, and reflection. Learning expands to become a visual dialogue. Seeing their work and words represented affirms and validates children's ideas and questions and their ongoing attempts to make sense of experiences.

5. *What is the teacher's role?* The teacher's role is much like that of an action researcher: asking questions about a project at various stages, determining appropriate means for, collecting, and analyzing "data," and drawing conclusions about what the project represents. While a project is underway, teachers identify key moments, stages, or changes in children's thinking over time as a project emerges, engage in study and inquiry experiences (facilitated by teachers), and create concrete representations of their learning. Teachers typically collect photos or videos of children in discussion and at work, audio recordings of conversations for later review and transcription, and samples of work both finished and in progress. Teachers also reflect with the children and other teachers about the work. Visual documentations can be constructed and shared while a project is in progress, or as a reflective process once a project ends.

6. *How is it different from or same as assessment?* Visual documentations do provide valuable information that can be used for assessment purposes. The main difference is in purpose and scope. While documentations include the work and words of individual children, those things are represented in the context of a more global narrative that is intended to provide insights about how children [and teachers] think and learn.

## CHILDREN [AND TEACHERS] THINK AND LEARN: CONCEPTUAL LEARNING THROUGH MUSIC AND MOVEMENT

The American Academy of Pediatrics reports that movement is essential to the physical and cognitive development of preschoolers. Children at this age master basic movement skills, such as running and skipping, as they explore their world. When using movement activities with these young children, we should remember that there is much individual variation in development. Movement experiences are a critical part of early childhood education (Paglin, 2000).

## Music and Movement as Communication

Movement, as a form of expression, is fundamental to conceptual development. For young children especially, movement is among the earliest forms of communication through which children explore and learn about their world because movement allows for the expression of ideas and imagination without words (Koff, 2000). Movement also helps children with their overall gross motor development. When children move, they explore their bodies in relation to space, which is valuable in developing body awareness. When combined with music, movement helps children acquire a feel for the rhythm and mood of the music. Children will use their whole body to explore changes in tempo or rhythm, and these kinesthetic actions facilitate muscle development and heighten awareness of the kinesthetic senses.

Movement is also a great source of joy and pleasure to children. They are eager to be physically free to move, to be spontaneous in their physical responses to music, and to show joy in movement simply for its own sake.

As all early childhood educators know, movement to music begins very early. Émile Jaques-Dalcroze (1865–1950), a Swiss composer, believed that movement was the best way to help children learn to love and appreciate music (1921). He believed that it was

"Miss Polly" is a wonderful song that encourages children to integrate play and music.

important to focus on the *process* of movement during the early years rather than on the *product* (Brewer, 1995). Movement experiences for young children should include both creative and structured movements. When children move in creative ways, they are interpreting the music and movement in their own ways; their movements may or may not match the beat of the music. For example, when children move in response to a teacher's suggestion, such as to move fast or slow or to move high or low, all of the children will not move the same way all of the time. Other excellent, tried and true methods for using music and movement to communicate are fingerplays and action songs. Fingerplays and action songs are usually poems and wordplays in which movement is critical to communication. "The contemporary rhythms and movements of fingerplays and action songs incorporate language, symbolism, and perception which help children to remember them" (Raines & Canady, 1990, p. 178). The following examples of fingerplays and action songs are a form of communication and are appropriate for 4-year-olds.

## FINGERPLAYS AND ACTION SONGS FOR 4-YEAR-OLDS

### TWO LITTLE APPLES

### THE OLD GRAY CAT

2. The little mice are creeping, creeping, creeping,
   The little mice are creeping through the house.
3. The little mice are nibbling . . . in the house.
4. The little mice are sleeping . . . in the house.

5. The old gray cat comes creeping . . . through the house.
6. The little mice all scamper . . . through the house.
7. The little mice are hiding . . . in the house.

# HEAD, SHOULDERS, KNEES, AND TOES

Action song

Head, shoul-ders, knees, and toes, knees and toes. Head, shoul-ders, knees, and toes, knees and toes and Eyes and ears and mouth and nose, Head shoul-ders, knees and toes, knees and toes.

# LOOBY LOO

Old English folk game

Arranged by K. BAYLESS

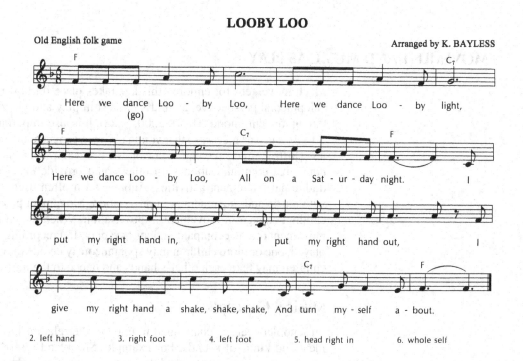

Here we dance Loo - by Loo, Here we dance Loo - by light,
(go)
Here we dance Loo - by Loo, All on a Sat - ur - day night. I
put my right hand in, I put my right hand out, I
give my right hand a shake, shake, shake, And turn my-self a - bout.

2. left hand  3. right foot  4. left foot  5. head right in  6. whole self

## FIVE LITTLE CHICKADEES

Old counting song

Five lit-tle chick-a-dees peep-ing at the door,
One flew a-way and then there were four. Chick-a-dee, chick-a-dee,
hap-py and gay, chick-a-dee, chick-a-dee, fly a-way.

2
Four little chickadees sitting on a tree,
One flew away, and there were three,
(Refrain)

3
Three little chickadees looking at you,
One flew away, and then there were two,
(Refrain)

4
Two little chickadees sitting in the sun,
One flew away, and then there was one,
(Refrain)

5
One little chickadee left all alone,
He flew away, and then there were none,
(Refrain)

## MOVEMENT AND MUSIC AS PLAY

Much movement for children this age takes place during free playtime. "From a developmental perspective, a child's interest in play and physical exploration continues throughout childhood" (Koff, 2000, p. 28). It is also important to provide unstructured activity, such as recess, so that young children can have the freedom to move their bodies. Unstructured time can foster physical development, aid self-exploration through nonverbal communication with others, and provide exciting reinforcement to more traditional movement activities. Another term often used when children are playing with music and movement is improvisation. Movement possibilities are endless when children engage in movement improvisation. When inside the classroom, music and movement often accompany indoor free play. If a recording with an inviting rhythm is played, one or more children may spontaneously decide they would like to dance. Two children may take each other's hands and dance to the music.

### Musical Concepts

Preschoolers can be challenged to explore the relationships between types of movement and kinds of sounds. For example, Strickland (2001) suggests that "a triangle produces a high-pitched sound that may encourage tiptoeing or prancing. A drumbeat produces a low-pitched sound that might encourage plodding movements or stomping" (p. 36). Teachers might collect a variety of animal pictures and match these to the sounds produced by rhythm instruments. Show the children the picture of an animal, play the corresponding instrument, and ask the children to move like that animal might move. Or play an instrument, and ask the children to look at several animal pictures and identify the animal that matches the sound.

Musical concepts can be taught quite easily. They are not taught in a highly structured manner during one session but are learned gradually over a period of time. For example, songs and singing games involving movement are very appropriate to use with children at this age. Initially, some children may not want to join in these sessions, but with time they will want to become a part of the group. *Remember to keep the group small.*

## Caribbean Ring Dances

The rhymes and songs of the Caribbean Islands can often be traced to their French, English, and African roots. The song "Brown Girl in the Ring" is sung as a circle game. One child stands in the middle of the ring and makes a motion that the other children mimic. The source for this song is a collection of Afro-Caribbean rhymes, games, and songs for children compiled by Grace Hallworth and illustrated by Caroline Binch (1996).

*Brown Girl in the Ring*

There's a brown girl in the ring
Tra la-la-la-la.
There's a brown girl in the ring
Tra la-la-la-la.
A brown girl in the ring,
Tra la-la-la-la.
For she's sweet like a sugar
And a plum, plum, plum.
Now show me your motion,

"Brown Girl in the Ring" is a delightful song and dance from the Caribbean Islands.

## MUSIC FROM AROUND THE WORLD

The early childhood classroom should reflect a variety of cultures integrated into all curriculum topics every day. The National Association for the Education of Young Children (NAEYC) recommends providing dolls, toys, wall decorations, books, and recordings that reflect diverse images children may not likely see elsewhere" (National Academy of Early Childhood Programs, 1998).

With the current emphasis on multiculturalism in education, it is critical that we provide young children the opportunity to learn the music of cultures other than their own. When we do this, we help young children better understand these other cultures. This must be a high priority for all early childhood teachers. The following section presents a delightful song and dance from the Caribbean Islands, "Brown Girl in the Ring," that can be used to promote just such understanding and sensitivity.

---

Tra la-la-la-la.
Now show me your motion,
Tra la-la-la-la.
For she's sweet like a sugar
And a plum, plum, plum.
Now hug and kiss your partner,
Tra la-la-la-la.
Now hug and kiss your partner,
Tra la-la-la-la.
Now hug and kiss your partner,
Tra la-la-la-la.
For she's sweet like a sugar
And a plum, plum, plum.

In addition, you might consider purchasing a recording by Marley and Booker of reggae and calypso songs for children. I highly recommend their *Smilin' Island of Songs: Reggae and Calypso Music for Children* (Redway, CA: Little People Music, 1992).

*People don't sing because they are happy, they're happy because they sing.*

—Goethe

## KEY IDEAS

1. Around 4 years of age, children are beginning to take a real interest in music activities.
2. At this age, children are almost continually in motion. This motion can often be channeled into productive ways of using music.
3. Children frequently chant and sing about what they are doing. This kind of play with words and music should be encouraged.
4. Teachers and parents can begin to help children understand that music has structure.

## SUMMARY

When music is presented within a cognitive framework that is appropriate for young children, meaning and understanding take place. Concepts should not be taught in a highly structured manner but introduced gradually over a period of time. Since children of this age are almost continually in motion, they should be given opportunities to act out stories, play singing games, and use movement in meaningful ways.

## QUESTIONS TO CONSIDER

1. Select four humorous songs appropriate for 4-year-olds. Develop activities for each song to promote conceptual awareness.
2. Select three everyday experiences common to this age level, and adapt each to a familiar melody. Present the songs to a child.
3. Develop a lesson plan for presentation using three songs from the chapter. Include activities, materials, and questions you wish to raise.

## SONG COLLECTIONS

*Excellent online source for songs for children*
Guthrie, W., & Guthrie, M. (1992). *Woody's 20 grow big songs*. New York, NY: HarperCollins.

Hudson, W., & Hudson, C. (1995). *How sweet the sound: African American songs for children*. New York, NY: Scholastic.

Manning, J. (1998). *My first songs*. New York, NY: Harper Festival.

*Recordings*
Brown, N., Culbertson, B., Braun, R., & Koz, D. (2002). *Golden slumbers: A father's lullaby* [CD]. Burbank, CA: Warner.

*Dreamland: World lullabies & soothing songs* [CD]. (2003). New York, NY: Putumayo World Music.

Palmer, H. (Composer), & Weintraub, A. (Director). (1999). *Baby songs: ABC, 123, Color & shapes*. [DVD]. Los Angeles, CA: 20th Century Fox.

Children's Book and Music Center
   *Activities designed for toddlers' fitness and development.*

*Lullabies from 'Round the World*
Children's Book and Music Center
   *Fourteen lovely international melodies for quiet time.*
   *Lullabies and Laughter*

Pat Carfra (A & M Records of Canada, Ltd.)
Children's Book and Music Center
   *For babies and small children, 33 lullabies and play songs that make it easy to sing to the young child.*

## REFERENCES

Brewer, J. (1995). *Introduction to early childhood education: Preschool through primary grades*. Needham Heights, MA: Allyn & Bacon.

Edwards, C., Gandini, L., & Forman. G. (Eds). (1998). The hundred languages of children. The Reggio Emilia Approach-Advanced reflections (2nd ed.). Greenwich. CT: Ablex Publishing.

Hallworth, G. (Ed.). (1996). *Down by the river: Afro-Caribbean rhymes, games, and songs for children* (C. Binch, Illus.). New York, NY: Scholastic.

Jaques-Dalcroze, É. (1921). *Rhythm, music, and education* (L. F. Rubenstein, Trans.). London, England: Hazell Watson and Viney for the Dalcroze Society.

Katz, L. G. & Chard, S. (2002). Engaging childrens' minds: The project approach, (2nd ed). Stamford, CT: Ablex Publishing.

Koff, S. R. (2000). Toward a definition of dance education. *Childhood Education, 77*(1), 27–31.

Laban, R. (1963). *Modern educational dance*. London, England: MacDonald and Evans.

Music Educators National Conference. (1994). *National standards for music education*. Reston, VA: Author.

National Academy of Early Childhood Programs. (1998). *Accreditation criteria and procedures of the National Academy of Early Childhood Programs*. Washington, DC: National Association for the Education of Young Children.

Paglin, C. (2000). Dance like a caterpillar: Movement is a big part of learning for little kids. *Northwest Education, 6*(1), 26–35.

Pica, R. (2004). *Experiences in movement: Birth to age 8* (3rd ed.). Clifton Park, NY: Delmar Learning.

Raines, S., & Canady, R. (1990). *The whole language kindergarten*. New York, NY: Teachers College Press.

Strickland, E. (2001). Move to the music. *Scholastic Early Childhood Today, 15*(4), 36–37.

# CHAPTER SEVEN

# Music and Movement for Kindergarten and Early Primary

*The most perfect expression of human behavior is a string quartet . . .*

Jeffrey Tate

*Music activities have traditionally been a part of kindergarten and early primary pro-grams. Friedrich Froebel (1878), "father of the kindergarten," believed in the value of musical experiences for young children. His book, Mother Play and Nursery Songs, brought this point to the attention of those who worked with children of this age. He believed that children should be given ample opportunity to sing songs and to play singing games. This thought has prevailed, and now making music is considered as integral a part of a child's day as eating or sleeping.*

## BUILDING A MEANINGFUL MUSIC AND MOVEMENT CURRICULUM

Educators at all levels tout the benefit of singing and playing musically with young children" (Wolf, 2000, p. 29). Music and movement are valued not only for potential intellectual benefits but for the enjoyment they give children. Music and movement are facets in the total education of the child that must be nurtured and experienced. It is important to remember that music and movement should not be limited to just sing-ing songs or dancing; music and movement are everything from crooning a lullaby to creatively interpreting the movement of swans or airplanes.

Keep these facts in mind, capitalize on them, and recognize that the early years are critical ones in forming favorable attitudes toward music and movement. A music and movement curriculum built on strong developmental theory combined with the national standards will provide a solid base for establishing and carrying out the goals of a well-developed, sequential kindergarten and early primary music and movement program.

### The Teacher's Role

The orientation and abilities of early childhood classroom teachers differ considerably. The teacher does not have to be classically trained in music or any of the other perform-ing arts. The most important thing for teachers to consider is their willingness to open their classroom to musical experiences for their children and to be willing to try, along with their children, new ways of exploring the many elements that music has to offer. With this in mind, Moravcik (2000) offers suggestions for teachers to consider when providing music activities for children. For example, it might be useful to reflect on the role of music in your own life. Specifically, Moravcik recommends that you reflect on what you feel and do when you hear:

- A lively piece of dance music
- A song you loved in school
- A slow processional
- A song your mother sang to you when you were a child
- A carol, hymn, or spiritual
- A song you listened to with a special friend (p. 27)

Thomas Moore, in an interview with *Early Childhood Today* (2000), says that children need to see adults who are open to music and music experiences in general. As we sing to children and with children, we open ourselves to each child's way of experiencing music. As Moore says, "It's a way of acknowledging that we are human" (p. 43).

# NATIONAL STANDARDS FOR MUSIC EDUCATION FOR 5-YEAR-OLDS

The Music Educators National Conference (MENC) identifies age-specific standards for 2-, 3-, and 4-year-old children (1994). These were discussed in previous chapters. The standards for 5-year-old children are included in the K–4 section of the national standards. The standards for K–4 describe the cumulative skills and knowledge expected of all students upon exiting grade 4. Children in the earlier grades should engage in developmentally appropriate learning experiences designed to prepare them to meet these standards at grade 4. Determining the curriculum and the specific instructional activities necessary to achieve the standards is the responsibility of states, local school districts, and individual teachers. It is important for early child-hood teachers to contact their state board of education to request a copy of specific state standards.

Although the national standards for music education for 5-year-olds are grouped with grades 1–4, it is possible to identify key standards that are appropriate for 5-year-olds. The Music Education Curriculum Standards for South Carolina, for example, are based on the national standards but have been grouped into categories for grades K–2, 3–5, 6–8/7–9, and 9–12. The following standards for K–2 are gleaned from the national standards and can be found at http://www.myschools.com/offices/cso/standards/vpa/.

## K–2 National Standards

### Content Standard: Singing
**Children use their voices expressively as they speak and sing. They also enjoy singing a variety of simple songs alone and with a group. The following standards identify the content and skills for singing.**

- Children sing in tune.
- Children use clear, free tone and correct breath support.
- Children sing alone or with others.
- Children sing a variety of simple songs in various keys.

### Content Standard: Performing on Instruments
**Children perform music using a variety of sound sources. The following standards address instrumentation.**

- Children play unpitched and pitched instruments.
- Children improvise simple rhythmic accompaniments.
- Children improvise simple rhythmic variations.

### Content Standard: Movement
**Children demonstrate an understanding of creative movement through self-expression.**

- Children demonstrate pulse and pitch direction of music with locomotor and nonlocomotor movements.
- Children demonstrate elements of space, time, and force through expressive movement.

*Content Standard: Listening*
**Children identify instruments and basic vocal types.**

- Children describe musical selections.
- Children use listening skills to describe elements of music.
- Children respond appropriately with correct etiquette in a variety of concert situations.

*Content Standard: Understanding Music in Relation to History and Culture*
**Children describe in simple terms how elements of music are used in music examples from various cultures of the world.**

- Children explain how music is a part of and a reflection of many cultures and ethnic groups.
- Children sing, play, and listen to music from a variety of periods and musical styles and from different geographic areas.
- Children recognize that music can be associated with other art forms.

Now that you have a conceptual knowledge of the content standards, it is important to look at the developmental characteristics of kindergarten and early primary children. The following section focuses on the general characteristics of kindergarten and early primary children and includes ideas to consider when planning musical and movement activities. These activities include a nice balance of singing, playing instruments, making sounds, and moving about in space.

## GENERAL CHARACTERISTICS OF 5- TO 8-YEAR-OLDS

Children at this age are generally conforming in nature, like to please, thrive on positive feedback, and are sensitive to praise and blame. Also at this age, children like to jump and climb and still need plenty of big muscle activity. Muscle coordination is improving. "Wigglers" and "bundles of endless energy" are good descriptors of this age group. They can skip on alternate feet and usually do quite well at galloping. These children like to talk a great deal and are interested in words and their meanings. For example, they will be happy to tell you how old they are and everything else about their lives they find interesting. They are also very curious; one of their favorite words is "why?" Kindergarten and early primary age children like to remain close to familiar surroundings; they are primarily interested in their home and community, not distant places, but they are interested in cities and states if they know someone who lives there, such as grandparents. Most children at this age understand and can carry out actions involving two or three similar commands and are learning the meaning of concepts such as small, smaller, and smallest. They are relatively independent and self-reliant, governed by rules, and often protective toward younger playmates and siblings. Figures 7–1 and 7–2 should aid in planning music and movement activities for 5-year-olds.

**Figure 7–1   Selected Characteristics of 5-Year-Olds**

- Are generally conforming in nature, like to please, thrive on positive feedback, and are sensitive to praise and blame
- Like to jump and climb and still need plenty of big muscle activity. Muscle coordination is improving
- Are described as "wigglers" and "bundles of endless energy"
- Can sometimes skip on alternate feet and do quite well at galloping
- Like to talk a great deal and are interested in words and their meanings
- Know how old they are and can generally tell how old they will be in another year
- Like to remain close to familiar surroundings; are primarily interested in their home and community, not distant places; are interested in different cities and states if they know someone who lives there, such as grandparents or previous playmates
- Understand and can carry out actions involving words like *forward* and *backward*
- Are learning the meaning of *small, smaller,* and *smallest*
- Are often very adept at rhyming words
- Are relatively independent and self-reliant, dependable, and protective toward younger playmates and siblings

**Figure 7–2   Characteristics to Consider When Planning Musical Activities for 5-Year-Olds**

- Are refining and exploring musical skills previously learned
- May be able to read words to songs
- Can generally play instruments accurately
- May begin to show an interest in piano and dance lessons
- Can better synchronize body movements with the rhythm of the music

## The Teacher's Role

The following three conditions will influence how well you fare in facilitating musical experiences for young children:

- *Psychological safety.* It is safe to try. Make sure children know your classroom is a safe place to try out new behaviors, to share ideas, and to make mistakes when learning new songs, dances, or movements or when playing instruments.
- *Comfort zone.* Assure children that the songs they are learning, the movements they are doing, and the instruments they are playing are easy and fun.
- *Encouragement.* All children should be encouraged to participate in musical activities. However, you should never force children to participate, even if you think they should. Shy children, especially, will enter into the musical activity when they feel comfortable and not a minute before. Remember that the musical activities are for the children's enjoyment, not to complete your lesson plan.

## LISTENING TO MUSIC

Listening (aural perception) is embodied in every phase of every activity that contributes to musical understanding and growth. It is considered to be the foundation for all musical experiences. Listening requires skills involved in focusing on the sound source, remembering sound sources, and responding (Anderson & Lawrence, 2001).

The ability to listen involves more than just hearing. It requires children to focus their minds on the sounds perceived. Haines and Gerber (2000) state, "This ability to pay attention is not innate but it is a learned skill, and the young child needs training and help to acquire it" (p. 9). Earlier in this book, we urged teachers to help young children become more sensitive to the sounds around them and to help them translate these sounds into meaningful experiences. These efforts should continue, as sound discrimination is vital to children's musical development. Unless someone has really made a point of helping a child sharpen his or her listening skills, the myriad sounds that must be confronted will often cause poor listening habits to be established prior to school.

Music activities provide an excellent means for increasing children's listening skills. Kindergarten and early primary age children can develop listening skills that will help them sing in tune, create melodies, accompany themselves on instruments, and move to music. They can be taught to listen to the expressive elements of music, such as melody, rhythm, and dynamics. As Flowers (1990) notes:

> In one way or another, music at all levels is focused on listening. The purposes and outcomes of listening may vary with the age of the listener and the musical setting, but there is perhaps no other music behavior so widely valued as good listening. (p. 21)

An important principle to keep in mind is that children cannot develop a high level of listening skill unless attentive listening is stressed. Listening is perceiving and requires thought and reasoning. Children's minds must be "filled" with musical images to build on what is new and unfamiliar to them musically. This takes time and can only be developed gradually through children's active participation in diverse and varied musical experiences.

### Conditions That Promote Good Listening

It is relatively easy to encourage children to listen to a variety of music. Children may need guidance in what to listen for, such as phrases, melody, and rhythm, but listening experiences are most effective if they include music that is pleasurable to the ear. Figure 7–3 explains how to create conditions that promote good listening.

Early childhood teachers must understand the relationship between music, music education, and the development of the whole child. Neely (2001) cites current research that supports this idea from David Elliott, a prominent music educator who reports that "whenever there is music, all kinds and levels of appraisals are going on at the same time" (p. 35). Neely also notes that listening to music involves children in "problem solving, decision making, and other complex processes that energize neuronal patterns similar to those exercised when playing chess or working complex math problems" (p. 35). Because listening is involved in all the musical skills, attention must be given to activities that improve the children's ability to listen. Thinking and reasoning should be enhanced.

**Figure 7–3  Promoting Good Listening**

During the early years, children need many opportunities to hear sounds and focus their attention on them. Listening and actively participating in musical experiences can enhance this ability.

1. Establish a happy, friendly atmosphere.
2. Make sure the children are physically comfortable. Rooms with acoustical tile ceilings and "soft" areas like carpet, pillows, and drapes tend to absorb sound and make for easier and more comfortable listening.
3. Put away any articles that might distract the children.
4. Provide a good variety of listening activities. These activities should require different comprehension levels and different interests.
5. Give children a reason for listening. That is, they should understand what to listen for.
6. Serve as a model. It is well recognized that the example the teacher sets is by far the single most important and influential factor in conditioning children to sensitive and discriminating listening. If you show enjoyment of music and actively participate, your children will generally feel the stimulation and will respond heartily and creatively.
7. Plan listening activities according to the maturity levels, abilities, and interests of your children. Gradually plan activities that encourage children to reach for the next level of understanding.
8. Provide an atmosphere in which your children can think creatively. For example, ask, "What instrument would you choose to make the sound of a ticking clock?"
9. Keep the experience short enough so that discipline problems will not intrude.

# SINGING

Singing brings much joy to children. We know that most young children love to sing and to be sung to. If you listen carefully as children go about their work and play, you will likely find them singing short, created songs that fit the rhythm of their movements. For example, on the playground, they might begin chanting, "Swing, swing, swing, swing, watch me go up and down." Recently, a group of 5-year-olds was observed coloring with purple crayons. As one child rhythmically made dots on her paper with her crayon, she started to sing over and over, "Purple-durple, purple-durple, purple-purple-durple." Soon the entire group joined in the singing, picking up the little girl's rhythm and dotting their papers as she did. They had just heard the story of *Harold and the Purple Crayon* (Johnson, 1998). Adults can sometimes sing back the chants and songs children improvise. These should occasionally be written down so children can see how songs are created and written.

At ages 5, 6, and 7, some children are unable to carry a tune. Therefore, one must be careful not to place too much emphasis on singing in tune and building musical skills at this age. Singing should not be taught formally at this time.

When teachers are unsure of the quality of their singing voice, they often use instruments to support their singing.

When you sit down to sing, watch the reactions of children. Usually their faces will light up as they gather around to ask for their favorite songs. We believe that an enthusiastic teacher singing in the classroom provides children with a more rewarding experience than even the best singer on a recording or a film. All teachers, whether or not they are naturally talented in singing, should sing to their children.

## Research and the Singing Voice

Research is beginning to help us better understand the child's singing voice and how to choose songs that will aid its natural development.

Anderson and Lawrence (2001) identify the vocal characteristics and the abilities of kindergarten and early primary children:

- Young children's voices are small and light.
- Children are generally unable to sing in tune.
- Children can sing play chants and easy tonal patterns.
- Children can sing short melodies in major, minor, or pentatonic scales.
- Children can sing melodies with one note to a syllable.
- Children can sing with an awareness of a steady beat.
- Children can sing repeated rhythmic patterns accurately.
- Children can sing softly and loudly.
- Children can sing melodies with or without a simple accompaniment. (p. 81)

## Suggested Singing Experiences

The following suggestions, based on research on vocal development, should help adults plan singing experiences for young children.

- Encourage children to improvise and sing about their everyday activities at home or at school.
- Record children's voices and play them back. It is essential to record individual voices so that each child can hear his or her own voice. A word of caution here: Use

a recording device that reproduces voices accurately and does not distort the quality of the child's voice. Do not record the children if they seem afraid of the experience. This could result in their withdrawing from singing. In most instances, youngsters thoroughly enjoy this activity.

- Provide many opportunities for children to make sounds using different pitches (e.g., the sound of a mewing kitten or a barking dog). These opportunities are essential in helping children learn to control their voices.
- Vary the beginning pitch of songs. All too often, adults find a comfortable starting pitch to fit their own voices and never change it for children. This "sameness" could be a contributing factor in the limited singing ranges of children as they grow older.
- Recite or say poems, nursery rhymes, or songs. Encourage children to use different voice inflections to "match" the meaning and sound. The song "If You're Happy and You Know It" has unlimited possibilities. Have the children say the words using inflection in their voices—for example, "If you're happy and you know it, toot your horn, toot, toot!" or "If you're happy and you know it, hum out loud!" This approach helps children find yet another way to learn to control both their speaking and singing voices.
- Songs that make use of repeated words, musical phrases, or repeated rhythmic patterns are good choices. An example of a good song is "Do You Know the Muffin Man?"

## Choosing Songs

It is extremely important to select song material that is appropriate for the age of the children. Teachers must take age into consideration when they write or choose songs for their class. Careful thought should be given to what children are like, what they can do, and what their interests are at their particular stage of development. This should be done before writing, selecting, or presenting songs for them.

When choosing songs, one should consider more than appropriate pitch range. Difficult pitch leaps and the speed at which intervals are sung can contribute to singing problems. Keep in mind also that short songs will probably be most successful.

Choose songs where the subject matter and words are closely related to the child's understanding and interests. Four- and 5-year-old children particularly enjoy action songs and singing games, contemporary and television-related songs, and songs about:

- Nature and the seasons
- Their own names
- Fun and nonsense
- School activities
- Families and friends
- Their bodies, parts of their bodies, and clothing
- Feelings, such as happiness
- Animals and pets

Other types, such as question-and-answer songs, help develop critical thinking. In addition, folk songs are considered one of the best sources of song material for young children.

• Nature and the seasons

## BARNYARD FAMILY

American folk song

Arranged by K. BAYLESS

1. I have a lit - tle roost - er by the barn - yard gate, And that lit - tle roost - er is my play - mate, And that lit - tle roost - er goes cock - a - doo - dle - doo, Doo - doo, ___ doo - doo, ___ doo - doo - dle doo.

**2**
I have a little hen by the barnyard gate,
And that little hen is my playmate,
And that little hen goes cluck, a-cluck-a-cluck,
Cluck-cluck, cluck-cluck, cluck-cluck-a-cluck.

**3**
I have a little duck by the barnyard gate,
And that little duck is my playmate,
And that little duck goes quack-a-quack-a-quack,
Quack-quack, quack-quack, quack-quack-a-quack, etc.

## MISTER WIND

Words and music by K. BAYLESS

1. Mis - ter Wind, you seem to be So mys - te - ri - ous to me. I can feel and ___ hear you too, But see - ing you I can - not do.

**2**
You are like a funny clown,
Twirling up and sometimes down,
But you help me fly my kite,
So Mister Wind, you are all right!!

## SPRING IS HERE

K. BAYLESS

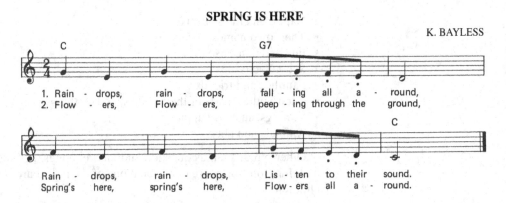

1. Rain - drops, rain - drops, fall - ing all a - round,
2. Flow - ers, Flow - ers, peep - ing through the ground,

Rain - drops, rain - drops, Lis - ten to their sound.
Spring's here, spring's here, Flow - ers all a - round.

• Their own names

### NAME YOUR STREET

Traditional tune

Adapted by K. BAYLESS

*Teacher:* Tell us what street you live on, you live on, you live on,
*Child or* I--- live on Sun - set Street, Sun - set Street, Sun - set Street,
*group:* Christine lives

Tell us what street you live on, (Chris - tine), please.
I--- live on Sun - set Street, Yes, I do.
Christine lives Yes, she does.

### HOW OLD ARE YOU?

K. BAYLESS

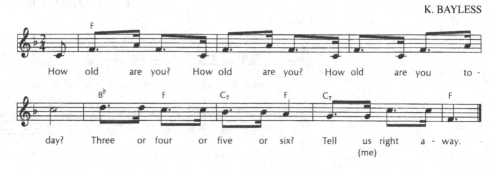

How old are you? How old are you? How old are you to -

day? Three or four or five or six? Tell us right a - way.
(me)

---

Most children like to be asked how old they are. Some will hold up their fingers for the number of years and then will smile and answer correctly. Note that the melody and rhythm in the song "How old are you?" are exactly alike in the first two measures. Sing "How old are you" and then pause before singing it the second time. Help the children discover that the two measures sound exactly alike. It will not take children long to discover these similarities and differences in melodies and rhythms if they are guided in a developmental, sequential way.

• Fun and nonsense

## I'VE GOT THAT HAPPY FEELING

Source unknown

I've got that hap - py feel - ing here in my heart,

Here in my heart, Here in my heart. I've got that hap - py feel - ing

here in my heart, Here in my heart to stay.

2. I've got that happy feeling here in my feet (march in place).
3. I've got that happy feeling here in my hands (clap hands).
4. I've got that happy feeling all over me.

## IF YOU'RE HAPPY

Traditional                                          Arranged by K. BAYLESS

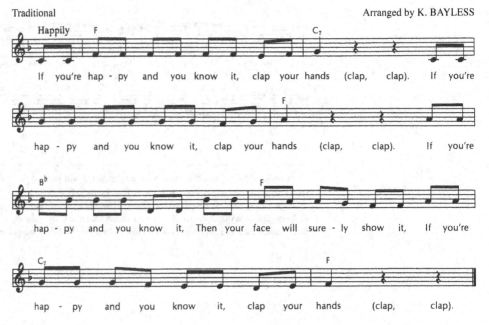

If you're hap - py and you know it, clap your hands (clap, clap). If you're

hap - py and you know it, clap your hands (clap, clap). If you're

hap - py and you know it, Then your face will sure - ly show it, If you're

hap - py and you know it, clap your hands (clap, clap).

2. If you're happy and you know it, stamp your feet.     4. If you're happy and you know it, swing around.
3. If you're happy and you know it, nod your head.       5. If you're happy and you know it, shout out loud!

• School activities

## HAPPY DANCING SONG

Words by Linda Card Edwards

Tune: Old Mac Donald

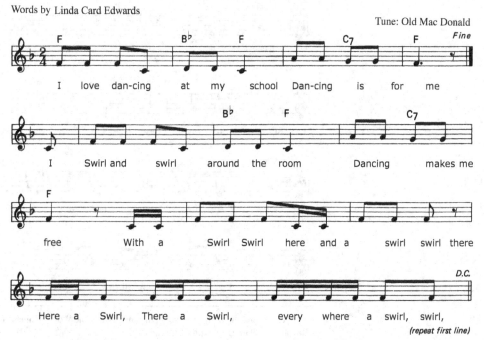

I love dan-cing at my school Dan-cing is for me

I Swirl and swirl around the room Dancing makes me

free With a Swirl Swirl here and a swirl swirl there

Here a Swirl, There a Swirl, every where a swirl, swirl,

*(repeat first line)*

suggested verses:
    I glide and glide around the room
    I skip and skip around the room
    I twirl and twirl around the room
    I skip and skip around the room

## AFTER SCHOOL

Chinese Folk Melody

*Source:* "After School" from page 43 of Sing Around the World. Chinese folk melody, translated by Grace Boynton © 1946. Used with permission.

- Families and friends
- Their bodies, parts of their bodies, and clothing

## SKIP SO MERRILY

Adapted and arranged
by K. BAYLESS

Skip so mer-ri-ly, skip so mer-ri-ly, all a-round the cir-cle.

Skip so mer-ri-ly, skip so mer-ri-ly, all you hap-py chil-dren.

Choose a part-ner quick as a wink. Take a hand, now don't you think

Skip-ping is fun, skip-ping is fun, All a-round the ring.

Children stand in a circle while one child skips around the inside. On the words "choose a partner quick as a wink," the skipping child chooses a partner and the two children skip around inside the circle. At the end of the song, the two skipping children return to their original places in the outer circle. Another child is chosen, and the song is repeated. (Skipping children do not sing, as it is too difficult to skip and sing at the same time).

- Feelings, such as happiness

## ROCKING YO HO

K. BAYLESS

Rock-ing and rock-ing, yo, ho, ho, ho. Fast-er and fast-er a-

way you go. Rock-ing and rock-ing, yo, ho, ho, ho.

Is-n't it fun to rock_____ just so!

• Animals and pets

## I CAUGHT A FISH

Traditional rhyme set to music
K. BAYLESS

One, two, three, four, five, I caught a fish a - live,
Six, seven, eight, nine, ten, I let him go a - gain.

Why did you let him go? Be - cause he bit my fing - er so!

## I HAD A CAT

Kentucky folk song
Adapted by K. BAYLESS

1. I had a cat and the cat pleased

me, I fed my cat un - der yon - der

tree. Cat goes fid - dle - i - fee.

(2. Refrain)
Hen goes chim - my chuck, Cat goes fid - dle - i - fee.

(3. Refrain)
Duck goes quack, quack, Hen goes chim - my chuck,

Cat goes fid - dle - i - fee.

2. I had a hen and the hen pleased me, I fed my hen by yonder tree.
3. I had a duck and the duck pleased me, I fed my duck by yonder tree.

## MAMMA KANGAROO

M. RAMSEY

K. BAYLESS

Bouncy

I am Mam-ma Kang-a-roo, Like to see me jump? I can take a great big leap

up a-bove this hump. I am Mam-ma Kang-a-roo, Peek in-to my pock-et___.

This is ba-by Kang-a-roo, Sleep-ing in my pock-et___.

*The Animals in the Zoo*
(To the tune of "Here We Go Round the Mulberry Bush")

Look at the animals in the zoo, in the zoo, in the zoo,
See the different things they do, and we can do them too.

The elephant walks and swings his trunk, swings his trunk, swings his trunk,
The elephant walks and swings his trunk, and we can do it too.

The tall giraffe can stretch her neck, stretch her neck, stretch her neck,
The tall giraffe can stretch her neck, and we can do it too.

Monkeys swing on limbs of trees, limbs of trees, limbs of trees,

Monkeys swing on limbs of trees, and we can do it too.

Camels march like soldiers brave, soldiers brave, soldiers brave,
Camels march like soldiers brave, and we can do it too.

Bears stamp their heavy feet, heavy feet, heavy feet,
Bears stamp their heavy feet, and we can do it too.

The kangaroos go jump, jump, jump; jump, jump, jump; jump, jump, jump.
The kangaroos go jump, jump, jump, and we can do it too.

(As the song is sung, have children do the actions. Encourage them to add other verses.)

## MR. TURKEY

Words and music by K. BAYLESS

1. See Mis-ter Tur-key strut a-round.

Gob-ble, gob-ble, gob-ble, gob-ble is his fun-ny sound.

2
See Mister Turkey, he's so fat.
Wibble, wobble, wibble, wobble, round he goes like that.

# MISTER RABBIT

Southern folk song

Arranged by K. BAYLESS

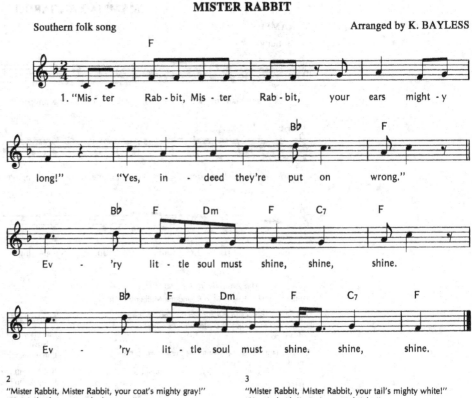

1. "Mis - ter Rab - bit, Mis - ter Rab - bit, your ears might - y long!" "Yes, in - deed they're put on wrong."

Ev - 'ry lit - tle soul must shine, shine, shine.

Ev - 'ry lit - tle soul must shine, shine, shine.

2

"Mister Rabbit, Mister Rabbit, your coat's mighty gray!"
"Yes, indeed, 'twas made that way."
Ev'ry little soul must shine, shine, shine.
Ev'ry little soul must shine, shine, shine.

3

"Mister Rabbit, Mister Rabbit, your tail's mighty white!"
"Yes, indeed, I'm going out of sight."
Ev'ry little soul must shine, shine, shine.
Ev'ry little soul must shine, shine, shine.

# SIX LITTLE DUCKS

Folk song from Maryland

Arranged by K. BAYLSS

1. Six lit - tle ducks that I once knew, Fat ones, skin - ny ones, fair ones too. But the one lit - tle duck with a feath - er on his back, He led the oth - ers with a quack, quack, quack! quack, quack, quack! quack, quack, quack! He led the oth - ers with a quack, quack, quack!

2

Down to the river they would go,
Wibble, wabble, wibble, wabble to and fro.
*Refrain*

3

Home from the river they would come,
Wibble, wabble, wibble, wabble, ho, hum, hum.
*Refrain*

---

*Source:* "Six Little Ducks" folk song from Maryland. Reprinted by permission of World Around Songs.

## SEE THE LITTLE DUCKLINGS

German folk tune

See the lit - tle duck - lings, swim - ming here and there,

Heads are in the wa - ter, tails are in the air.

## FOUR LITTLE MONKEYS

Traditional

Arranged by LINDA EDWARDS

Four lit - tle mon - keys jump - ing on the bed.

One fell off and bumped his head.

Mom - ma called the doc - tor, the doc - tor said:

"Get those mon - keys off that bed!"

**TWO LITTLE BLACKBIRDS**

Traditional

Arranged by K. BAYLESS

Two lit-tle black-birds sit-ting on a hill, One named Jack, And one named Jill.

Fly a-way Jack! Fly a-way Jill! Come back Jack! Come back! Jill.

Actions for "Two Little Blackbirds":

| | |
|---|---|
| Two little blackbirds | (Hold up both hands, |
| Sitting on a hill, | thumbs erect, fingers bent) |
| One named Jack, | (Wiggle one thumb) |
| And one named Jill. | (Wiggle other thumb) |
| Fly away, Jack! | (Bend down one thumb) |
| Fly away, Jill! | (Bend down other thumb) |
| Come back, Jack! | (Raise one thumb erect) |
| Come back, Jill! | (Raise other thumb erect) |

Haines and Gerber (2000) offer excellent criteria to use when selecting songs for young children:

1. The song must appeal to the children through:
   a. its clear rhythm.
   b. its pleasing, simple melody that is based on chord tones and stepwise progressions.
   c. its singable range.
   d. its content (good poetry, natural word order, and topics of interest to the children).
2. It must be well known and well liked by the teacher.
3. It must have a close relationship between words and the melody. The meaning of the words should be reflected in the style of the music. The phrasing of the words and the melody line should coincide. The words and the melody should fit together like a hand in a glove. (p. 132)

## Presenting New Songs

New songs can be introduced spontaneously when the situation seems just right or at a planned group time. They may be introduced to a small group of children who are informally gathered together or to the entire class. It is important to keep the situation as natural as possible.

Almost all children are eager to learn new songs as well as to sing their favorite ones. Children like to repeat their favorites, but interest will begin to wane if songs are overworked. Variety is necessary, as the same song will not appeal to the entire group. To keep interest high, you need to have a number of songs at your fingertips that you know well. Keep these tips in mind:

When you first introduce songs to young children, they will probably not sing every word or follow every phrase. If the song has repetition or a chorus, children will usually join in on the words or lines they hear most often. Do not be discouraged when you first introduce a song and your children sing just a word or two and do not match your pitch or sing with your tune. By the time you have sung it several times, your children will begin to pick up the lyrics and melody and will say, 'Let's sing it again!' (Edwards, 2006, p. 123)

Whenever possible, memorize the words and melody of a song so you can use the nonverbal cues and eye contact that are so necessary when sharing a song with children. If your voice is accurate and of good quality, it is best to introduce the song without any accompaniment. It is easier for children to match their tones with the human voice than it is for them to match the melody played on an instrument. If your voice is somewhat shaky, or for the sake of variety, an instrument like a piano, guitar, or Autoharp® can be used.

Some songs will need a short introduction; others will not. You might introduce a song by showing a picture or a diorama (a three-dimensional scene showing objects and figures representative of a particular song or situation), asking a leading question, sharing a related incident, or giving some helpful background information. When presenting songs, this introduction is extremely important and must not be overlooked. Such motivation promotes interest and helps the children understand the "message" of the song.

Teachers who are eager to share songs with young children but are unsure of their singing talent or the musical quality of their singing voice should not hesitate to offer singing opportunities to children. It is not essential that you have a good singing voice. If you are unsure, let go of your musical inhibitions and enjoy the activities with the children. See yourself as a participant and not as a performer. All that children require is a responsive, encouraging teacher who knows how to interact with them and how to stimulate them to learn songs and enjoy singing (Van Der Linde, 1999).

## Reluctant Singers

Do not be disturbed if all the children do not join in the singing. Once in a while you will find a child who will not sing with the others. These children may sing freely at home or when they are alone but not in the school setting. Their reluctance to participate may be because they are totally absorbed in watching the other children sing or because they simply are not ready to join in. These cases are rather uncommon, since most children like to sing whether or not they can carry a tune accurately. Many children of this age are still trying to find their singing voices. In dealing with reluctant singers, encourage but do not force them to participate. Give them time to respond. The length of time will depend on each child's personality and previous experiences.

In addition, emphasis should be placed on those music activities and experiences that will encourage the shy child and the "off-key" singer to join in the singing without fear and self-consciousness. Children can best improve the quality of their singing voices only after they have had many opportunities for singing in social groups that give meaning to their efforts. We must not forget that good attitudes about singing are as important as good singing voices.

Because children are highly motivated by action songs, reluctant singers will often become involved in songs that call for moving the hands, feet, or other parts of the body. As children become involved in the physical sense, the words of the song seem to emanate and become part of the activity. Soon these children begin to take part.

Props for a song also lend interest and invite participation. For example, for the song "Two Little Blackbirds," two blackbirds made of construction paper and mounted on lightweight sticks can be the motivating factor in getting children involved. Children enjoy holding the blackbirds, carrying them around, and acting out the song. There is also a great sense of security that goes along with having something in one's hands.

## Teaching New Songs

Knowing how to teach a song effectively to young children can influence whether the children will like the song. Smile as you sing. Rotate your head so you make facial contact with every child. Do not make the mistake of asking the children if they like the song. They may say, "No!" When they like a song, children will generally say, "Let's sing it again!" Remember that singing songs should be a joyful experience that provides opportunities for successful participation.

Sing the song slowly (but not *too* slowly) and distinctly at first, keeping in mind the rhythmic flow. Haines and Gerber (2000) recommend that teachers start a song and sing it all the way through, repeating it until the children begin to sing. If interest is high, it will not be long before the children begin to sing right along. This method, called the *whole method*, is encouraged. It gives children the opportunity to "chime in" with a word or a phrase that is easy for them to grasp and remember. The phrases become longer, and soon the entire song is learned in a relatively short time. Songs that get children involved quickly and naturally are songs that invite participation. An example is "Old MacDonald Had a Farm."

Teaching a song line by line is not good practice. This method, if used repeatedly, can destroy the entire effect of a song and can cause children to dread learning a new song. However, this does not mean that a teacher should never sing a line of a song or a certain word of a song and have the children repeat it. In fact, this practice may be necessary so that children learn the pronunciation of a word or how to fit the words and melody together correctly. When children are not matching the teacher's singing, Haines and Gerber (2000) suggest "echo singing" selected phrases until the children learn the song as a whole. The problem arises when teachers use the line-by-line method in teaching every new song.

Brewer (2001) reminds us that we do not have to teach a new song in just one lesson. A new song may have to be taught over a period of days and maybe weeks before the children are comfortable with it. As new songs are repeated on successive days, it will not be long before you know if the children like the song. If, after a careful introduction, they do not seem to respond to a particular song, do not use it again for a while. Because there is so much good song material, do not feel upset if children do not seem to care for a particular song. Once in a while, after the children have learned a song well, sing along very softly or not at all so the children can hear themselves singing and strengthen their ability to carry the melody all by themselves.

Singing together can be a pleasant, happy experience for teachers and children. Above all else, keep in mind that the joy of singing should hold the highest priority.

# INSTRUMENTS

Children are fascinated by devices and instruments that produce sound. Around 1 year of age, a child's attention is quickly drawn to the movement and sound of a musical toy. If one tries to divert the child's attention, almost invariably the youngster will return to watch the movement and sounds of the toy.

Children are such natural inventors! As they move through the infant stage, one of their favorite activities is taking a wooden spoon and striking it against a pot or on a cup or cereal dish. We often hear parents say that their children prefer pots, pans, and spoons to commercial sound-making toys.

Have you ever watched older children jump mud puddles, landing on both feet? Have you watched them pound nails in rhythm or stomp their feet to band music? This is movement and body percussion combined. This is the "stuff" of which good rhythmic experiences are built.

## Body Percussion

Children delight in using different parts of their bodies to produce sounds, which is referred to as *body percussion*. They soon discover, as they shuffle their feet back and forth in rhythm, that this kind of movement makes an interesting sound. Experimentation of this kind often helps them express how a train starts up and slows down, for example. Encourage children to experiment in making other sounds with their bodies, such as snapping their fingers, thumping on their chests, and making hisses, clicks, and other sounds with their mouths. Ask them to make the softest body percussion sound they can make, then the loudest, the highest, the lowest, and the heaviest. As children explore sound making through body percussion, ask them how different things might sound. For instance, what sound would a boiling tea kettle make? A spacecraft taking off? Jet airplanes flying by? Rhythmic patterns should then become a part of the sound making. Children need time and guidance to help them explore and learn to control body percussion. It is important that instrumental patterns be reinforced in body percussion first and then extended to sound-making objects like instruments.

## Percussion Through Sound-Making Devices

Percussion using objects logically follows experimentation with body percussion. At this point, adults and children can begin to bring together all sorts of interesting sound-making devices. Children, guided by the teacher, can begin to sort out and classify these devices according to the kinds of sounds they produce. Collecting and experimenting with things that make sounds is a crucial step in introducing instruments to children.

## Introducing Instruments

You may remember the chaos associated with the traditional "rhythm band." Fortunately, there is a trend away from this approach to using instruments and toward a more relaxed and personally selected use of rhythm instruments. Under this approach, children can select an individual instrument and discover what tones it produces, what its dynamic range is, and what musical textures can be developed. They can experiment

Rhythm sticks and jingle bells are easy to play.

with different ways of playing the instrument and notice how differently a drum sounds when they play it with a mallet and tap it with their fingers. Children can compare the duration of the bell sound when they strike a triangle that is suspended from a string or held in their hands. They can discover the music hidden in the instrument and create rhythmic patterns of their own. The more children experiment with rhythm instruments, the more sensitive they will become to the delightful patterns, combinations, and possibilities these instruments hold for making music. Bringing a child and an instrument together with ample opportunity to explore can help eliminate the stereotypical "rhythm band" where all the instruments sound at once. Certainly, few things are more frustrating for a teacher and more confusing for a child than having to march to the beat of the drum as all the instruments crescendo to the maximum of their dynamic range (Edwards, 2002).

Brewer (2001), reviewing studies of children's use of musical instruments, recommends the following guidelines for teachers:

- Children should have many opportunities for free exploration with instruments before any structured activities are attempted.
- Teachers should attend to the child's interests and needs when providing any instruction on how to play an instrument.
- Children need to express rhythm through physical movement before instruments are introduced.
- Exploration with instruments can help children learn about pitch, timbre, rhythm, and melody. (pp. 398–399)

When children are old enough to respect instruments and to care for them, they should have the opportunity to use them. Both commercial and homemade instruments can be introduced. Children enjoy making some of these instruments. Adults can make others for use with children. Whole families and classes can become involved in making some of the instruments and will enjoy sharing the sound making together. When children go through the process of making instruments, they have a much better understanding of how the sound is produced, and problem solving and creative thinking are enhanced. It is extremely important to remember that the better the tone quality of the instrument, the more satisfying and more valuable the experience will be for the child. Instruments of genuine tone quality like resonator bells, wood and tone blocks, and xylophones are good instruments to use for sound exploration and discrimination.

Introduce one type of instrument at a time. As you introduce the instrument, explain it and then pass it around for the children to handle and explore. Some teachers prefer to introduce an instrument on one day and then reintroduce the same instrument on the next day before the children are permitted to explore and play it. It is important for the children to hear and see the instrument played enough times so that they can distinguish its sound and know its name and how to play it. Once this is accomplished, another instrument can be introduced, until children have had the opportunity to hear and explore many different instruments. This process takes time, and children need to be patient, but the results are rewarding.

It is also wise at this point to establish a few rules for handling the instruments to prevent some of the problems that usually occur if expectations are not set. Keep the rules simple. Once children have explored different types of instruments, they can begin to use them creatively in different ways.

As children explore how to play different instruments, in addition to having fun, they are also developing important skills. As with singing, playing instruments allows children to be directly involved in making music. During this process, they are developing the musical concepts of a steady beat, differences in dynamics, musical form, and pitch and melody (Anderson & Lawrence, 2001).

## ESTABLISHING A LISTENING MUSIC CENTER

A listening music center for children is a definite asset for any classroom if it is carefully prepared and regulated. Certain rules must be set up and expectations carefully explained to the children. A good listening/music center creates an environment where children are free to make choices. When children are playing in these centers, they are in charge of their own learning as they explore independently and make their own decisions about the activities in which they engage. Listening/music centers should give children the freedom to explore rhythm, melody, form, and expressive music qualities. The teacher creates the environment, and the children dictate the learning (Kenney, 1997).

A good center could include a piano, a CD player, a recording device, headsets, and melody and rhythm instruments like a xylophone (Orff-type), drums, resonator bells, wood blocks, and an Autoharp®. When the budget permits, a double series of Montessori bells would be an excellent addition to the center. Montessori bells are used in training the ear to perceive differences between musical sounds. There are two sets of bells that look alike but produce successive tones of a chromatic scale. In using the bells, the task is for children to match the pair of bells that produce the same pitch. One set of bells in chromatic scale order remains stationary. The child strikes the first bell, which is the "do" of the stationary series, and then finds its match from the second, mixed set. When the correct bell is found, it is then placed beside its match. Each note of the scale is found in this manner. After much experimentation, children are then encouraged to place the bells in the order of the scale, guided only by the sound. This reinforcement aids children greatly in helping them sing the syllables of the scale, "do," "re," "mi." Some of the instruments and listening activities within the center should be changed periodically to provide new interest and new challenges. Many teachers have found that the most profitable time to use the listening/music center is during children's work and playtime activity periods.

## Inviting Resource Visitors

As children's interest in instruments grows, it's a great idea to invite professional musicians to the classroom to demonstrate their instruments. In this way, children can learn firsthand what each instrument is like, how it is played, and how it sounds. The musician might encourage the children to touch the instrument and, in some cases, to play it. This needs to be done under careful supervision. With woodwind and brass instruments, it is good hygienic practice not to allow the children to blow into the instrument. Children will be pleased if the musician plays familiar melodies and songs they know. If the songs are familiar, the children will generally chime in singing. It is also a good idea to have the visitor play a selection that is particularly well suited to the instrument being introduced. The following is an excerpt from a conversation with a kindergarten teacher and the musicians who visited her class.

### TALKS WITH TEACHERS

Mary White is the Master Teacher of 5-year-olds at the N. E. Miles Early Childhood Development Center at the College of Charleston. After teaching English at the high school level, she earned her MEd degree in Early Childhood Education from the College of Charleston. She has done collaborative research with Dr. Ann Wallace on the way that children's mathematical thinking is expressed in their play with sand and water. Mary is an amateur historian with a particular interest in the African contributions to the history and culture of the South Carolina low country.

The kindergartners in Mary's classroom have a weekly visual and performing arts concert. Mary describes the process here in her own words.

We invite musicians, such as parents, students, music majors from the School of the Arts, custodians, and any other musicians we happen to hear about who live in the community. The goals of the Early Childhood Development Center weekly concert are to introduce the children to different types of instruments and music. The concerts typically last from 10 to 15 minutes. As a follow-up to the concert, we listen to recordings of the same types of instruments that we heard live. For example, a student from the School of the Arts showed us his acoustic guitar and played some of his own compositions for us. As a follow-up we listened to recordings of Eric Clapton playing his acoustic guitar and singing his original songs. The children talked about what music they liked, why they liked it, and how the live performance by the music major was different or similar to the Eric Clapton recordings. Recently, we heard some young, college students playing music on the grass across from our building. I took a couple of the children with me and went over to them and asked if they would be willing to come and play for us. One of the students later told me that when I approached them, they thought I was coming to ask them to quiet down. They were both relieved and happy that I didn't want them to stop; I wanted to invite them to come play for the children in our school. They came and played that day and loved the children so much that they came back several times that year.

*(continued)*

(Continued)

The College of Charleston offers a unique experience for young children and College of Charleston students at the Miles Early Childhood Development Center (ECDC). This nationally accredited program has served as the demonstration program and laboratory preschool for the college since 1974.

In Charleston, South Carolina, we are also fortunate to have two world class arts festivals: Spoleto USA Festival and MOJA Arts Festival. For 17 days and nights each spring, Spoleto Festival USA fills Charleston's historic theaters, churches, and outdoor spaces with more than 120 performances by renowned artists as well as emerging performers in disciplines ranging from opera, music, theater, dance, and chamber, symphonic, choral, and jazz music, as well as the visual arts. MOJA, a Swahili word meaning "One," is the appropriate name for this festival celebration of harmony among all people in our community. The festival highlights the many African-American and Caribbean contributions to Western and world cultures. MOJA's wide range of events includes visual arts, classical music, dance, gospel, jazz, poetry, R&B music, storytelling, theater, children's activities, traditional crafts, ethnic food, and much, much more. During these festivals, the ECDC also celebrates the arts. Once a week we feature a musician, a dancer, or someone involved in theater arts. These featured artists are often student workers, parents, friends of the children, or the children themselves. This past year, our featured musicians included a hip-hop artist, a belly dancing troupe, a harmonica player, and a cellist and violinist. One of our parents came and sang African folk songs. At the end of the festival, we presented our own version of "Stomp," the Off-Broadway musical. We love the arts and the children truly come alive during our ECDC weekly concerts and our version of Spoleto USA Festival and MOJA Arts Festival.

## Imaginative Teachers

Young children move and respond naturally with an imaginative and sensitive teacher. Teachers who are willing to experiment can develop a vital, creative rhythmic program for their children. You can develop a good movement program by paying close attention to children as they move—as they skip down the hall, run with the wind, pound with their hammers, twirl around in circles, or stamp their feet in puddles. *There is no set way to begin.* One possible way to start would be to group children informally on the rug or gym floor. Have the children lie flat on their backs or stomachs. Can they wiggle their bodies without moving from their spaces? Can they wiggle their bodies

When music brings this kind of joy to our lives, the world becomes an even better place.

away from their spaces? Can they move parts of their bodies that no one else can see? Can they move two or perhaps three parts of their bodies at the same time? Can they puff up their stomachs like a cake that is rising in the oven?

Keeping in mind that most children are very inventive, adults can encourage them to do all kinds of "tricks" with their bodies. It is not surprising that a child can roll up into a tiny ball, make himself so rigid that no part of his body wobbles or bends, push the clouds high into the sky, or crawl into a very, very tiny box. If they are motivated by a creative teacher, it won't be long before children's ideas begin to flow. Many times, the whole group picks up another child's idea and extends it. Trying out the movements of other children often encourages the more reticent youngster to try out movements of his own. Teachers can help with words of encouragement. For example, if the children are discovering different ways to move across the floor, the teacher might say, "Look! Tommy is moving sideways. Let's all try to move the same way as Tommy." After the children have tried Tommy's way, the teacher might say, "Who would like to show us another way to move across the room?" Once the children have begun to share their ideas freely, the teacher can play an important part by expanding on the ideas that children began.

Here is an example. A kindergarten boy eagerly told his teacher and classmates about a trip he had just taken with his family through Pennsylvania. He told them that at times his father had to turn on the headlights because it had suddenly become too dark to see. After considerable discussion as to what that dark place was called, a child sang out, "That dark place is called a tunnel." Other children agreed, "Yes, that's what you call it—a tunnel!" The children then asked their teacher if they could darken the room and pretend that they were going through a long, dark tunnel like the ones in Pennsylvania. The teacher asked, "What shall we use for a tunnel?" Some of the children suggested lining up a long line of tables and then crawling underneath them. Tables were quickly put together. The children pretended to be automobiles. They crawled through the tunnel, each in their own way. They had captured the mood of moving through a darkened space. More discussion followed. They began to tell what it was like to try to do things in dark places. The conversation and play lasted all morning.

We could cite many other examples in which a creative movement idea developed into a series of expanded learning experiences. If you observe your children in an environment that encourages movement and music activity, they will give you all the ideas you need!

## FUNDAMENTALS OF MOVEMENT

The fundamentals of movement were defined in Chapter 2. The activities presented here have been developed especially for kindergarten and early primary age children. For the purpose of review, movements can be divided into three categories: locomotor movements, axial movements (nonlocomotor), and a combination of movements. *Locomotor movements* are those movements that propel the body through space. They are classified as walking, hopping, jumping, running, and leaping. Movements like galloping, sliding, and skipping are variations or combinations of locomotor movements. *Axial movements* are nonlocomotor movements originating from a stationary position of the body. They include bending and twisting.

As you also learned in Chapter 2, movement can be further divided into three additional categories: space, time, and force. *Space* simply refers to the manner in which we use an area for movement, either "personal space" or "general space." *Time* is a quality of tempo or rhythm. A movement can be slow or fast. *Force* is involved when children experiment with light, heavy, sudden, or sustained qualities of movement requiring varying degrees of muscular tension.

## Activities for Exploring Space, Time, and Force

As you continue exploring space, time, and force with your children, you can develop activities based on the suggestions presented in this section. Extend the experiences by adding recorded music or other rhythmic accompaniment. Both of these will add immensely to the movement and dance experience.

Do not initiate these activities all at one time or on a day that is designated as "movement day." If you think the traditional rhythm band creates chaos, you will certainly see your children transform themselves into an uncontrollable whirlwind should you decide to introduce all of these activities at once. Group the ideas as they fit into the natural progression of your plans, or select one each day to introduce your children to the creative and unique ways they can move their bodies.

Remember, there is no copyright on children's creative movements. As the teacher, you will provide children with "starter" ideas like the following, but the extension and stretching of those ideas is left up to the children and their own creativity.

### Space

1. What is space? (Begin by describing space, or ask your children to tell you their definition of space.)
2. Can you find a space on the floor where you will not touch anyone and that will be your very own?
3. How tall can you make yourself?
4. How many different directions can you reach by stretching different parts of your body?
5. Can you make a long, low bridge using only two parts of your body?
6. Can you move forward in your space? Backward? Sideways? In a circle? Can you change your direction from upward to downward?
7. Lying on the floor, can you make a round shape in your space? Straight, crooked, twisted?

### Time

1. How fast can you move about without bumping into anyone? How slowly?
2. Can you move about, changing your speed from fast to slow?
3. Can you move very fast without leaving your space?
4. Can you move one part of you very fast and another very slowly?
5. Can you combine a kick, a catch, and a throw in a smooth motion?

### Force

1. How quietly can you walk? How heavily?
2. How would you walk against a strong wind?
3. Can you make your muscles feel very strong? Weak?
4. How would you lift a heavy object? A light object?

The ideas in Figure 7–4 will help you explore space, time, and force with your children. All of these ideas encourage children to create dramatic and creative movements to either imitate familiar things in their environment or to use their bodies to perform specific movements. Examine these movement ideas to determine which are developmentally appropriate for the age and skill of your children. I encourage you to add musical accompaniment such as recordings or musical instruments, both of which can add immensely to the movement and dance experience. When in doubt, refer to "Basic Stages of Early Musical and Movement Development and the National Standards" in Chapter 1.

In addition, you should find some of the following books that can provide many additional ideas for movement and dance.

- Gelsanliter, W., & Christian, F. (1998). *Dancin' in the kitchen*. New York, NY: Putnam.
- Hopkins, L. B. (Ed.). (1997). *Song and dance: Poems*. New York, NY: Simon & Schuster.
- Morgan, M. (1999). *Wild Rosie*. New York, NY: Hypernion.
- Shannon, G. (2000). *Frog legs: A picture book of action verse*. New York, NY: HarperCollins.
- Wood, A. (1992). *Silly Sally*. New York, NY: Harcourt Brace.

**Figure 7–4   Ideas for Movement**

- Make yourself as small as you can.
- See how much space you can fill by using different parts of your body.
- Make your body into a straight, long shape, and crawl like a snake or wiggle like a worm.
- Make your body as tall as you can, and move in and out of empty spaces.
- Try different ways of moving through space.
- Can you move straight?
- Can you move in a zigzag?
- Can you move forward and backward?
- Can you move sideways?
- Can you move upward, downward, or in a circle?
- Can you move very near to someone else without touching them?
- Move your arms and body as high as they can go and then as low as they can go.
- Lie on the floor on your back, and let your feet and legs fly in their space.
- Lie on your stomach and stretch your head back, kick your feet in the air, and wave your arms out to your sides.
- Move around the room as slowly as you can.
- Move around the room as fast as you can without touching or getting into anyone else's space.
- Without leaving your space, move as fast as you can. Without leaving your space, move as slowly as you can.
- Move as quietly as you can. Can you move as quietly as a mouse?
- Can you quietly creep and crawl like a spider?
- Can you dance through the air like a butterfly?
- How heavily can you move? Can you move like an elephant?
- Can you make your muscles very strong and swing and sway like a bear?

## Establishing the Beat

Once children have had plenty of opportunity for free movement and can move about without bumping into others, more locomotor and body movements like walking, running, and jumping can be used. You can strike up a steady beat on a drum, a tambourine, or a piano to accompany the children's movements. As children gain more experience, ask for a response to the steady beat being played. The ability to maintain a steady beat comes easily to some children but not to others.

After children have attained skill in walking, running, jumping, and leaping, they are ready to have more complicated experiences, such as galloping and skipping. Have the children gallop at different tempos: some fast, some slow. You will need to use lots of "word pictures" to stimulate children as they try out new and different movements.

Skipping is much more difficult to do than galloping because it is a bilateral movement that combines the movements of walking and hopping. The song "Skip to My Lou" is good to sing when children are attempting to learn how to skip. The words to the song can be chanted slowly as the children try out the new movement. This song has helped many children get the "feel" of how to skip. We often find that the music used for skipping (once the movement is learned) is too slow, thus causing some children to have difficulty coordinating their skipping movements with the tempo of the music. Observe the children skipping. Then adjust the music's tempo to their movements. When children discover that they can make their bodies skip, it often becomes one of their favorite movements.

Folk songs and singing games also provide opportunities for children to move. These are particularly good for young children, since most of the songs are within their singing range. Pete Seeger's recording *American Folk, Game, and Activity Songs for Children* (2000) is perhaps the best-known collection of folk songs in the country. Most of the songs invite participation and improvisation. Three-fourths of the tunes in this collection focus on action and are easy to dance, clap, and move to. As children listen to these folk songs, they will begin clapping on their own and performing other body movements, such as skipping, jumping, and kicking their feet. It is not uncommon for children at this age to make up new and inventive motions as the spirit of the music moves them (Seeger, 2000).

## MUSIC FROM AROUND THE WORLD

Music is a universal language, and it brings excitement, joy, and satisfaction to children of all ages. Whether in the city or the country, China, the Caribbean, Dallas, or Rome, children are chanting, humming, and making up songs, as well as dancing, clapping, shaking, and moving to the rhythms of others and themselves. Culturally diverse music, dance, and expressive movement provide different lenses for conveying cultural traditions and ideas.

Many languages have no word that means "dance," while other languages have multiple words for different dances without having a single generic term (McCarthy, 1996). For example, the dance activity included in this section, the hula, has many referents—the dance, the dancers, and the song or chant used. Aina (personal communication, July, 2005) notes that in Nigeria, the drum is an essential part of dance, so the word *dance* also refers to drumming.

The cultural traditions of Hawaii are reflected in the hula. From a global view, music, movement, and dance are indeed a universal language, "an embodiment of culture, a way of knowing, a way of communicating, a kinetic human history" (Frosch-Schroder, 1991, p. 62).

## The Hawaiian Hula

The children of Hawaii learn the hula at a very young age. The hula includes a variety of hand and body motions that tell a particular story. The basic steps are easy to learn and are introduced here. All you need is a recording of Hawaiian music or ukulele music. You might consider making and giving your children flower garlands called *leis* to wear while dancing. "Pearly Shells," introduced as follows, is a traditional hula known and loved around the world. The dance movements are simplified here to be appropriate for young children.

*Basic Hula Steps*

Hands on waist.

Step to the right and follow with the left.

(Hands and arms lift to the right.)

Repeat.

Step to the left and follow with the right.

(Hands and arms lift to the left.)

Repeat.

Bend knees with hands on knees and sway to the right and then to the left.

Repeat.

*Hand Motions*

Smile motion: Put hands on cheeks, and smile.

Coconut tree: Put one elbow on top of the other hand, and sway arms.

Ocean roll: Make a rolling motion with both arms in front of you.

Shining in the sun: Bring both arms up above head to make a sun.

Love and heart: Touch chest with hands.

*Pearly Shells*

(Words can be sung or chanted)
Pearly shells (motion to pick up pearly shells from the sand)
From the ocean (ocean roll)
Shining in the sun (sun motion)
Covering the shores (extend arms and hands to touch sandy shore)
When I see them (hands to eyes)
My heart tells me (love and heart motion)
That I love you (love and heart motion)
More than all those little pearly shells (motion to pick up shells from the sand)

An excellent resource to share with children is *Hula for Children*, a video recording that shows young Hawaiian children dancing the hula. If your library doesn't have a copy, you can purchase it through Taina Productions, Inc.

Taina Productions, Inc.
1127 11th Ave., Suite 204
Honolulu, HI 96816
(808) 739–5774
www.galaxymall.com/hawaii/hula

## Using Recordings and Props

Many fine recordings on the market invite movement participation. These do not need to be recordings made especially for children. Some of the works of our finest composers, such as Grieg, Pierné, Saint-Saëns, Mendelssohn, Bartók, Debussy, and Stravinsky, are excellent for stimulating free movement. More contemporary selections like the bluegrass tune "Orange Blossom Special" and Copland's "Hoe-Down" from *Rodeo* are also good choices for encouraging children to move their bodies freely.

Homemade CDs have also been used with good results. If you record one piece of music several times on each CD, the desired piece of music is always at the beginning and can be used as long as needed. You can stop or extend the music as desired. This technique saves time and helps with classroom control.

Props like scarves, fans, strips of crepe paper fastened onto cardboard tubes, balloons, and rhythm instruments, such as maracas, can be used to enhance movement. Props can aid in making children less inhibited. The opportunity to hold something in their hands often gives them balance and lends variety. Keep in mind, however, that overuse of props can become distracting and may overshadow the purpose of the activity.

As children continue to move and to sharpen their listening skills, they can begin listening for special parts in the music. As music is played, you need to help children listen for changes of tempo, mood, and dynamics. Here again, word pictures help children interpret the many combinations of musical sounds.

## OVER IN THE MEADOW

South Appalachian folk song

Accompaniment by K. BAYLESS

1. O - ver in the mead - ow in a nest in the tree Lived an
2. O - ver in the hol - low in a pool in the bog Lived an

old moth - er bird - ie and her lit - tle ba - bies three.
old moth - er frog - gie and her ba - by pol - li - wog.

"Sing," said the moth - er, "We sing," said the three And they
"Kick," said the moth - er, "I kick," said the wog. Then he

sang and were hap - py in the nest in the tree.
kicked and he kicked him - self in - to a lit - tle frog.

## MARY HAD A LITTLE LAMB

SARA JOSEPHA HALE

Traditional
Arranged by K. BAYLESS

1. Ma - ry had a lit - tle lamb, lit - tle lamb, lit - tle lamb,

Ma - ry had a lit - tle lamb, Its fleece was white as snow.

2
And ev'ry where that Mary went,
Mary went, Mary went,
Ev'rywhere that Mary went,
The lamb was sure to go.

3
It followed her to school one day,
School one day, school one day,
It followed her to school one day,
Which was against the rule.

4
It made the children laugh and play
Laugh and play, laugh and play,
It made the children laugh and play,
To see a lamb in school.

## OVER THE RIVER

Traditional American song

1. O-ver the riv-er and through the wood, To Grand-fa-ther's house we
2. O-ver the riv-er and through the wood, Trot fast, my dap-ple

go,_____ The horse knows the way to car-ry the sleigh Through the
gray!_____ Spring o-ver the ground like a hunt-ing hound, For

white and drift-ed snow. O-ver the riv-er and
this is Thanks-giv-ing day! O-ver the riv-er and

through the wood, Oh how the wind does blow!_____ It
through the wood, Now Grand-mother's face I spy!_____ Hur -

stings the toes and bites the nose, As o-ver the ground we go._____
rah for the fun, Is the pud-ding done? Hur-rah for the pump-kin pie!_____

## LOVE SOMEBODY

American folk song

1. Love some-bod - y, yes I do; Love some-bod - y, yes I do;
Love some-bod - y, yes I do; Love some-bod - y, but I won't tell who.

2. Love somebody, yes I do;
   Love somebody, yes I do;
   Love somebody, yes I do;
   Love somebody, but you can't guess who.

## A TISKET, A TASKET

Traditional
Adapted by K. BAYLESS

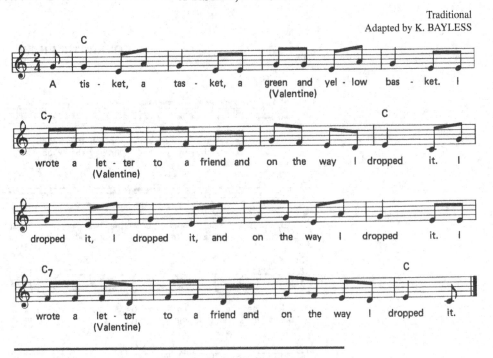

A tis-ket, a tas-ket, a green and yel-low bas-ket. I
(Valentine)

wrote a let-ter to a friend and on the way I dropped it. I
(Valentine)

dropped it, I dropped it, and on the way I dropped it. I

wrote a let-ter to a friend and on the way I dropped it.
(Valentine)

This favorite play or party game can be adapted in many ways. For Valentine's Day,
use a Valentine basket and have the child who is "It" drop a Valentine behind a child
in the circle. The game proceeds like "Duck, Duck, Goose."

## THIS OLD MAN

English singing game

This old man, he played one, He played nick-nack on my thumb,

Nick-nack pad-dy whack Give a dog a bone This old man came roll-ing home.

2
This old man, he played two,
He played nick-nack on my shoe;
Nick-nack, paddy whack, Give a dog a bone,
This old man came rolling home.

3
This old man, he played three,
He played nick-nack on my knee;
Nick-nack, paddy whack, Give a dog a bone,
This old man came rolling home.

4
This old man, he played four,
He played nick-nack on my door; (Point to forehead.)

5
This old man, he played five,
He played nick-nack on my hive; (Fight the bees.)

6
This old man, he played six,
He played nick-nack on my sticks; (Hold up index fingers.)

7
This old man he played sev'n,
He played nick-nack up in heav'n; (Fly like angels.)

8
This old man, he played eight,
He played nick-nack on my pate; (Point to top of head.)

9
This old man, he played nine,
He played nick-nack on my spine; (Tap between shoulders.)

10
This old man, he played ten,
He played nick-nack once again;
Nick-nack, paddy whack, Give a dog a bone,
Now we'll all go running home.

## FIVE LITTLE DUCKS WENT SWIMMING ONE DAY

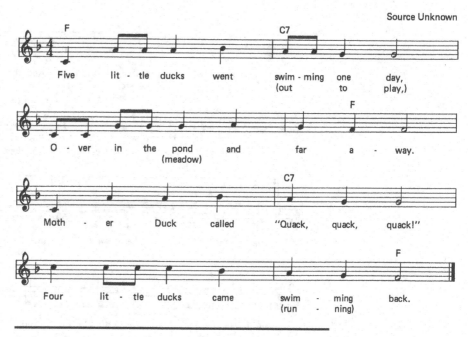

Source Unknown

Five lit-tle ducks went swim-ming one day,
(out to play,)

O-ver in the pond and far a-way.
(meadow)

Moth-er Duck called "Quack, quack, quack!"

Four lit-tle ducks came swim-ming back.
(run-ning)

Continue singing the song until no little ducks come swimming (running) back.

Then, Father Duck said, "Quack, quack, quack" *(in a strong voice)* And five little ducks came swimming (running) back!

# FAVORITE SONGS AND RHYTHMS

Growing children need to keep moving. This is very much a part of the learning process, which continues throughout a lifetime. Keep in mind that movements expressed by children are often accompanied by their innermost feelings and ideas. Wise adults will do everything within their power to find a way to help children express their feelings and ideas.

The following selections are examples of songs that invite participation. Many of these songs motivate children to use different locomotor and nonlocomotor movements. Additional songs and singing games involving movement and rhythm can be found in other chapters of this book.

## ROLL OVER

Traditional American song

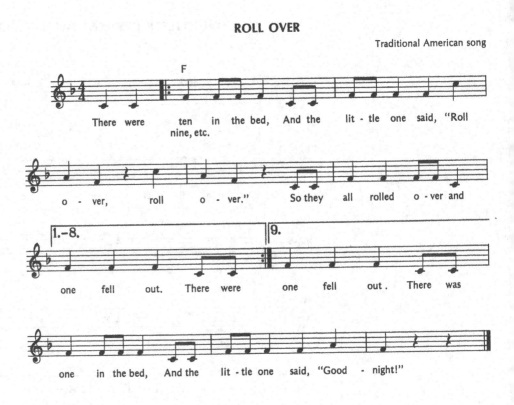

There were ten in the bed, And the lit - tle one said, "Roll
nine, etc.

o - ver, roll o - ver." So they all rolled o - ver and

**1.–8.**  **9.**

one fell out. There were one fell out. There was

one in the bed, And the lit - tle one said, "Good - night!"

*Jazz tickles your muscles, symphonies stretch your soul.*

—Paul Whiteman

## KEY IDEAS

1. Listening is considered the foundation of all music experiences.
2. Listening is perceiving and requires thought and reasoning.
3. Regardless of natural talent, teachers should sing with children.
4. Research is helping us to better understand the child's singing voice and to choose songs that help develop it in a natural way.
5. In choosing songs for children, select those in which the subject matter and the words are closely related to the child's understanding and interests.
6. Knowing how to present a song effectively to children can influence whether or not they will like the song.
7. Percussion using objects logically follows experimentation with body percussion.
8. When children are old enough to respect and care for instruments, they should have the opportunity to use them.
9. As children learn to control their body movements, they build feelings of satisfaction, self-worth, and confidence that will grow and carry over into mastery of other areas.

## SUMMARY

By the time children are in kindergarten and the early primary grades, they are ready for more planned music experiences. These should include a balance of activities, such as listening and appreciation, singing, playing instruments and sound makers, creating songs and melodies, and moving about extensively.

A balance of good listening activities is important for growth in music appreciation. Children need to be exposed to, to listen to, and to try out different types of music so that they can begin to develop musical tastes and preferences. If their appreciation for music is to grow, children need to be introduced to music of enduring quality. Naturally, the music selected must be appropriate for their level of experience and understanding.

Singing together can be a pleasant, happy experience for teachers and children. The joy of singing should be given the highest priority.

Children delight in using parts of their bodies to produce sound. If children are given time to explore body percussion, it will be easier for them to reproduce rhythmic and melodic patterns with instruments.

Movement exploration gives children an opportunity to become aware of their own abilities and what their bodies can do. It is important that, as children are guided in this critical area, they have no fear of failure as they learn to control their bodies in movement exploration.

## QUESTIONS TO CONSIDER

1. As budgetary constraints in school systems create the need to eliminate programs, music instruction is often limited or curtailed. Develop a position statement on this issue.
2. Defend this contention: "Every teacher of young children should be a teacher of music."
3. Isolate yourself in an environment. In a 15-minute span, record all of the sounds of which you are aware. Repeat this activity with a group of two or three children. Compare the results. What conclusions can you draw?
4. Select four favorite songs that could be used to enhance movement. Describe the activities that invite participation.

## RECORDINGS

Moore, T. (2000). *Songs children love to sing* [CD]. Charlotte, NC: Thomas Moore Records.

Raffi. (1996). *Rise and shine* [CD]. Cambridge, MA: Rounder Records.

Scelsa, G., & Millang, S. (1995). *Kids in motion: Songs for creative movement* [CD]. Huntington Beach, CA: Young Heart Music.

Scelsa, G., & Millang, S. (1995). *We all live together* [CD]. Huntington Beach, CA: Young Heart Music.

*Birds, beasts, bugs, and fishes (little and big)* [CD]. Washington, DC: Smithsonian Folkways Recordings.

Seeger, P. (2000). *American folk, game, and activity songs for children* [CD]. Washington, DC: Smithsonian Folkways Recordings.

## SONG COLLECTIONS

Moomaw, S. (1997). *More than singing: Discovering music in preschool and kindergarten*. St. Paul, MN: Redleaf Press. Musical activities for young children, including singing and movement.

Nylander Ebinger, V. (1993). *Niñez: Spanish songs, games, and stories of childhood*. Santa Fe, NM: Sunstone Press.

## REFERENCES

Anderson, W. M., & Lawrence, J. E. (2001). *Integrating music into the elementary classroom* (5th ed.). Belmont, CA: Wadsworth/Thomson Learning.

Brewer, J. A. (2001). *Introduction to early childhood education: Preschool through primary grades* (4th ed.) Boston, MA: Allyn & Bacon.

Edwards, L. C. (2002). *The creative arts: A process approach for teachers and children* (3rd ed.) Upper Saddle River, NJ: Pearson.

Edwards, L. C. (2006). *The creative arts: A process approach for teachers and children* (4th ed.). Upper Saddle River, NJ: Pearson.

Flowers, P. J. (1990). Listening: The key to describing music. *Music Educators Journal, 77*(4), 21–23.

Froebel, F. (1878). *Mother play and nursery songs.* Boston, MA: Lee & Shepard.

Frosch-Schroder, J. (1991). A global view: Dance appreciation for the 21st century. *Journal of Physical Education, Recreation, and Dance, 63*(7), 61–68.

Haines, B. J. E., & Gerber, L. L. (2000). *Leading young children to music* (6th ed.). Upper Saddle River, NJ: Pearson.

Johnson, C. (1998). *Harold and the purple crayon* (50th anniversary ed.). New York, NY: HarperCollins.

Kenney, S. (1997). Music in developmentally appropriate integrated curriculum. In C. H. Hart, D. C. Burts, & R. Charlesworth (Eds.), *Integrated curriculum and developmentally appropriate practice: Birth to eight.* Albany: State University of New York Press.

McCarthy, M. (1996). Dance in the music curriculum. *Music Educators Journal, 82*(6), 17–21.

Moore, T. (2000). On music and young children. *Scholastic Early Childhood Today, 14*(8), 43–45.

Moravcik, E. (2000). Music all the livelong day. *Young Children, 55*(4), 27–29.

Music Educators National Conference. (1994). *National standards for music education.* Reston, VA: Author.

Neelly, L. P. (2001). Developmentally appropriate music practice: Children learn what they live. *Young Children, 56*(3), 32–36.

Seeger, P. (2000). *American folk, game, and activity songs for children* [CD]. Washington, DC: Smithsonian Folkways Recordings.

Van Der Linde, C. (1999). The relationship between play and music in early childhood: Educational insights. *Education, 119*(4), 610–615.

Wolf, J. (2000). Sharing songs with children. *Young Children, 55*(2), 28–30.

# CHAPTER EIGHT

# Music and Movement:
# An Interdisciplinary Approach

*The history of a people is found in its songs . . .*

*George Jellinek*

*Music is an integral part of contemporary American life. Think of your day. How often do you listen to music, hum a favorite melody, or observe children caught up in rhythms of popular TV programs or playground activities?*

*We do not need to be reminded of the joy of music or its importance to our mood or well-being. We have discussed the development of children in the early months and years, as well as the impact of parents and other adults on musical development. Attitude is important, as is opportunity. Music learning is inseparable from other learning; it is interwoven into the fabric of the child's day. We delight in singing; we sway, we clap, we tap our toes, we sing along with a companion. We sing in many places, often in the shower or as we drive. No matter what our age, music lightens the spirit.*

- Music is basic.
- Music is a part of our being.
- Music is a part of our total education.
- Music is a part of romance.
- Music is a part of diplomacy.
- Music adds to our understanding of the cultures of the world.
- Music is a part of our family traditions.

*Music can be interwoven into the pattern of daily living for children. Consider the possibilities for the integration of music using the boundless enthusiasm and spontaneity of children. Encourage imagination, creativity, and the action art of music rather than assigning children to be spectators at a performance.*

## INTERDISCIPLINARY FOCUS ON MUSIC AND MOVEMENT

The national standards for the performing and visual arts have been covered in previous chapters. State curriculum frameworks, guidelines, and standards also encourage teachers to integrate curricula and find common strands that weave through different subject areas. Music and movement offer many opportunities for integration of other content areas across all grade levels (Rogers, 2004). The connections between music

These girls are graphing their classmates' responses to a story question.

and mathematics, movement and science, and music, movement, and the language arts and social studies are already integrated in the minds of young children; it is just us teachers who need to develop curricular models to fit the needs of what children already know. Music and movement may be separate content areas, but if we look at the ways in which young children construct knowledge, we will understand that they are not as separate from other content areas as sometimes we may proclaim.

## MUSIC AND MOVEMENT AND THE LANGUAGE ARTS

For most young children, language unfolds naturally as part of the growth process. Maximum development comes only through careful nurturing of language opportunity by adults.

### Language Development

Language development is essential in the child's total development. Singing is an excellent aid in promoting good language patterns. Many songs contain repetitive sounds that can help children with speech problems. Pronunciation of the words helps distinguish initial, medial, and final consonant sounds. The child can more easily understand sentence structure by singing musical phrases. Young children can complement all areas of their language learning with music and can enhance their musical activities with language. Music and movement provide wonderful ways for young children to extend their language:

> [When] emergent readers hear, sing, discuss, play with, and write songs, they are building important background knowledge that they will draw upon during later reading and writing experiences. With each new song, students learn concepts and word meanings that they will encounter in print. (Smith, 2000, p. 647)

Researchers have long hypothesized that music, movement, and language learning are closely connected. Butzlaff (2000) presents several possible reasons why instruction in music may help children acquire reading skills.

1. Music and written text both involve formal written notation that must be read from left to right.
2. Skill in reading requires a sensitivity to phonological distinctions and a sensitivity to tonal distinctions.
3. Learning song lyrics engages children in reading written text.
4. Motivational agreement can be made because when children form parts of a musical group, they must learn to work together. This instills a sense of personal responsibility, which leads to heightened academic responsibility and performance. (p. 167)

Early childhood educators generally agree that there is a positive relationship between music and reading and that musical learning has positive effects on reading skills. However, the evidence that "music helps you do English and math better" could miss the main point of studying music. The study of music for its own sake is an ideal that music educators work to preserve through rich and comprehensive music education programs (Hansen & Bernstorf, 2002). Still, early childhood educators know that music, language, and reading work together. The more songs a child learns, the wider his vocabulary and more accurate his pronunciation. The better a child is at language, the more easily she will understand the words of a song and sing them with enthusiasm. In fact, songs can be one of the best vehicles for vocabulary development and language acquisition.

## MUSIC AND READING SKILLS

As the young child matures, so does language, and the vocabulary expands as reading becomes a natural extension of language. We sometimes find the paradox of a child who ostensibly cannot read words but who can "read" music and respond to familiar words and melodies. Music is an excellent way to explore words and the concept of print.

Feierabend, Saunders, Getnick, and Holahan (1998) report that there is "evidence to suggest that listening to songs repeatedly over an extended period of time contributes to an integration in long-term memory of words and music among preschool children" (p. 358). Researchers theorize that perhaps it is the multisensory approach—through movement, eyes, ears, and body coordination—coupled with the improvement in self-concept that makes the difference. It is the whole child who learns! Both reading and making music call for concentration, memory, and understanding of abstract concepts, and both are skills children prize and know are highly valued. The wise teacher capitalizes on opportunities to spark reading.

To begin, we can set nursery rhymes or simple poetry to music, or place them in simple chants or choral verse. Country songs, ballads, pop tunes, and even carefully selected commercials are legitimate when reading enjoyment and skill are the goal. Words have meanings; words open doors; words have power; words are personal; words are humorous; words tell us what we are. Words are ribbons of the future, and words set to music lead us there.

From nursery rhymes and simple poems we might progress to jingles, fingerplays, short prose stories, chant stories, jump-rope chants, and even haiku, which might use music as accompaniment. Or we might select a favorite tune of the children and fit original lines to that tune. We seek to build rhythm, fluency, and attention-holding activity. Whatever the ability of the child, participation is guaranteed. It is the rare adult who can resist the combinations described, and sharing enjoyment with children brings an added dimension to our participation. The following two chants focus on things children like to eat and children's birthdays. Change the words to include what your children think is best of all and insert the age of the children in your classroom into "Me."

*Best of All*

Lollipops and gum drops,
Choc'lets, bubble gum.
Lemon drops and licorice,
Oh, yum, yum!
Lollipops and ice cream,
Choc'let cake and pie,
Butterscotch, vanilla,
Oh, yum, yum!
Choc'let chips and M&Ms,
Gum balls, big and small,
Jello, pudding, sundaes, rolls,
Oh, I love them all!

*Me*

Today's my birthday;
I am four;
Growing bigger, too;

Cake and ice cream, gifts, and toys.
How old are you?
Today's my birthday;
I am five;
Growing taller, too;
Cookies, ice cream, cars, and boats.
How old are you?
Today's my birthday;
I am six;
Growing stronger, too;
Ice cream, chocolate, books and school.
How old are you?

All teachers and caregivers of young children need a well-stocked shelf of easy books, poetry, choral verse, and jingles. From these, they can choose selections to support vocabulary activities throughout the day, emphasizing the importance of the interrelationship of music, language, and reading in children's daily lives. Reading skills are extended by simply learning a new song. Rote memorization, proper inflection, accenting, and syllabication are strengthened. As Lapp and Flood (1983) indicate, for syllabication in particular, children can clap the beat of a song, separating the words into correct syllables, then sing part of the song, leaving out certain syllables, words, or phrases. DeMicco and Dean (2002), Fisher and McDonald (2001), Moravcik (2000), and Hildebrandt (1998) emphasize the importance of the interrelationship of music, language, and reading in the daily life of the child.

> The music in language and the language in music support each other and young children's learning. Weaving language and music activities together through the use of quality children's literature provides an integrated, natural setting for meaningful learning. Language and music concepts develop simultaneously, along with creativity, imagination and critical thinking skills. (McGirr, 1994/1995, p. 76)

Remember that recordings, tapes, jingles, and the like cannot take the place of an adult who enjoys both reading and music and displays this enjoyment to children. Children want to be like the primary adult in their lives. If that adult reads, sings, and is enthusiastic about these activities, the mood and example are contagious.

## The Mozart Effect

I think it's appropriate at this point to say a few words about the "Mozart Effect." The question made famous in the 1993 report in *Nature* by Rauscher, Shaw, and Ky was: "Does listening to music for brief periods temporarily enhance performance on spatial tasks?" The authors concluded that college students' scores on the spatial subtest of the Stanford-Binet IQ test increased 8–9 points for 10 to 15 minutes after listening to a 10-minute section of Mozart's *Piano Sonata for Two Pianos in D Major*. Consequently called the "Mozart Effect," this finding led to a national frenzy of media attention. Some well-meaning educators and politicians touted the benefits of classical music as an "educational silver bullet." The Mozart Effect was studied only in adults, lasted only a few minutes, and was found only for spatial-temporal reasoning. No scientific evidence supports the claim that listening to music improves children's intelligence. Two studies tested the Mozart Effect and found no experimental support for the effect in children, concluding that "it is questionable as to whether any practical application will come from it" (McKelvie & Low, 2002, p. 241). The Mozart Effect may be of scientific interest, but its educational implications appear to be limited.

## Whole Language

Much discussion today concerns psycholinguist Ken Goodman's "whole language," which places a strong focus on oral language experiences and reading aloud as a means of encouraging children to use their knowledge. The main structure of whole language is based on speaking, reading, and writing activities that are most naturally nurtured when children use words and concepts from their own experiences. Teachers avoid overemphasizing correct spelling and grammar. Instead, the emphasis is placed on supporting the child's self-expression. When working with emergent readers, teachers can record the child's words to share later or can write them on a chart or bulletin board. Teachers using the whole language approach do not change a child's words or dialect. The focus is always on the unique ways children express meaning within context or social situations. In other words, teachers do not break language into bits and pieces for study. Words in isolation or sounds in isolation have no meaning. Children do not need to practice isolated components of language, nor do they need to learn the parts and then put them back together and use them. They do need to learn language in many situations and with a variety of speakers (Brewer, 2001). Whole language programs are built on this belief that children should learn to read and write in the same natural way they learned to speak. Curriculum-related music, listening, songs, poems, and chants are used. Songs and poems are read aloud to internalize the rhythm and intonation of language. As we listen, we realize how musical speech is.

## Stories and Singing

There are so many books in the world of children's literature that include songs, opportunities for movement and dance, and sometimes instrumentation. The literature selections in Figure 8–1 are recommended as developmentally appropriate for young children.

Singing and rhyming words can play an important role in the total language program for young children. They give children an opportunity to practice the correct and distinct pronunciation of words, the stress of vowel sounds, and the rhythmic flow of syllables and words. Humorous folk songs, in particular, with their nonsense syllables sung repetitively, provide a group activity in which children use their voices freely as they roll the sounds over their tongues. The songs in this text extend language skills as well as musical skill and enjoyment.

## Simple Tunes

Awareness is the key to language and music stimulation. Singing is often better than talking. The adult can make simple tunes:

- "Mary, put the box away."
- "Tommy, you can stand up tall."
- "Billy, let's dance together."
- "Mary, Mary, brush your hair."

**Figure 8–1 Stories That Sing**

The following stories are recommended for young children.

*Mama Don't Allow* by Thatcher Hurd
Live Oak Media, book and cassette edition, 2001

*The Sound That Jazz Makes* by C. B. Weatherford Walker and Company, 2000

*Peanut Butter and Jelly: A Play Rhyme* by Nadine Bernard Westcott/Bt Bound, 1999

*Three Little Kittens* by Paul Galdone Houghton Mifflin, book and cassette edition, 1999

*Oh, A-Hunting We Will Go* by John Langstaff/Bt Bound, 1999

*Musicians of the Sun* by G. McDermott Simon and Schuster, 1997

*The Lady with the Alligator Purse* by Nadine Bernard Westcott Little, Brown, 1998

*On Top of Spaghetti* by Tom Glazer Goodyear, 1995

*Making Sounds* by J. Rowe and M. Perham Children's Press, 1993

*Lizard's Song* by George Shannon Mulberry Books, 1992

*London Bridge Is Falling Down* by Peter Spier Yearling Books, reissued 1992

*I Make Music* by E. Greenfield Black Butterfly Children's Books, 1991

*Grandpa's Song* by T. Johnston Dial Books for Young Readers, 1991

*Old MacDonald Had a Farm* by Glen Rounds Holiday House, 1989

*The Wheels on the Bus* by Maryann Kovalski Scott Foresman, 1990

*Cat Goes Fiddle-i-fee* by Paul Galdone Houghton Mifflin, 1988

*Pop Goes the Weasel and Yankee Doodle* by Robert Quackenbush

Lippincott/Williams and Wilkins, 1988

*I Know an Old Lady Who Swallowed a Fly* by Colin and Jacqui Hawkins G. P. Putnam's Sons, 1987

*The Complete Story of the Three Blind Mice* by Paul Galdone Ticknow and Fields, 1987

*The Balancing Act: A Counting Song* by Merle Peek Clarion, 1987

*Go In and Out the Window* by the Metropolitan Museum of Art Henry Holt, 1987

*If You're Happy and You Know It: Eighteen Story Songs Set to Pictures* by Nicki Weiss Greenwillow Books, 1987

*Over in the Meadow* by Paul Galdone Prentice Hall for Young Readers, 1986

*Go Tell Aunt Rhody* illustrated by Aliki Macmillan, 1986

*Sing a Song of Sixpence* by Tracey Campbell Pearson E. P. Dutton, 1985

*Hush Little Baby* by Jeanette Winter Pantheon, 1984

*Music, Music for Everyone* by Vera Williams Greenwillow Books, 1983

*Frog Went A-Courtin'* by John Langstaff School and Library Binding, 1983

*Roll-Over: A Counting Song* by Merle Peek Houghton Mifflin/Clarion Books, 1981

*The Friendly Beasts* by Tomie de Paolo G. P. Putnam's Sons, 1981

*Six Little Ducks* by Chris Conover Thomas Y. Crowell, 1976

*Skip to My Lou* by Robert Quackenbush J. B. Lippincott, 1975

*Over the River and Through the Wood* by Lydia Maria Child Coward, McCann and Geoghegan, 1974

Children are true and avid imitators. After hearing an instruction, a simple melody, or a line from a book, their language exhibits fluency, ease, and color. For many children, words hold a special attraction. When blended with music and movement, the enchantment expands. Figure 8–2 lists several simple songs. These songs include repetition, songs that tell a story, and other topics that children enjoy.

**Figure 8–2   Examples of Simple Tunes**

- "Polly Put the Kettle On" and "Here We Go 'Round the Mulberry Bush" are songs that include repetition and a chorus.
- "Miss Mary Mack, All Dressed in Black" and 'She'll Be Comin' 'Round the Mountain" have repeated words and phrases that can be used to create an echo effect.
- "If You're Happy and You Know It" and "Old MacDonald Had a Farm" encourage children to make sound effects or animal noises.
- "Hush Little Baby" and "Humpty Dumpty" tell a story.
- "Do You Know the Muffin Man" engages children in a question-and-answer song or name game (Jackson, 1997).

## Big Music Books

Another valuable resource available to teachers and children are *Big Music Books*. There are many delightful *Big Music Books* that are appropriate for young children and that will help you incorporate the concept of print into your music program. The following are excellent:

- Kovalsky, M. (1987). *The wheels on the bus*. New York, NY: Trumpet Club.
- Peek, M. (1985). *Mary wore her red dress and Henry wore his green sneakers*. New York, NY: Trumpet Club.
- Sweet, M. (1992). *Fiddle-i-fee: A farmyard song for the very young*. New York, NY: Trumpet Club.
- Weiss, N. (1987). *If you're happy and you know it*. New York, NY: Greenwillow.
- Wescott, N. B. (1989). *Skip to my Lou*. New York, NY: Trumpet Club.

Early childhood educators who wish to create a stimulating and challenging environment for young children must include many opportunities for them to be thoroughly engaged in music and literacy activities. You will discover that music and reading are mutually supportive and beneficial to young learners. Imagination and creativity establish the bridge between the realms of music and reading.

## MUSIC, MOVEMENT, AND MATHEMATICS

The world is mysterious to young children. Their curiosity is limitless, and the need to know is imperative. "Why?" is a common question among young children. Everything must be experienced to be learned—being told does not suffice.

Teachers who teach in an elementary education setting often consider each subject area as a separate part of the curriculum. Early childhood teachers know better. They understand that children's thinking is not compartmentalized into "I'm learning math now" or "I'm learning language arts right now." Early childhood educators understand that the nondifferentiated thinking of young children is naturally compatible with an integrated curriculum. For example, when children are singing songs such as "One two, buckle my shoe," they are forming beginning understandings of number concepts. Mathematics for young children is not abstract. The foundations of mathematics are required when children "sort, stack, and compare manipulatives; play with sand and

Puzzles and manipulatives help children develop math skills.

water; measure or set-up the table in the housekeeping center; or learn nursery rhymes and songs" (Essa, 2003; Mayesky, 2002) such as "Ten in Bed" or "This Old Man." Mayesky also suggests a list of words that should be included in daily classroom activities. Among the words suggested are:

| | | |
|---|---|---|
| big and little | few | bunch |
| long and short | tall and short | group |
| high and low | light and heavy | pair |
| wide and narrow | together | many |
| late and early | same length | more |
| first and last | highest | most |
| middle | lowest | twice |
| once | longer than | |

Music and movement activities that involve levels such as those discussed in Chapter 2 (high, low, medium) provide concrete opportunities in which children can move their bodies in ways that define many of the words that compose the language of mathematics. For example, children can work in pairs, children can make their bodies big and little, and they can form groups and play together. Children can work together as they; for example, stand in front of or behind each other. They can use their bodies to demonstrate how to move over, around, or under each other. Children can form the shape of numbers with their bodies. They can use props such as jump ropes or streamers to form number shapes. These kinds of activities are very appropriate for combining music, movement, locomotor, and nonlocomotor skills. Another idea is to ask children to place a certain number of body parts on the floor. For example, "Put two hands and one foot on the floor and raise the other foot as high as you can."

In short, music, movement, and math go hand in hand. This is a natural combination for children. As we think about the integrated curriculum, it is important to remember all of the educational possibilities of weaving music, movement, and mathematics throughout children's experiences and all parts of the classroom environment. The integration of music and movement into the general curriculum encourages children to become actively involved in their learning. Rhythm, meter, measure, and pattern of familiar lyrics can help provide concrete ways for children to develop mathematical concepts and skills while enhancing many other aspects of the curriculum. As Gill (1998) suggests:

> Music is filled with patterns and that's what mathematics is really about. You're not going to explain the intricacies of notes and scales to a three-year-old, but exposing a child to music now will help him learn these concepts later. (p. 40)

One of the keys to success is exposing children to a wide variety of music, including country, classical, jazz, blues, folk, pop, rock and roll, rap, reggae, soul, and other genres that they may find interesting. As children listen to and respond to the different rhythms they hear, the more patterns they are exposed to the more they will recognize when they begin a structured study of mathematics (James, 2000).

During the early years, the study of mathematics can be perfectly integrated into the music curriculum. Children love to play with number words, number concepts, and number actions. Children enjoy chanting:

- "One, Two, Buckle My Shoe"
- "This Little Pig Went to Market"
- "Ten in a Bed"
- "Sing a Song of Sixpence"

Children gain a sense of power and feel a part of the adult world when they understand numbers. According to Gardner (1993), this integration is especially effective with children who have a strong sense of hearing and musical intelligence. When children are engaged in music activities, they are also developing reasoning skills, which are crucial for later learning as they develop concepts in areas like proportional reasoning and geometry (Grandin, Peterson, & Shaw, 1998). It is important for teachers to remember that activities that integrate music and mathematics do not require any specialized musical training. All you need is a set of rhythm instruments, a CD player, an object that can serve as a baton, and musical recordings that have different beats and rhythms (Johnson & Edelson, 2003).

The omnipresence of numbers in daily life may surprise you. Children notice signs, billboards, and their messages. Perhaps as adults we block them out—but young children do not! Theirs is a world of number, color, and newness. Look for numbers in your world, and transfer them to the world of the child through music.

## MUSIC, MOVEMENT, AND SCIENCE

Science education is all about exploring, investigating, problem solving, and discovering. Does this sound like activities in which young children continuously engage? Yes, indeed! From the moment of birth, children are exploring, investigating, problem solving, discovering, and making monumental strides toward understanding their world. Observe kindergartners as they play at the water table. They will discover on their own (if the teacher will leave them alone) which objects float and which objects sink, while actually experimenting with the object and the water. Or, observe children getting ready to blow up balloons. They may not realize it at the time, but they are actually making a prediction that if they blow up the balloon, they can bounce it around from one person to the other.

In science play, just as in music and movement play, young children learn by doing. It's important at this point in the discussion on music, movement, and science to at least review the basic science process skills that you have already covered or will cover in your science course. These are: observing, classifying, measuring, inferring, predicting, communicating, and using number relationships. Obviously this section on integrating curriculum cannot cover all the possibilities for exploring scientific concepts through music and movement. However, we will present suggestions for activities that you can provide as ways for children to do so.

When selecting music and movement with which to integrate science into the child's day, look for the concepts you want to reinforce, such as animals, and develop music and movement activities around songs, fingerplays, creative movement, and instrumentation upon which you can build the integrated curriculum. For example, when learning about animals, make sure that you teach children songs with accurate and useful information. Consider the fingerplay "There Was a Little Turtle." The words and actions to this fingerplay introduce vocabulary such as "box," "puddle," "rock," "snapped," "minnow," and "flea." The word "box" used in this context refers to the little turtle's shell. This can bring a whole new meaning to the word "box" when it is explained through the lyrics of a fingerplay. Encourage children to pretend to be different types of animals. For example, "Pretend you are moving across the floor like a frog," or "Pretend to slither like a snake."

Consider the topic "My Body," which is a content area that closely aligns with most second grade Science Process State Standards. During a music and movement integrated curriculum, "My Body" concepts can be addressed through body-part identification with activities such as "Simon Says" or "Head, Shoulders, Knees, and Toes." On the opposite side of the coin are nonlocomotor movement activities such as relaxation.

Relaxation exercises that encourage children to be more aware of their muscles are equally as important as they continue to discover what their bodies can do. Breathing is an essential bodily function. Teaching children how to relax, contract and relax their muscles, and be aware of their breathing can help create an awareness of their lungs: "Can you lie very still, squeeze your muscles as tight as you can, relax your muscles, and listen to your breath as it goes in and out of your body?"

The basic science process skill of observing focuses on the five senses (see, hear, touch, smell, and taste). Design a nonlocomotor movement activity in which the children close their eyes and concentrate on what they hear.

Children are usually captivated by stars, comets, space, alien beings, space vehicles, bugs, worms, and reptiles, just to mention a few. Use your imagination and those of the children to apply new lyrics and movements about these things to a familiar melody or rhyme. Other songs may be based on these ideas:

- Seasons
- Colors
- Plants
- Insects
- The child
- Food
- Machines
- Indoors/outdoors
- Senses
- Travel

- Tools
- Growing up
- Sounds

When we think of rainbows and prisms, "Pop Goes the Weasel," "Curious George," "Caps for Sale," and Rimsky-Korsakov's *Flight of the Bumblebee* comes to mind. When planning your integrated curriculum on animals, don't forget wonderful books such as *Kitten's First Moon*, *Make Way for Ducklings*, *My Friend Rabbit*, *The Three Pigs*, *Officer Bundle and Gloria,* and *Owl Moon*. While we recognize all the new literature on the market for children, the beloved classics should remain at the top of our list when developing curricula for young children. There is a wonderful recording by Folkways Records titled *Songs of the Philippines*. There are the sounds of nature: the music of birds, the wind in the trees, night sounds, and flowing water, all lovely additions to an integrated science, movement, and music unit.

One of my colleagues, Dr. Calium Johnston, was a kindergarten teacher when we first met. As a part of a unit on hygiene, he was trying to teach the children the abstract "concepts of germs-on-dirt." This was in the days before "developmentally appropriate practice" and Cal developed a movement-music-science (hygiene) activity that had as its focus "Rub-a-Dub-Dub, Three Men in a Tub." The children pretended they were in a tub of water and they rub-a-dub-dubbed as they washed their hair, washed their clothes, and washed many imaginary objects in the imaginary tub with the imaginary water.

Science is everywhere. This grandmother is answering a question asked by her granddaughter: "Do the crabs sleep under this pier?"

At the end of the activity, Cal had them all rinse their hands in a real basin with real water. You should be able to guess the outcome. They looked at the dirty water under the microscope to discover real, live moving things. Cal used this activity to reinforce what had previously been an abstract concept of germs-on-dirt by giving the children opportunities to have fun, splash in imaginary water, and then end the activity with a very concrete set of microscopic organisms. All of this happened through a music and movement activity with children "rubbing-a-dubbing."

Many other science concepts are candidates for music and movement exploration, such as simple machines, household appliances and machines, magnets, electricity, gravity, balance, and action and reaction. And don't forget the classical "The Child Grows from a Seed to a Plant" movement activity. When I do this activity with young children, I play a recording of the Pachelbel *Canon in D*. My particular favorite recording is *Pachelbel's Greatest Hits: The Ultimate Canon*. This recording is on the RCA label and can be purchased online for a mere $7.95. If you do not yet own a recording of this canon, order it now!

The Music Educators National Conference (MENC) recommends several resources that are helpful to teachers when developing interdisciplinary lessons or units in music, mathematics, and science. Visit the MENC website (www.menc.org) or call 800-828-0229.

*The Charlie Horse Music Pizza Teacher's Guide* features a free online music and science activity for grades K–4. Go to www.menc.org/guides/.

## MUSIC, MULTICULTURALISM, AND SOCIAL STUDIES

Music and social studies mesh easily. Perhaps in no other area of the curriculum is there such an abundance of songs that can add richness to the day. The National Standards for Music Education support the relationship between music, social studies, and other content disciplines. Content Standards 8 and 9, "Understanding relationships between music, the other arts, and disciplines outside the arts" and "Understanding music in relation to history and culture" (Consortium of National Arts Education Associations, 1994, pp. 28–29), address music and social studies in ways that apply to early childhood education (Barrett, 2001). The curriculum standards for social studies in the early grades "describe ways in which language, stories, folktales, music, and artistic creations serve as expressions of culture and influence behavior of people living in that culture" (National Council for the Social Studies, 1994, p. xiii).

One of the easiest ways for children to develop an appreciation of cultural diversity is through music. Children can learn songs from other cultures and the words from the languages used in the songs. Children can look at pictures of instruments from different cultures, read about the instruments, and listen to the recordings of instruments of other cultures. For example, if you're fortunate enough to have children from India in your classroom, you certainly want to introduce them to the sitar, a traditional stringed Indian instrument. By the time the children in your classroom have reached age 8, they should have already learned to appreciate differences between themselves and others and should have been exposed to music from a variety of cultures. If this is not the case for your students, you've got a lot of catching up to do. Most classrooms have children from Christian, Jewish, Muslim, Buddhist, and nonreligious families. It is not atypical for classrooms to enjoy having children from many different countries as well. Several selections of music from around the world include: *The Planet Sleeps* from

Sony Wonder Records (1997), *Global Lullabies* by Freyda Epstien (1995), and *The World Sings Goodnight* (Wasingar, 1993). It is important to remember that movement as a part of music curriculum can include music from other cultures. Introduce your children to Israeli folk dance music, an African drum song, or cross-cultural dances such as Mexican folk dances or line dances such as the "Virginia Reel."

Multicultural music can include songs, singing games and dances, instrumental music, stories, and poetry. Every area of social studies—history, geography, civics, economics, sociology, and anthropology—can be illustrated through music. The geography of our country is revealed through song. Our historic milestones are carried from generation to generation with music as we sing.

The term *social studies* also implies teaching children social information, such as valuing cultural diversity and accepting people who are different from us. Social information can also be taught through music; for example, "Be Kind to Your Parents" recorded by Linda Arnold on her album *Make Believe* (1986). Red Grammer (1986) recorded the song "Use a Word" on his album *Teaching Peace*. The lyrics go something like this: "When someone makes you slip and you want to bruise their hip, Use a word!"

Teachers communicate values to children every minute of every day. This is sometimes referred to as the "silent curriculum." One of my favorite classics is the song written by William Backer, "I'd Like to Teach the World to Sing." This is a song about peace and family love, two things we all hold and value for children. And let's not forget Michael Jackson and Lionel Richie's "We Are the World." This wonderful song proclaims: "We are the world, we are the children, we are the ones who make a brighter day, so let's start giving. There's a choice we're making, we're saving our own lives. It's true; we'll make a brighter day, just you and me."

Songs from around the world help us learn about individuals, our similarities and differences, and what makes us all special. Counting songs, songs about color, musical stories, choral speaking, and action songs can be found in all the languages of the world and from all the cultures that speak these languages. Our enthusiasm, participation, flexibility, and willingness to learn songs from other cultures will encourage children to enlarge their musical repertoire.

It is important to understand music in relation to culture.

## MUSIC FROM AROUND THE WORLD

Jenkins (1995) reminds us that every culture speaks through music: "Songs are rich with stories about the world, who people are, and how they live" (p. 41). With all the emphasis that is put on multiculturalism in education, early childhood educators must give young children the opportunity to hear and learn music of cultures other than their own. When teachers encourage children to listen to, experience, and sing traditional music of various cultures, children cannot help but gain new insight into those cultures through music (Hopton-Jones, 1995). This also helps children begin to develop a sense of cultural sensitivity. This does not come easily, nor does it come from being exposed to the "tourist approach" to multicultural music, as discussed in earlier chapters. Teachers must be sure to include music from around the world as a part of their regular, daily music curriculum. Ethnic music resources are plentiful and increasingly available. Following is a Yoruba folk chant provided by our colleague Dr. E. Olaiya Aina. He used it with his children when he taught preschool in Nigeria. "This chant teaches children to love nature and animals," he explains. "It teaches color, comparison, and vocabulary. Children role play/dramatize by 'jumping and flying' like a bird as they chant the song. There is usually a lead person or child who chants the refrain of the song while others chant the chorus. Children love it!" (E. Aina, personal communication, 2003).

*Yoruba Children's Chant*

Yoruba Version:

Eye meta tolongo waye
*Chorus:* Tolongo
Okan dudu bi aaro
*Chorus:* Tolongo
Okan riri bi osu,
*Chorus:* Tolongo
Soso firu bale
*Chorus:* Sooo
Soso firu bale
*Chorus:* Sooo

English Version:

Three birds were descending to Earth
*Chorus:* Tolongo
One of them as dark as the black dye
*Chorus:* Tolongo
One as white as the moon
*Chorus:* Tolongo
One has a tail so long
*Chorus:* Sooo
So long touching the ground!
*Chorus:* So oo

Most early childhood classrooms have children from a number of different racial and ethnic backgrounds, but in some areas of the country, the classrooms are more homogeneous. Regardless of the cultural and ethnic makeup of your classroom, give your children the opportunity to develop a sensitivity to and understanding of the cultural diversity of today's world. Here in the United States, culturally diverse music can readily be found, so be careful that you don't overlook these rich sources of our musical heritage.

### Gospel Music

Traditional gospel songs are sung by choirs, and solo voices are often accompanied by a variety of instruments ranging from piano or organ to rhythm instruments like drums and tambourines. Some of the more familiar gospel songs for Americans are "O Mary, Don't You Weep, Don't You Mourn," "Steal Away," "Wade in the Water," and "Nobody Knows the Trouble I've Seen." Figure 8–3 lists recommended recordings of African American music and African American gospel music. I also recommend visiting the website www.negrospirituals.com for a complete list of songs, complete with lyrics.

Before we switch directions and move on to other topics, let's not forget that music is a global phenomenon and that no culture is without music (Blacking, 1973). Let's also remember Jenkins's concept of the global village (1995).

## PLANNING MUSICAL EXPERIENCES FOR YOUNG CHILDREN

The following plans have been developed as an aid for teaching music to children. You will note that the concept to be taught is stated first, followed by anticipated learning, a list of materials, and possible approaches. These plans are merely guides and can be used either where music is taught separately or as a part of the children's day. Feel free to introduce and carry out the lesson to suit your particular group of children.

**Figure 8–3   Gospel Music Recordings**

- *Africa to America: The Journey of the Drum.* Sounds of Blackness. Perspective Records.
- *Amazing Grace.* Aretha Franklin (with James Cleveland). Atlantic Records.
- *Peace Be Still.* Vanessa Bell Armstrong. Onyx International Records.
- *21 Greatest Hits.* Mahalia Jackson. Kenwood Records.
- *You Brought the Sunshine.* The Clark Sisters. Sound of Gospel Recordings.

When invited, adults can enter into the movement play of children.

## Body Senses and Body Parts Awareness

### *Concept*
Children can become more aware of body senses and body parts through songs and movement.

### *Objective*
The children will:

1. Identify some of the body senses and body parts
2. Sing about some of the functions of the body senses and body parts
3. Become more aware and appreciative of their bodies and what they can do

**Standard K–3: The student will demonstrate an understanding of the distinct structures of human body and the different functions they serve. (Life Science)**

### *Materials*
1. Song "The Hokey Pokey"

### *Approach*
Discuss the importance of the body senses. Name parts of the body involving the senses, such as the eyes, ears, nose, and mouth. Ask children, "Why are these so important to us?"

*Procedure*
1. Sing the song "The Hokey Pokey."
2. Have children perform the appropriate movements to the song.
3. Ask children to name and discuss other body parts and their functions. For example, the fingers can feel (touch); the tongue can taste (sense of taste).
4. Sing the song, and perform the movements. (This may be extended over several days.)

---

## Jack-in-the-Box (A wind-up toy available in most toy stores.)

*Concept*
The power of springs to make sudden and bouncy movements

*Objective*
The children will:

1. Discover that a mechanical spring, after being compressed and released suddenly, will produce a bouncy movement
2. Duplicate the same kind of springing action with their bodies
3. Discover that the muscles in their legs serve as springs to their bodies

**Standard 1–5: The student will demonstrate an understanding of the positions and motions of objects. (Physical Science)**

*Materials*
1. Jack-in-the-box toy that plays the tune "Pop Goes the Weasel"
2. A spiral whisk, a Slinky©, or other objects having springs

*Approach*
Show the children the jack-in-the-box toy. Allow one of them to turn the handle and play the tune. (Jack pops up at the end of the song.) Ask, "What do you think makes Jack pop up? Let's find out."

*Procedure*
1. Permit each child to push Jack down in the box with his or her hand and then let him jump up again. Let the children feel the springing movement. Ask, "What do you think is inside Jack that makes him pop up?" Some child will probably guess that Jack has something inside his body that makes him spring up.
2. Show the children different kinds of springs. A whisk composed of a spiral spring on a handle is a good example to use. Children can push down on the handle, let go suddenly, and see the springing action.
3. Have the children pretend that they are jacks-in-the-box.
4. Have them spring up at the same time as the toy "Jack."

*Follow-up*
1. "What did you do to make your body spring up like a jack-in-the-box?"
2. "Why did some of you go higher than the other boys and girls?"

### Enrichment

*Poem*

Do you have something well hidden from view
That helps you jump when you tell it to?
Sometimes it helps you jump so high
You think you'll almost reach the sky!

---

### Pairs Together

#### Concepts
Pairs and sets of two

#### Objective
The children will:

1. Identify a set of two and discover that a pair is a set of two things
2. Apply the concept of pairs and discover that a pair is a set of two similar items
3. Apply the story of *One Mitten Lewis* to their own experiences.

**Standard K–2: The student will demonstrate through the mathematical processes an emerging sense of quantity and numeral relationships, sets, and place values.**

#### Materials
1. Book: *One Mitten Lewis* by Helen Kay, published by Lathrop, Lee, and Shepard
2. Song: "Pairs Together," by Linda Carol Edwards
3. Smart Board characters from the story of *One Mitten Lewis*
4. Smart Board
5. Several pairs of mittens (different sizes and colors)

#### Approach
Tell the children, "I have a story to tell you about a little boy whose name is Lewis. Lewis had a big problem. Perhaps some of you have had the same kind of problem that Lewis had. Let's find out."

#### Procedure
1. Tell the story of *One Mitten Lewis*, showing the characters on the Smart Board as the story is told.
2. After telling the story, discuss with the children some of their experiences of losing mittens.
3. Ask the children how many mittens it takes to cover both hands.
4. Tell the children there is a special word to describe two mittens that are alike and that it is used in a song they are going to learn. "Listen to the song while I sing it for you."
5. Sing the song, "Pairs Together." Encourage the children to participate in singing the song after you have sung it a few times.
6. Ask the children if they can think of another pair of something.

7. Continue to add new verses.
8. Remove Smart Board figures. Take the real mittens from the box.
9. Choose children to find two mittens that make a pair.
10. Continue to do this until all the mittens are matched in pairs.

### Evaluation
The children will demonstrate their understanding of a pair and a set of two by (1) recalling pairs of things they are familiar with and (2) matching the real mittens. The children may recall experiences of losing their own mittens and will understand how other people feel when they have lost something that belongs to them.

### Enrichment
Place all the mittens in the math center so children can play the game independently.

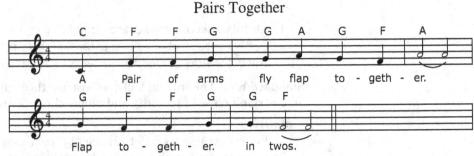

Pairs Together

A pair of knees bump bump together.
A pair of feet stomp stomp together.
A pair of hands clap clap together.
A pair of eyes blink, blink together.

*Source:* "Pairs" arranged by K. Bayless, written by Linda Edwards. Based on original composition written by Nancy Mack.

## Head, Shoulders, Knees, and Toes

### Concept
Naming and identifying parts of the body

### Objective
The children will:

1. Identify and name parts of the body as each part is mentioned in the song
2. Experience fast and slow tempo.

**Standard K–3: The student will demonstrate an understanding of the distinct structures of human body and the different functions they serve. (Life Science)**

### Materials
1. Smart Board
2. Action song: "Head, Shoulders, Knees, and Toes"

*Procedure*
1. Make up a short descriptive story about a boy or girl, naming the parts of the body as you assemble them on the Smart Board. (The body parts mentioned in the song are head, shoulders, knees, toes, eyes, ears, mouth, and nose.)
2. Sing the song, pointing to body parts as they are mentioned in the song.
3. Sing the song again, and have the children point to their own body parts.
4. As the children become familiar with the song, increase the tempo. They will enjoy singing the song faster and faster as they point to their body parts.

*Evaluation*
Were the children able to identify the parts of the body mentioned in the song? Were they able to name each part?

*Enrichment*

*Poem*

I look in the mirror and guess what I see,
My head, my ears, they're part of me.
And every day I wiggle my toes,
And sometimes you'll find me wiggling my nose.

---

## Mister Wind

*Concepts*
Rhythmic movement; wind

*Objective*
The children will:

1. Discover that wind is air set in motion, has the power to carry and push things, and can be felt and heard but not seen
2. Use their imaginations to create their own movements stimulated by discussions about the wind.

**Standard 2–3: The student will demonstrate an understanding of daily and seasonal weather conditions. (Earth Science)**

*Materials*
1. Pictures showing "winds" of different strengths at work. Include flying kites, wind blowing against an umbrella, storms, sailboats sailing in the water, branches of trees bending in the wind to blowing snow.
2. Poem: "Who Has Seen the Wind?" by Christina G. Rossetti
3. Rhythmic participation record: *My Playmate the Wind*, Young People's Records. (This recording, which is presently out of production, is a valuable resource.)
4. Song: "Mister Wind" by K. Bayless and M. Ramsey

*Approach*
Read or recite the poem "Who Has Seen the Wind?"

*Procedure*
1. Show and discuss the wind pictures.
2. Have children blow on their hands. Help them discover that by using their mouths, they are making a small wind.
3. At another time, permit children to find their own spaces and create their own movements stimulated by word pictures, music, visuals, poems, and recordings about the wind.

   a. "Pretend that you are a tree. Your arms are the branches. How would you move your branches if the wind were blowing slowly and gently? If it were blowing very hard?"
   b. "Now pretend you are holding on to an umbrella. Suddenly a gust of wind comes along. How would you hold your umbrella so it wouldn't get away from you?"
   c. "The wind is strong and pushing hard on your back. How would you walk?"
   d. "Pretend you are a kite. Use your arms and hands to show how the wind might blow you about in the sky."

*Evaluation*
1. Were the children able to create their own rhythmic movements illustrating the effect of wind on people and things?
2. Did the children give examples of feeling and hearing the wind?

*Enrichment*

*Poems*

• "Wind Song" by Lillian Moore
• "The Wind" by Robert Louis Stevenson
• "Clouds" by Christina G. Rossetti
• "The North Wind Doth Blow"
• "To a Red Kite" by Lillian Moore

*Songs*

• "The North Wind" by K. Bayless

---

*The creativity of the arts and the joy of music should be central to the education of every American child.*

—Richard Riley, former U.S. Secretary of Education

## KEY IDEAS

1. Music is basic to the young child's day.
2. Enjoyment and appreciation are primary goals for including music in the young child's day.
3. Music enhances the flow of language as well as fluency and extension of language.
4. Research evidence indicates that there is a relationship between music and the development of reading skills.
5. Through careful selection of songs, science concepts can be extended and clarified.

6. Number learning can be enjoyed through the use of nursery rhymes and songs, jingles, and poetry.
7. Every area of the social studies curriculum can be expanded and illustrated through the use of songs.

8. Musical opportunities abound throughout the day and the curriculum. Seek them out.
9. Adults establish a musical environment through enthusiasm, participation, and flexibility.

## SUMMARY

Music is a part of the daily lives of all children. Teachers and caregivers have virtually unlimited opportunity to seek out music resources to enhance the study of language, science, numbers, and social studies.

Research evidence supports the use of music to develop language, expand vocabulary, and enhance reading skills. Music naturally attracts the attention of children and leads to increased fluency in communication as they sing their favorite melodies.

Adults working with young children should seek out a wealth of music resources to incorporate into activities for children in their daily lives. Begin a collection of a broad variety of songs, chants, and poetry, and a collection of tapes, records, and texts.

## QUESTIONS TO CONSIDER

1. List several songs that illustrate the basic concepts presented in the opening paragraphs of the chapter.
2. Music offers unique possibilities to expand and extend vocabulary. Select six songs that present unusual vocabulary that would appeal to children.
3. Write a lesson plan that integrates music and language arts.
4. Select at least two songs that might be used to integrate each of the following: music and math,

music and science, music and social studies, music and reading skills, and music and art.
5. Prepare a bulletin board featuring music and one of the curriculum areas.
6. In your opinion, what is the best children's television program that incorporates music? Explain.
7. List your 10 favorite children's songs. What children's book could extend each one?

## RECORDINGS

Moore, T. (2000). *Songs children love to sing* [CD]. Charlotte, NC: Thomas Moore Records.
Raffi. (1996). *Rise and shine* [CD]. Cambridge, MA: Rounder Records.

Scelsa, G., & Millang, S. (1995). *Kids in motion: Songs for creative movement* [CD]. Huntington Beach, CA: Young Heart Music.
Seeger, P. (1998). *Birds, beasts, bugs, and fishes (little and big)* [CD]. Washington, DC: Smithsonian Folkways Recordings.

## SONG COLLECTIONS

Cohn, A. L. (1993). *From sea to shining sea: A treasury of American folklore and folk songs.* New York, NY: Scholastic.

Weikart, P. S. (1997). *Movement plus rhymes, songs and singing games* (2nd ed.). Ypsilanti, MI: High/Scope Press.

## REFERENCES

Barrett, J. R. (2001). Interdisciplinary work and musical integrity. *Music Educators Journal, 87*(5), 27–31.

Blacking, J. (1973). *How musical is man?* Seattle: University of Washington Press.

Brewer, J. A. (2001). *Introduction to early childhood education: Preschool through primary grades.* Boston, MA: Allyn & Bacon.

Butzlaff, R. (2000). Can music be used to teach reading? *Journal of Aesthetic Education, 34*(3/4), 167–168.

Consortium of National Arts Education Associations. (1994). *National standards for arts education: What every young American should know and be able to do in the arts.* Reston, VA: Music Educators National Conference.

DeMicco, D., & Dean, T. (2002). Mostly Mother Goose. *Journal of Youth Services in Libraries, 15*(2), 31–35.

Essa, E. (2003). *Introduction to early childhood education.* Clifton Park, NY: Delmar.

Feierabend, J. M., Saunders, T. C., Getnick, P. E., & Holahan, J. M. (1998). Song recognition among preschool-age children: An investigation of words and music. *Journal of Research in Music Education, 46*(3), 351–359.

Fisher, D., & McDonald, N. (2001). The intersection between music and early literacy instruction: Listen to literacy! *Reading Improvement, 38*(3), 106–115.

Gardner, H. (1993). *Multiple intelligence: The theory in practice.* New York, NY: Basic.

Gill, J. (1998). Add a little music. *Parent and Child, 5*(4), 40–45.

Grandin, T., Peterson, M., & Shaw, G. (1998). Spatial-temporal versus language-analytical reasoning: The role of music in training. *Arts Education Policy Review, 99,* 11–15.

Hansen, D., & Bernstorf, E. (2002). Linking music to learning to reading instruction. *Music Educators Journal, 88*(5), 17–21.

Hetland, L. (2000). Listening to music enhances spatial-temporal reasoning: Evidence for the "Mozart Effect." *Journal of Aesthetic Education, 34*(3–4).

Hildebrandt, C. (1998). Creativity in music and early childhood. *Young Children, 53*(6), 68–74.

Hopton-Jones, P. (1995). Introducing the music of east Africa. *Music Educators Journal, 82*(3), 26–30.

Jackson, H. L. (1997). *Early childhood curriculum: A child's connection to the world.* Albany, NY: Delmar.

James, A. R. (2000). When I listen to music. *Young Children, 55*(3), 36–37.

Jenkins, E. (1995). Music is culture. *Scholastic Early Childhood Today, 9,* 40–41.

Johnson, G. L., & Edelson, R. J. (2003). Integrating music and mathematics in the elementary classroom. *Teaching Children Mathematics, 9*(8), 474–479.

Lapp, D., & Flood, J. (1983). *Teaching reading to every child* (2nd ed.). New York, NY: Macmillan.

Mayesky, M. (2002). *Creative activities for young children.* Clifton Park, NY: Delmar.

McGirr, P. I. (1994/1995). Verdi invades the kindergarten. *Childhood Education, 77*(2), 74–79.

McKelvie, P., & Low, J. (2002). Listening to Mozart does not improve children's spatial ability: Final curtains for the Mozart effect. *British Journal of Developmental Psychology, 20*(2), 241–258.

Moravcik, E. (2000). Music all the livelong day. *Young Children, 55*(4), 27–29.

National Council for the Social Studies. (1994). *Expectations of excellence: Curriculum standards for social studies.* Washington, DC: Author.

Rauscher, F. H., Shaw, G. L., & Ky, K. N. (1993). Music and spatial task performance. *Nature, 365,* 611.

Rogers, G. (2004). Interdisciplinary lessons in musical acoustics: The science-math-music connection. *Music Educators Journal, 91*(1), 25–30.

Smith, J. (2000). Singing and song writing support early literacy instruction. *Reading Teacher, 53,* 646–649.

# Music Terminology and Approaches to Music Education

## MUSICAL CONCEPTS

The musical concepts presented here will help parents and teachers as they expand on and enrich the music experiences of their preschool or kindergarten-age and early primary children. For most children, this will be just the beginning of their understanding of music. Children's awareness of musical concepts should grow out of their natural experiences with music. Parents and teachers can plan for and guide these discoveries. Most of the musical selections throughout this book include one or more of the following concepts.

I. Melody
   a. Direction: discover whether the melody of a song moves up or down
   b. Pitch differences (high–low): respond to high or low sounds

II. Rhythm
   a. Steady beat: respond to a steady beat of music by tapping, clapping, or playing percussion instruments
   b. Tempo (fast–slow): experience songs, both fast and slow; move in response to music that gets faster or slower
   c. Rhythm patterns: echo simple rhythm patterns and repeat them by clapping or playing a percussion instrument; recognize repeated patterns in a song
   d. Rhythmic activities: walk, run, gallop, skip, and hop (locomotive movements) and bend, push, pull, reach, and sway (nonlocomotive movements) to music

III. Form
   a. Beginning and ending: learn to respond to beginnings and endings of music; start when the music begins, and stop when it comes to an end; draw a "map" of the song in the air, from beginning to end
   b. Two-part song (AB or ABA): respond in one way to one section or part of the music and in a different way to the other
   c. Individual or group (call and response): imitate musical tone calls or phrases
   d. Verse and refrain: recognize the difference between a verse and a refrain

IV. Tone color
   a. Instruments: begin to identify instruments by sight and sound; begin with strings, winds, and percussion; be exposed to different methods of playing instruments, such as blowing, striking, and bowing
   b. Natural and environmental sounds: experience clapping, snapping, whistling, and tongue-clicking. Identify different environmental sounds, such as trains, sirens, machines, owls, and other animals.
   c. Voices: recognize the difference in men's, women's, and children's speaking and singing voices
   d. Dynamics (soft–loud): recognize the difference between loud and soft in music; recognize when music gets louder and softer

V. Texture-harmony
   a. Have the experience of adding harmony to a song by playing simple bell parts or strumming on an Autoharp®
   b. Have opportunities to hear songs with and without accompaniment

## GLOSSARY

**accent**   A stress or emphasis given to certain notes.

**beat**   The audible or visual markings of the metrical divisions of music; also, a pulse that can be heard or felt in music.

**direction**   The upward or downward movement of a melody.

**duration**   The length of time that sound persists (short or long).

**dynamics**   The loudness or softness of sounds in music.
   **crescendo**   Gradually growing louder.
   **diminuendo**   Gradually growing softer.
   **forte (f)**   Loud.
   **fortissimo (ff)**   Very loud.
   **mezzo forte (mf)**   Moderately loud.
   **mezzo piano (mp)**   Moderately soft.
   **pianissimo (pp)**   Very soft.
   **piano (p)**   Soft.
   **sforzando (sf)**   Forcefully.

**fermata**   (⌢) The sustaining of a note, chord, or rest for a duration longer than the indicated time value, with the length of the extension at the performer's discretion.

**form**   Scheme of organization that determines the basic structure of a composition; often designated by letters (AB form, ABA form, etc.).

**harmony**   The simultaneous combination of tones (sounding at one time).

**interval**   The difference in pitch between two tones.

**measure**   Music contained between two vertical bars.

**melody**   The succession of single tones (moving upward or downward) in a musical composition.

**ostinato**   A short rhythmic or melodic pattern that is repeated.

**pentatonic scale**   A five-tone scale (do, re, mi, sol, la). It can begin on any tone.

**phrase**   A division of a composition—a "musical sentence"; commonly, a passage of four or eight measures.

**pitch**   The highness or lowness of a tone.

**rest**   A sign (symbol) in music indicating an interval of silence.

**scale**   A succession of ascending or descending tones arranged according to fixed intervals.

**staccato**   Short, detached sound.

**steady beat**   Regular, even pulsation.

**tempo**   The speed or rate of beats in music.
   **accelerando**   Gradually getting faster.
   **allegretto**   Moderately fast.
   **allegro**   Fast.
   **andante**   Moderately slow.
   **andantino**   Slightly faster than andante.
   **largo**   Very slow.
   **lento**   Slow.
   **presto**   Very fast.

**timbre**   The quality of a sound (voice or instrument).

**tonal music**   Music that has a "home base"—that is, music that is written in a particular key.

**tone color**   The sound that makes an instrument or voice different from another.

## GRAND STAFF AND PIANO KEYBOARD

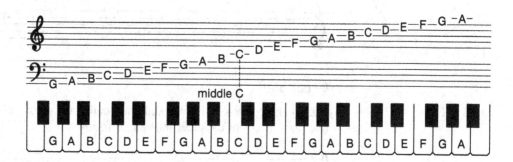

## MUSIC FUNDAMENTALS

### Staff

Music is written on a staff that consists of five lines and four spaces. Notes are placed upon the staff to indicate *pitch,* which is the highness or lowness of tone.

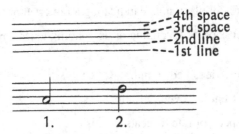

To indicate where a note is located, the lines and spaces are always counted from the bottom of the staff up to the top, as shown on keyboard graphic.

1. This note is in the second space.
2. This note is on the fourth line.

When a note is below the third line, the stem goes up on the right side of the head. When the note is on the third line, the stem can go in either direction, but if the note is above the third line, the stem extends down on the left side, as follows:

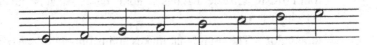

### Letter Names

The first seven letters of the alphabet are used to name the lines and spaces. These are used consecutively and repeatedly to correspond with all the white keys on the piano.

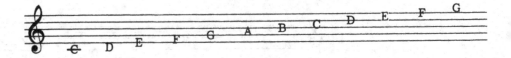

### Great Staff

The combined bass and treble staffs are called the great staff. The letter names of the lines and spaces of the great staff are as follows:

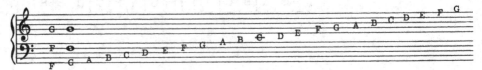

## Clefs

For vocal and piano music, the treble and bass clefs are used almost exclusively. Middle C has the same pitch in each of these clefs.

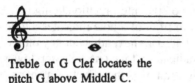

Treble or G Clef locates the pitch G above Middle C.

Bass or F Clef locates the pitch F below Middle C.

When making the treble clef sign, be sure the two lines of the sign cross on the fourth line of the staff and the G line or second line is crossed three times.

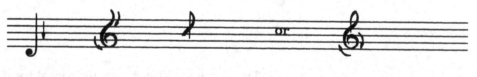

## Other Terms

1. *Bars.* Lines drawn vertically through the staff are called *bars.*
2. *Double bars.* These are used at the end of a composition to indicate the completion of a composition.
3. *Measure.* The music contained between two bar lines is one measure. The rhythm of the music is measured.
4. *Accent marks.* These are used for accent or emphasis.
5. *Tie.* The curved line connecting two or more notes of the same pitch (in the same place on the staff) is called a *tie.* The note is sounded or played once and held for the duration or value of all the notes.

6. *Slur.* The curved line connecting two or more notes of different pitch is called a *slur.* One word or syllable of a word is sung on the two or more tones.

7. *Repeat signs.* Two dots before a bar indicate that the music of the preceding section is to be repeated. Go back to the preceding double bar or, in case there is no double bar, go back to the beginning and continue to the end or the sign "Fine."

8. *Fermata (hold).* The note under this sign is to be held longer than usual, the length of time dependent on the interpretation being given the music.

9. *Sharp.* This sign in front of a note indicates a tone one-half step, higher than the normal pitch of that tone (next adjacent key on the piano or bells).

10. *Flat.* This sign indicates a tone one-half step lower than the normal pitch.

11. *Natural.* This sign removes the effect of a sharp or flat or takes away the sharp or flat.

a. Placed before a flatted note, the natural has the same effect as a sharp and raises that tone one-half step higher than the pitch represented by the flatted note.

b. Placed before a sharped note, the natural has the same effect as a flat and lowers that tone one-half step below the pitch represented by the sharped note.

12. *Half step.* A step is a unit for measuring distance in music. The tone nearest to any given tone, either above or below, is a half step from the given tone. The half steps that occur normally on the staff are between B and C (*12a*) and E and F (*12b*). As another example, on the keyboard the half steps are from white key G to black key G# (*12c*) and from white key A to black key $A_b$ (*12d*).

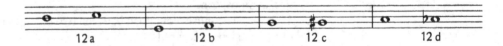

13. *Whole step.* A whole step consists of two half steps. On the keyboard the whole steps are from a white key to the next white key or from a black key to the next black key (except from B to C and from E to F).

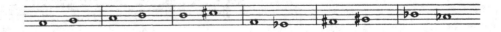

14. *Chromatic.* Sharps, flats, or naturals (other than those in the signature) placed before notes in a composition are called *chromatics* or *accidentals*. When sharps, flats, or naturals are used in a measure of music, they affect only the same note when repeated in the same measure. The measure bar automatically cancels these accidentals.

**Notes and Their Corresponding Rests**

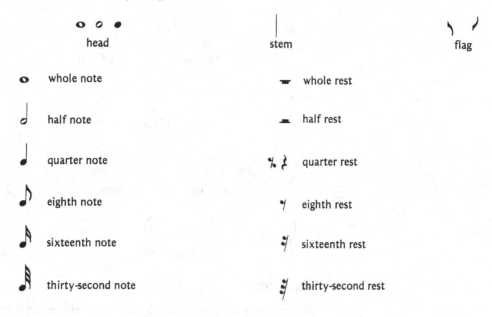

## Placement of Rests on the Treble Staff

| 1. | 2. | 3. | 4. | 5. |
|----|----|----|----|----|
| Whole | Half | Quarter | Eighth | Sixteenth |

1. The whole rest is placed down from the fourth line of the staff.
2. The half rest is made up from the third line.
3. The quarter rest is started in the third space and goes down into the second space.

4. The flag of the eighth rest is made in the third space and on the left side of the stem.
5. The flags of the sixteenth rest are made on the third and fourth lines and on the left side of the stem.

## Dotted Notes

A dot following a note adds one half of the value of the note. The most commonly found dotted notes are:

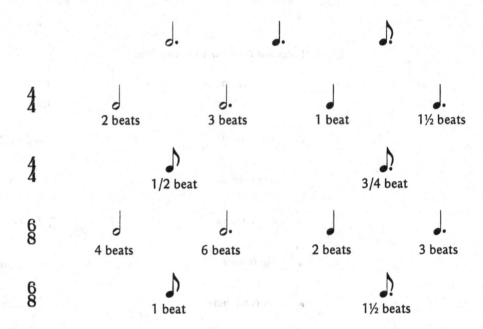

## Signature

The term *signature* includes the clef sign, sharps or flats, and numbers. The sharps or flats indicate the *key signature*. The numbers indicate the *time* or *meter signature*.

1. Treble clef key of D
   6/8 meter

2. Bass clef key of E♭
   4/4 meter

## Rules for Meter (Time) Signatures

Meter signatures are numerical indications of the regular recurrence of a beat or pulse. They are composed of two numbers placed one above the other. The upper figure tells the number of beats in a measure. The lower figure tells the kind of note that receives one beat.

### Examples of Meter Signatures

$\frac{4}{4}$  $\frac{3}{4}$  $\frac{2}{4}$   The 4 on the bottom means that the <u>quarter</u> note gets one count or beat.

**C** means common time, the same as $\frac{4}{4}$ time.

| 𝅝 | 𝅗𝅥 | 𝅘𝅥 | 𝅘𝅥𝅮 | 𝅘𝅥𝅯 | 𝅗𝅥. | 𝅘𝅥. | 𝅘𝅥𝅮. |
|---|---|---|---|---|---|---|---|
| 4 beats | 2 | 1 beat | 1/2 | 1/4 | 3 | 1½ | 3/4 |

$\frac{3}{8}$  $\frac{6}{8}$   The 8 means that the <u>eighth</u> note gets one count or beat.

| 𝅗𝅥 | 𝅘𝅥 | 𝅘𝅥𝅮 | 𝅘𝅥𝅯 | 𝅗𝅥. | 𝅘𝅥. | 𝅘𝅥𝅮. |
|---|---|---|---|---|---|---|
| 4 beats | 2 | 1 beat | 1/2 | 6 | 3 | 1½ |

Typical complete measures of these meter signatures are:

## Finding the Key of a Song

Songs are written in various keys. The key of a song is determined by the scale tones used. Thus, a song in the key of C uses the tones in the scale of C:

**Key of C**

In this scale, the pitch of C is considered to be the key center or the pitch that begins and ends the scale series, and in this scale it is given the number 1. In the C scale, the pitch of D is number 2, E is number 3, F is number 4, G is number 5, A is number 6, B is number 7, and C again is number 8, or the octave of 1. In the scale of C, none of the pitches is either sharped (#) or flatted (b), so in a song in the key of C no sharps or flats are shown at the beginning of the song.

Songs in other keys show key signatures that use sharps or flats because they are based on scales that have to use pitches either sharped or flatted. Thus, a song in the key of G, the tones of which are derived from the scale of G, has to use a sharp (F#) in its signature because in the scale of G, this pitch (F) has to be sharped:

Key of G

This sharp is placed on the staff after the clef sign. In each case, the key signature denotes the pitch considered to be the key center for the song. The pitch so considered is always given the number 1.

To play or sing a song in its proper key setting, it is important to be able to tell from the key signature in what key the song is to be played or sung. The technique of determining the key from a given key signature is not difficult.

In songs having flats in their signatures, call the line or space of the staff on which the last flat (the one to the far right of any others shown) is placed "four" (4) and count downward each consecutive line or space of the staff until the line or space number one (1) is reached. The pitch for that line or space of the staff is then the key center (*x*) or key tone (keys of Bb, Eb, Ab, and Db):

Key of F          Bb          Eb          Ab          Db

In songs having only one flat in their signature, call the line of the staff on which it is placed "4," and count down to 1 (key of F above).

To find the key of songs with sharps, move up one line or space of the staff from the last sharp, which is the one to the far right of any others shown in the key signature. If the last sharp is located on a line, the key center will be located on the next space. If the last sharp is located in a space, the key center will be located on the next line:

Key of G          D          A          E          B

## APPROACHES TO MUSIC EDUCATION

### The Orff Approach

The Orff, or Orff-Schulwerfe, approach was introduced by Carl Orff (1895–1982), a well-known German composer. This musical approach emphasizes the use of specially designed percussion and keyboard instruments for young children.

Orff was influenced by Dalcroze's thinking, by the surge of interest in physical education and gymnastics, and by the advent of a new kind of dancing that has since become known as modern dance. Orff, like Dalcroze, had a great interest in the theater. He opened a school for gymnastics and dance in 1924 and combined the study of music with gymnastics. This fusion became the key to his concept of music education. Orff began to create music for the young dance students in his school. By 1948, he had developed an educational system specifically for music.

The contrast and variation of rhythm are the primary elements in Orff's style of musical composition, and percussion instruments that produce this rhythm naturally play a primary role in these works. Thus, Orff invented new percussion instruments to meet his demand for novel effects. These unique instruments distinguish Orff's approach from others. They are easy to play and are of excellent quality. Since rhythmic responses are so natural to the young child, Orff was convinced that these melodic percussion devices would allow children the opportunity for creative improvisation and ensemble experience. The child memorizes pitch and rhythmic patterns with facility and without inhibition.

Orff felt that children should play instruments from memory and that the study of piano should come only after the development of other musical skills. Drill is to be avoided. Orff believed that a gradual progression from speech patterns to rhythmic activities to song was the best and most natural for the child. The playing of instruments follows. Children try out and play various rhythm patterns and melodic and ostinato figures on instruments. Orff felt the instruments provide a comprehensive and sound musical foundation for the child.

Originally, Orff based his approach on German folklore and children's music. (Orff's music for children is now available in English-language adaptations.) Teachers might substitute American folk music and children's songs in the pentatonic mode. These songs can be accompanied by the Orff instruments. The prized Orff instruments are manufactured in Germany but can be readily obtained in the United States. Although the teacher must be fairly well trained and the instruments are rather expensive, the Orff approach is used successfully throughout the United States.

We have been impressed with the range of possibilities in using the Orff instruments. Teachers are encouraged to pursue the Orff approach in more depth. Today, the Orff Institute, established in 1963 in Salzburg, offers training in the Orff approach for teachers from many parts of the world. Music schools throughout America can provide information on the Orff approach.

## The Suzuki Method

The Suzuki method, or talent education, was developed by Dr. Shinichi Suzuki, a violinist and Japanese language teacher. The approach received worldwide recognition and acclaim when 3-, 4-, and 5-year-old children demonstrated their ability to play demanding sonatas and concertos on their miniature violins. Suzuki's method of instruction employs a psycholinguistic approach. The child learns to respond to and repeat music in the same manner that he learns to speak his native tongue, playing first by ear rather than by reading notes. Suzuki regards two elements as being very important in his method: "(1) The child must be helped to develop an ear for music. (2) From the very beginning, every step must by all means be thoroughly mastered" (Suzuki et al., 1973, p. 12).

The Suzuki method requires close supervision by the parent and the teacher. The student must listen, practice, and perform. The parent is asked to attend each weekly lesson and to supervise daily practice sessions. Parental involvement not only ensures that the student follows the teacher's instructions but gives encouragement and praise for the child's efforts. The children have the opportunity to play for each other in informal recitals. Frequent opportunities to play before an audience build a child's self-confidence.

The Suzuki method now encompasses the instruction of piano, cello, flute, and viola as well as violin. Although each particular instrument has its own music repertoire, Suzuki's basic techniques, principles, and philosophy still apply. Many schools today are employing the Suzuki method and instrumental technique, which relies primarily on the human ear.

Obviously, each approach discussed here offers a unique musical experience to the young child. Whatever approach feels most comfortable to the teacher will be the most successful one for the students.

---

**Dr. Shinichi Suzuki (1898–1998):** Renowned Japanese violinist and teacher, Dr. Shinichi Suzuki studied how children learn for more than fifty years. Encouraged by their ability to assimilate the "mother tongue," he saw a great opportunity to enrich children's lives through music. His primary goal was not only to teach young people to play musical instruments. Rather, he recognized the unique contribution music can make in the total learning process. His goals for all children included development of the whole child, unfolding the natural potential to learn and becoming a good and happy person.

In 1993, Dr. Suzuki and the Board of Directors of the International Suzuki Association (ISA) approved the curriculum developed by Dorothy Jones and named her school in London, Ontario as the first World Centre for Suzuki Early Childhood Education Teacher Training.

# Resources for Teachers in Early Childhood Classrooms

## PROFESSIONAL ORGANIZATIONS, NEWSLETTERS, AND JOURNALS

## ORGANIZATIONS

Association for Childhood Education International (ACEI)
11141 Georgia Ave. Suite 200
Wheaton, MD 20902
http://www.udel.edu/bateman/acei/

Educational Resources Information Center/Early
  Childhood Education (ERIC/ECE)
805 W. Pennsylvania Ave.
Urbana, IL 61801
http://eric.ed.gov/

National Association for the Education of Young
  Children (NAEYC)
1834 Connecticut Ave., N.W.
Washington, DC 20009
http://www.naeyc.org/

National Association for Music Education
Music Educators National Conference (MENC)
1902 Association Dr.
Reston, VA 22091
http://www.menc.org/

## Journals

*Child Development*
Society for Research in Child Development
University of Chicago Press
5801 Ellis Ave. Chicago, IL 60637
http://www.blackwellpublishing.com

*Childhood Education*
Association for Childhood Education International
11141 Georgia Ave. Suite 200
Wheaton, MD 20902
http://www.springer.com

*Children Today*
U.S. Department of Health, Education, and Welfare
Office of Child Development
Children's Bureau
Superintendent of Documents
U.S. Government Printing Office
Washington, DC 20402
http://www.crwflags.com

*Merrill-Palmer Quarterly of Behavior and
Development*
Merrill-Palmer Institute
71 E. Ferry Ave.
Detroit, MI 48202
http://muse.jhu.edu/

*Music Educators Journal*
Music Educators National Conference
1902 Association Dr.
Reston, VA 22091
www.menc.org

*Young Children*
National Association for the Education of Young Children
1834 Connecticut Ave., N.W.
Washington, DC 20009
www.journal.naeyc.org/search/

## SOURCES FOR ORDERING INSTRUMENTS

Lyons Band
P.O. Box 1003
Elkhart, IN 46515

Oscar Schmidt/Music Education Group
230 Lexington Dr.
Buffalo Grove, IL 60090

Rhythm Band, Inc.
P.O. Box 126
Fort Worth, TX 76101

## BOOKS ON MAKING INSTRUMENTS

*Making Music: Create and Play 70 Musical Instruments Using Stuff From Around Your House!*
John Langstaff and Ann Sayre Wiseman
Storey Publishing ISBN: 9781580175128

*Penny Nick: Making Musical Instruments From Junk*
Penny Nick
A & C Black Publishers Ltd. (United Kingdom) ISBN: 9780713672466

*Making Gourd Musical Instruments*
Jim Widess
Sterling Publishing Co. Inc. ISBN: 9781402745034

*Make Your Own Musical Instruments*
Muriel Mandell and Robert E. Wood
Sterling Publishing, 419 Park Ave. S., New York, NY 10016

*Music and Instruments for Children to Make and Rhythms, Music, and Instruments to Make*
John Hawkinson and Martha Faulhaber
Albert Whitman, 560 W. Lake St., Chicago, IL 60606

*Simple Folk Instruments to Make and Play*
Ilene Hunter and Marilyn Judson
Children's Book and Music Center,
2500 Santa Monica Blvd.,
Santa Monica, CA 90404

## SONGS FOR LISTENING AND MUSIC APPRECIATION

It has often been said that the tastes of young children can be shaped by the music we play for them. For children to appreciate music of quality, they need to hear the music played repeatedly. A list of recordings that develop listening skills and music appreciation follows.

"Air on the G String" (Bach)
"Aragonaise" from *Le Cid* (Massenet)
"Ballet of the Unhatched Chicks" (Moussorgsky)
"Barcarolle" from *Tales of Hoffman* (Offenbach)
"Berceuse" (Chopin)
"Bridal Chorus" from *Lohengrin* (Wagner)
*Carnival of the Animals* (Saint-Saëns)
*Children's Corner Suite* (Debussy)
"Clown" from *Marionettes* (MacDowell)
"Country Gardens" (Granger)
"The Dancing Doll" (Poldini)
"Danse Macabre" (Saint-Saëns)
"Dance of the Ballerina" from *Petrouchka* (Stravinsky)
"Entrance of the Little Fauns" (Pierné)
"The Flight of the Bumblebee" (Rimsky-Korsakov)
"Golliwog's Cakewalk" (Debussy)
*Grand Canyon Suite* (Grofé)
*Hansel and Gretel* (Humperdinck)
"The Happy Farmer" (Schumann)
"Hornpipe" from *Water Music* (Handel)
"Knight of the Hobby Horse" (Schumann)
"Leap Frog" from *Children's Games* (Bizet)
"March Militaire" (Schubert)
"March of the Little Lead Soldiers" (Pierné)
"March of the Toys" (Herbert)
*Mother Goose Suite* (Ravel)
*Nutcracker Suite* (Tchaikovsky)
"Of Tailor and a Bear" (MacDowell)
*Peer Gynt Suite No. 1* (Grieg)
*Peter and the Wolf* (Prokofiev)
"Pizzicato" (Delibes)
"Polka" (Shostakovich)
*Scenes from Childhood* (Schumann)
"The Skater's Waltz" (Waldteufel)
"Sleighride" (Anderson)
*The Sorcerer's Apprentice* (Dukas)
"The Swan" from *Carnival of the Animals* (Saint-Saëns)
"Sweet Dreams" (Tchaikovsky)
*Symphony No. 94 in G Major* ("Surprise") (Haydn)
"To a Water Lily" (MacDowell)
"Toy Symphony" (Haydn)
"Waltzing Doll" (Poldini)

## MUSIC THAT HIGHLIGHTS MUSICAL INSTRUMENTS

The following selected recordings highlight particular instruments.

*"Anvil Chorus" from Il Trovatore* (Verdi)
*Tambourine, triangle*
*Carnival of the Animals* (Saint-Saëns)

*Piano, double bass, strings, flute, clarinet, xylophone*
"Dance of the Sugar Plum Fairy" (Tchaikovsky)
*Celesta*
*New World Symphony*, second movement
   (Dvořák)
*English horn*
"Nocturne" from *A Midsummer Night's Dream*
   (Mendelssohn)
*French horn, cello, bassoon*
*Peter and the Wolf* (Prokofiev)
*Oboe, bassoon*
"Prelude and Fugue in G Major" (Bach)
*Organ*
"Stars and Stripes Forever" (Sousa)
*Piccolo*
"The Swan" (Saint-Saëns)
*Cello, piano*
"Trumpet Voluntary in D" (Purcell-Clark)
*Trumpet*
"Waltz of the Flowers" (Tchaikovsky)
*Harp*
"The White Peacock" (Griffes)
*Flute*

# MUSIC FOR MOVEMENT

The following classical recordings are recommended for use with movement.

## Creative Dancing

"Danse Macabre" (Saint-Saëns)
*Nutcracker Suite* (Tchaikovsky)

## Hopping

"Ballet of the Unhatched Chicks" (Moussorgsky)

## Jumping/Leaping

"Aragonaise" from *Le Cid* (Massenet)
"Leap Frog" from *Children's Games* (Bizet)

## Marching

"American Salute" (Gould)
"Children's March" (Goldman)
"Entrance of the Little Fauns" (Pierné)
"March" from *Nutcracker Suite* (Tchaikovsky)

"March Militaire" (Schubert)
"March of the Little Lead Soldiers" (Pierné)

## Running

"The Ball" from *Children's Games* (Bizet)
"Catch Me" from *Scenes from Childhood*
   (Schumann)
"Tag" (Prokofiev)

## Skipping/Galloping

"Gallop" from *The Comedians* (Kabalevsky)
"Knight of the Hobby Horse" from *Scenes from Childhood*
   (Schumann)
"The Wild Horseman" from *Album for the Young* (Schumann)

## Sliding/Gliding

"The Skater's Waltz" (Waldteufel)
"The Swan" from *Carnival of the Animals* (Saint-Saëns)
"Waltz on Ice" from *Winter Holiday* (Prokofiev)

## Swaying/Rocking

"Barcarolle" from *Tales of Hoffman* (Offenbach)
"To a Water Lily" (MacDowell)
"Waltz" from *Six Piano Pieces for Children*
   (Shostakovich)
"Waltz of the Dolls" (Delibes)

## Tiptoe

"Dance of the Little Swans" from *Swan Lake*
   (Tchaikovsky)

## Walking

"Bourree" (Telemann)
"Gavotte" (Handel)
"Walking Song" from *Acadian Songs and Dances*
   (Thomson)

## Whirling

"Clowns" (Kabalevsky)
"Impromptu—The Top" from *Children's Games* (Bizet)
"Tarantella" from *The Fantastic Toy Shop*
   (Rossini-Respighi)

## CHILDREN'S BOOKS ABOUT MUSIC

Bassett, C. (2003). *Walk like a bear, stand like a tree, run like the wind: Cool yoga, stretching and aerobic activities for cool kids.* New York, NY: Nubod Concepts. This book includes many fun ways to get children to move.

Bramhall, W. (2004). *Hepcat.* New York, NY: Philomel Books. Hepcat gets scared before a piano performance and loses his groove. He finds his groove from the Beatles, Elvis, and Little Richard. Now when he performs, he's the coolest cat around.

Carle, E. (1997). *From head to toe.* New York, NY: Harper Collins. Animals invite children to imitate them as they stomp, wriggle, thump, and clap.

Cauley, L. B. (1992). *Clap your hands.* New York, NY: Putnam. Rhyming text instructs the listener to find something yellow, roar like a lion, give a kiss, tell a secret, spin a circle, and more.

Child, L. M. (1974). *Over the river and through the wood.* New York, NY: Coward, McCann and Geoghegan. A favorite Thanksgiving song is presented with illustrations.

Conover, C. (1976). *Six little ducks.* New York, NY: Crowell. One little duck leads his friends into mischief in this adaptation of an old camp song.

Conover, C. (2004). *Over the hills & far away.* New York, NY: Farrar Straus Giroux. Tom the otter plays only one song as he travels the country side playing his pipe.

Cox, J., & Brown, E. (2003). *My family plays music.* New York, NY: Holiday House. This picture book is about a very musical family in which each member plays a different instrument. Everything from jazz to polkas is discussed.

Crozon, A. (2004). *What am I? Music!* Paris, France: Editions du Seuil. This book offers learning concepts and ideas that come to light in an interactive format.

Dewan, T. (2005). *Bing: Make music.* New York, NY: Random House. This book uses everyday materials to make instruments.

Dillon, L., & Dillon, D. (2002) *Rap a tap tap: Here's Bojangles—Think of that!* New York, NY: Blue Sky Press. In this book, the legendary dancing spirit of Mr. Bojangles is celebrated, with the repetitive phrase, "Rap a tap tap—think of that!"

Gammell, S. (1989). *Song and dance man.* New York, NY: Knopf. Grandpa demonstrates for his visiting grandchildren some of the songs, dances, and jokes he performed when he was a vaudeville entertainer.

Geras, A., & McNicholas, S. (2003). *Time for ballet.* New York, NY: Dial. This adventure of a little girl taking ballet lessons illustrates learning some of the ballet poses and preparation for a recital in which she plays a cat.

Hanke, K., & Gollub, M. (2000). *The jazz fly.* Santa Rosa, CA: Tortuga Press. This book and CD tell the tale of a musician fly who is inspired by animals he meets on his way to a performance.

Helldorfer, M. C., & Nakata, H. (2004). *Got to dance.* New York, NY: Random House. A young girl with nothing to do in the summer decides to dance—at the zoo, under the bus seat, in sneakers, and in shoes with wings. Dancing helps to relieve her summer blues.

Hoffman, M. (1993). *Amazing Grace.* New York, NY: Scholastic. With encouragement from her grandmother, Grace discovers that she can play Peter Pan in the school play.

Isadora, R. (1979). *Ben's trumpet.* New York, NY: Mulberry. Ben has an imaginary horn that he plays for his family and friends. One day the trumpet player from the Zig Zag Jazz Club introduces Ben to a real horn.

Johnson, D. W. (1975). *The willow flute: A north country tale.* Boston, MA: Little, Brown. Lewis Shrew goes out into the white woods to gather twigs for his stove. He finds a musty old room in a house. As he searches throughout the house, he finds a willow flute amid the wreckage on the floor. As he begins to play, winter disappears and spring returns.

Johnson, T. (1991). *Grandpa's song.* New York, NY: Dial Books. A little girl helps her forgetful grandfather by singing him a favorite song.

Kraus, R. (1990). *Musical Max.* New York, NY: Simon & Schuster. When Max decides to put away his instruments, it drives the neighbors as crazy as when he was practicing.

Krementz, J. (1991). *A very young musician.* New York, NY: Simon & Schuster. A boy learns to play the trumpet in a story illustrated with photographs.

Krull, K. (2003). *M is for music.* San Diego, CA: Harcourt. This alphabet book introduces musical terms, from allegro to zarzuela.

Kuskin, K. (1986). *The Philharmonic gets dressed.* New York, NY: Harper Collins. The musicians of the orchestra are shown going about their daily routine and preparing for an evening concert.

Landy, J. M., & Burridge, K. R. (2000). *Ready to use fundamental motor skills and movement activities for young children*. West Nyack, NY: Center for Applied Research in Education. This book contains fundamental motor skills and movement activities for young children (PreK–3).

Langstaff, J. (1955). *Frog went a-courtin'*. New York, NY: Harcourt, Brace and World. Langstaff made one story out of the different versions of the ballad that are sung in various parts of America.

Langstaff, J. (1957). *Over in the meadow*. New York, NY: Harcourt, Brace and World. The text is Langstaff's version of an old rhyme for children; not a traditional folk song.

Lasker, D. (1979). *The boy who loved music*. New York, NY: Viking Press. This book, based on the true story of a boy who played horn in the orchestra of Prince Nicolaus Esterhazy, is beautifully illustrated and filled with humor.

McCloskey, R. (1940). *Lentil*. New York, NY: Viking Press. Lentil wants to sing but cannot. When he opens his mouth, only strange sounds come out. He cannot whistle either. Lentil saves up enough money to buy a harmonica and saves the day when the band members' lips all pucker up and they can't play their instruments for Colonel Carter. The people give Lentil a warm welcome.

McDermott, G. (1997). *Musicians of the sun*. New York, NY: Simon & Schuster. In this retelling of an Aztec myth, Lord of the Night sends Wind to free four musicians that the Sun is holding prisoner, so they can bring joy to the world.

Newcome, Z. (2002). *Head, shoulders, knees, and toes: And other action counting rhymes*. Cambridge, MA: Candlewick Press. This book contains more than 50 verses, with energetic illustrations that get kids moving.

Pica, R. (2003). *Teachable transitions: 190 activities to move from morning circle to the end of the day*. Beltsville, MD: Gryphon House. This book makes everyday transitions fun and valuable learning experiences.

Prokofiev, S. S. (1971). *Peter and the wolf*. Tokyo, Japan: Gokkin; Morristown, NJ: Silver Burdette (U.S. distributor). In this classic of music literature, each character is represented by an instrument.

Sage, J. (1991). *The little band*. New York, NY: McElderry. Everyone is delighted by the little band as it marches through town.

Saint-Saëns, C. (1971). *Carnival of the animals*. Tokyo, Japan: Gokkin. Various instruments impersonate animals; for example, the double bass impersonates an elephant, and the cello, a swan.

Schook Hazen, B. (1973). *Frère Jacques*. New York, NY: Lippincott. A monk has a terrible problem with oversleeping, especially when it is his turn to ring the morning bells. The problem is finally solved by a young choir boy. Includes words and music to the song.

Sendak, M. (Lyrics), & King, C. (Composer). (1999). *Really Rosie* [CD]. New York, NY: Ode/CBS Records. This reissued CD includes "Chicken Soup with Rice" and other songs.

Spier, P. (1961). *The fox went out on a chilly night*. Garden City, NY: Doubleday. This old folk song is beautifully illustrated.

Sturgers, P., & Wolff, A. (2004). *She'll be comin' round the mountain*. Boston, MA: Little Brown. This Southwest adaptation of the classic folk song includes animals awaiting the arrival of a mysterious guest, who turns up in a bookmobile.

Taback, S. (1997). *There was an old lady who swallowed a fly*. New York, NY: Simon and Schuster. This illustrated version retells the cumulative song in cutout book form.

Wetherford, C. B. (2000). *The sound that jazz makes*. New York, NY: Walker. This illustrated story of the origins of jazz links its African and American roots.

Williams, V. (1984). *Music, music for everyone*. New York, NY: Mulberry. Rosa earns money to help out her mother when her grandmother is sick. Rosa's accordion is a great addition to the Oak Street Band.

Williams, V. B. (1983). *Something special for me*. New York, NY: Greenwillow. The story of Rosa, who takes money from a jar and can't decide what she wants to buy. She finally decides on a small, used accordion and loves it.

Zemach, M. (1976). *Hush, little baby*. New York, NY: Dutton. This beautifully illustrated book brings the popular folk song to life.

# Learning Autoharp® and Guitar for the Classroom

## A PRACTICAL APPROACH TO LEARNING TO PLAY THE AUTOHARP

The Autoharp® is a relatively easy instrument to learn to play. The best way to become proficient in playing it is to learn the location of the bars and chords and then spend a great deal of time just playing and singing.

### Care and Tuning

The Autoharp should receive the same kind of treatment that one would give a fine piano or other instrument. Dampness and sudden changes of temperature will affect its playing qualities. When it is not in use, keep it in a box or case and store it in a dry place of even temperature.

The instrument should be tuned frequently to keep it in perfect tune. This is not difficult to do if one has a good sense of pitch. It should either be tuned to a well-tuned piano, to some other instrument with a fixed pitch (such as an accordion), or to a pitch pipe. If one person plays the corresponding key on the piano while the other person tunes the Autoharp, the tuning can be done in approximately 10 minutes.

Middle C should be tuned first, and the lower and higher octaves tuned in unison with it. In the same manner, continue to tune the other strings. The tuning tool should be placed on each peg and turned *slowly* with either the right or left hand, either clockwise or counterclockwise, until the tone produced by the string matches the tone of the corresponding key of the piano or other instrument. With the other hand, pluck the string with the thumbnail while turning the tuning tool. By turning the tool clockwise, the pitch of the string will be raised.

Turning the tool counterclockwise lowers the pitch. When one is first learning to tune the Autoharp, it is most helpful to have one person playing the note on the piano while another person does the tuning. Continued practice in tuning the Autoharp should make one's ear more sensitive to changes in pitch.

When checking to see if the Autoharp is out of tune, press down the bars, one at a time, and slowly draw the pick across the strings to locate the string or strings that are out of tune with the chord. Usually, only a few strings will be out of tune at one time.

For optimum results, it is extremely important to keep the instrument in tune. If one does not have a good ear for pitch, ask a music teacher or some other musical person for help.

### Autoharp Chording

This chart indicates the primary chords as they appear in the various Autoharp keys:

| Key* | Tonic I | Subdominant IV | Dominant $V_7$ | Tonic I |
|------|---------|----------------|----------------|---------|
| C major | C | F | $G_7$ | C |
| F major | F | $B^b$ | $C_7$ | F |
| G major | G | C | $D_7$ | G |
| D minor | $D_m$ | $G_m$ | $A_7$ | $D_m$ |
| A minor | $A_m$ | $D_m$ | $E_7$ | $A_m$ |

\* Play the chord progressions in each key until you feel familiar with their individual qualities.

The primary chords on the Autoharp—the I, the IV, and the $V_7$ in any of the keys—are played in the following manner. When the index finger is placed on the I chord of a given key, the middle finger falls on the $V_7$ chord and the ring finger on the IV chord of that key. For example, place the index finger on the F major bar. This would be the I chord in the key of F. The middle finger would fall on the $C_7$ bar (the $V_7$), and the ring finger would fall on the $B^b$ major bar (the IV chord).

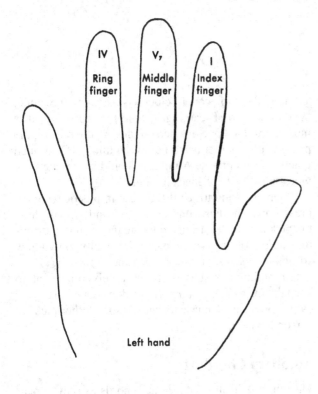

Left hand

The accompanying chart indicates the chord markings for the 12-bar Autoharp, the system used in this appendix.

## Variations in Strumming Technique

Variations in rhythm or accent can be accomplished by strumming in different ways.

To strum rhythmically, one must be acquainted with the time or meter signature found at the beginning of every song. Some of the more commonly used meter signatures are 2/4, 3/4, 4/4, and 6/8. The top number always indicates the number of beats or counts in each measure; the lower number indicates what kind of note or rest receives one beat or one count. For example, in

| Bar label* | Chord produced | See note† |
|---|---|---|
| G Min. | G minor | $G_m$ |
| $B^b$ Maj. | $B^b$ major | Bb |
| A Sev. | A seventh | $A_7$ |
| C Sev. | C seventh | $C_7$ |
| D Min. | D minor | $D_m$ |
| F Maj. | F major | F |
| E Sev. | E seventh | $E_7$ |
| G Sev. | G seventh | $G_7$ |
| A Min. | A minor | $A_m$ |
| C Maj. | C major | C |
| D Sev. | D seventh | $D_7$ |
| G Maj. | G major | G |

\* On the Autoharp, "Maj" stands for the word *major* and "Min" stands for the word *minor*. In a song, a chord marking followed by a small *m* indicates that the chord is a minor one. A chord is considered major if it is not followed by a small letter.

† The letters and signs shown in this column are the same ones that are generally found in guitar chords on sheet music.

2/4 time the top number 2 shows there are two beats in each measure, and the lower number 4 shows that a quarter note (q) receives one count. In 6/8 time, the top number 6 shows there are six beats in each measure; the lower number 8 shows that an eighth note (;) receives one count.

Chord markings for the songs in this book, placed above the music staff, are changed when the melodic line requires it. Additional chords are to be strummed between chord changes according to the rhythm of the song and the strumming patterns desired by the player. Press down one of the bar buttons with the index finger of the left hand, and strum with the right. Following are several suggested variations in strumming patterns:

- *2/4 time.* One or two strokes per measure, depending on the tempo and style of the song. For one stroke per measure, strum on beat 1 and count silently on beat 2. For two strokes per measure, strum on both beats, 1 and 2.
- *3/4 time.* One long, accented stroke or one long, accented and two short strokes, depending on tempo and style of the song. Strum one long, accented, full stroke, and count silently on beats 2 and 3, or strum one long, accented, full stroke from the bass strings

up and two short, unaccented strokes on the higher-pitched strings.

- *4/4 time*. One, two, or four strokes to the measure, depending on the tempo and style of the song. For one full stroke to a measure, strum on beat 1 and count silently on beats 2, 3, and 4. For two full strokes to a measure, strum on beats 1 and 3 and count silently on beats 2 and 4. For four strokes to a measure, use short strokes on all 4 beats.

Guitars can also be strummed to mimic the banjo and harp.

- *Banjo quality*. Sharp, short strokes from the bass strings up or the higher-pitched strings down or stroking in both directions. The player can best decide on the desired length of stroke. A plastic pick is sometimes desirable to obtain the banjo effect.
- *Harp quality*. Full, long strokes from the bass strings up, using most or all of the strings. One may also achieve the harp quality by strumming in both directions on the strings for certain desired effects. By strumming on the left side of the bars, one can obtain a realistic harplike effect. Play smoothly without accent and only fast enough to keep the rhythmic pattern flowing.
- *Broken rhythms*. A combination of short and long strokes in either direction. If one can "feel" certain rhythmic patterns, it is usually not difficult with experimentation and practice to strum these patterns on the Autoharp.

When practicing the strumming patterns, press down firmly one bar button at a time with the fingers of the left hand. Strum with the right hand, using an easy, flowing action. The left-handed person may find it easier to reverse these positions. It is possible to obtain an endless variety of rhythm patterns by experimentation.

When playing the Autoharp, always try to strum it in such a way to help create a mood that is appropriate to the song being played or sung.

## FINGERING CHART FOR THE GUITAR

### The Guitar and Its Parts

The accompanying guitar drawing and fingering chords will help you figure out how to begin learning to play the guitar.

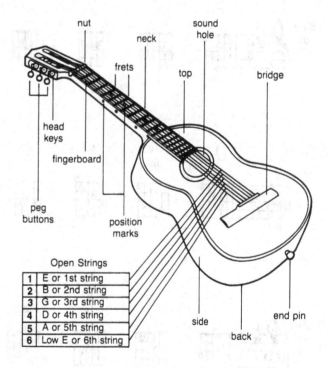

| Open Strings | |
|---|---|
| 1 | E or 1st string |
| 2 | B or 2nd string |
| 3 | G or 3rd string |
| 4 | D or 4th string |
| 5 | A or 5th string |
| 6 | Low E or 6th string |

## Guitar Fingering Chords Common to the Music in This Book

1   means first finger (forefinger)
2   means second finger
3   means third finger
4   means fourth finger
T   means thumb

The small circle (o) used on the diagrams indicates that those strings are to be played "open"—that is, they are not fingered.

A string that has no marking is not played. A slur ⌒ connecting two or more numbers on the diagrams means that those strings are to be pressed by one finger.

# Instruments for the Classroom

## PERCUSSION, MELODY, AND CHORDING INSTRUMENTS

The following percussion, melody, and chording instruments are suitable for use with young children:

*Percussion Instruments*

| | |
|---|---|
| Rhythm sticks | Gong |
| Tone blocks | Drums, small and large |
| Wood blocks | Bongo drums |
| Temple blocks | Tom-tom drums |
| Tambourines | Maracas |
| Triangles | Claves |
| Finger cymbals | Coconut shells |
| Cymbals | |

*Melody Instruments*

| | |
|---|---|
| Piano | Step bells |
| Melody bells | Xylophone |
| Resonator bells | |

*Chording Instruments*

Autoharp®

Guitar

Ukulele

## Drums

A drum is a versatile instrument to have in the home and classroom. A good drum is basic to any rhythm program for young children. One can make it do so many things. It can be played to tell when it is time to clean up the room or to call the children in from play. The syllables of a name can be tapped out on a drum. One can play loudly or softly, fast or slowly, on this "friendly" instrument.

Drums can be purchased or made, and it is recommended that a variety of sizes and kinds be made accessible. Each drum should differ in pitch so that children have the opportunity to hear and distinguish different levels of pitch. If possible, arrange several different drums close together, in a semicircle for example, so that children can discover the different sounds the drums produce as they tap one, then another. Children will soon discover that the drum produces different sounds depending on how, where, and with what they strike it. In good weather, the children can collect the drums and take them outside to experiment with them. When this kind of opportunity is provided, children can accompany their rope-skipping games and create rhythms of their own. Parents and teachers are beginning to use some of the interesting drums from different parts of the world, such as Asia, Africa, and some of the Latin American countries.

## Rhythm Sticks

Rhythm sticks, two slender pieces of hardwood approximately 12 inches long, are good basic instruments for keeping time when marching, singing, or accompanying another instrument or a record. One stick from the pair is usually notched. A scraping sound can then be produced when the smooth stick is scraped across the stick that is notched. Sticks can be made from doweling. When making rhythm sticks, be sure the type of wood used produces a good tone quality.

## Wood Blocks

Two pieces of square- or rectangular-shaped wood with handles are used for this instrument. The size and weight of the wood should fit the age of the children using the instrument. Some wood blocks are too heavy and large for younger children. The instrument can be played by tapping or sliding one wood block against the other.

## Sand Blocks

Sand blocks are made from sandpaper attached by staples to the sides of two wooden blocks, approximately 2½ [times] 4 inches each. Choose size and weight according to the age of the children using them. Sand blocks are much easier to use if they are equipped with handles or holders. They are played by rubbing one sandpaper block against the other.

## Tone Blocks

A small block of wood, hollowed out with a cut on each side, and a wooden mallet make up the tone block. It is played by striking the mallet above the cut opening. This produces a hollow, resounding tone. When played correctly, the instrument provides a good underlying beat for musical selections.

## Wrist Bells

Sleigh bells, which should be of good quality, are mounted on a strap. The instrument is worn on the wrist or ankle and produces an effective sleigh bell sound to accompany songs and dances.

## Jingle Bells on Handles

Generally, a single bell is mounted on the end of a handle. The instrument is held in one hand and shaken in time to music.

## Tambourines

Six or more pairs of jingles are mounted in the instrument's shell. The plastic shell head comes in different sizes. The instrument may be shaken or struck with the hand, knee, or elbow, producing an interesting jingling effect.

## Triangles

The triangle consists of a steel rod bent into a triangular shape, open at one corner, and struck with a small, straight, steel rod. We suggest that this instrument be purchased, since most homemade triangles have rather poor tone quality. The instrument is held by a holder and struck with a metal rod. It may also be played by placing the rod inside the triangle and striking it back and forth against the sides.

## Maracas

Maracas are gourd or gourd-shaped rattles filled with seeds or pebbles. The instruments are shaken to produce rhythmic effects and can be played singly or by holding one maraca in each hand.

## Castanets

Castanets are a pair of concave pieces of wood, which may be held in the palm of the hand and clicked together or attached to a handle for easier use by small children. The sound makes an interesting accompaniment for dancing.

## Finger Cymbals

Two small cymbals with finger holders are held with each hand and struck together. The instrument also may be played by placing the loop holder of one cymbal over the thumb and the loop of the other cymbal on the middle finger. The two finger cymbals are then struck together.

## Hand Cymbals

Concave plates of nickel, silver, bronze, or brass produce a sharp, ringing sound when struck. Cymbals may be played in pairs by striking one against the other or singly by striking one cymbal with a drumstick.

## Autoharp®

This string instrument has buttons or bars that, when depressed by the finger; dampen all the strings needed for the desired chord. It can be played by strumming or plucking. The number of bars on Autoharps varies; the most common types have 12 or 15. People with little or no musical training can learn to play the Autoharp in a relatively short time. (See Appendix C.)

## Melody Bells

Melody bells are arranged like notes on the piano keyboard and are mounted on a frame. The bells are played with mallets. Sets come in various ranges.

## Step Bells

These bells are mounted on an elevated frame, include chromatic tones, and come in various ranges. Some frames are collapsible, allowing easy storage.

Children can easily see whether the melody moves up or down.

## Resonator Bells

Mounted individually on a block of wood or plastic, these bells are arranged in a luggage case. Mallets are used to play the bells. The keyboard is similar to the piano keyboard. Each bell may be removed from its case and played individually. These are excellent for use by both child and teacher.

# Song Index

# Index